Lecture Notes in Computer Science $\quad$ 8993

Commenced Publication in 1973
Founding and Former Series Editors:
Gerhard Goos, Juris Hartmanis, and Jan van Leeuwen

More information about this series at http://www.springer.com/series/7409

Asma Al-Saidi · Rudolf Fleischer
Zakaria Maamar · Omer F. Rana (Eds.)

Intelligent Cloud Computing

First International Conference, ICC 2014
Muscat, Oman, February 24–26, 2014
Revised Selected Papers

 Springer

Editors
Asma Al-Saidi
Sultan Qaboos University
Muscat
Oman

Zakaria Maamar
Zayed University
Dubai
Utd.Arab.Emir.

Rudolf Fleischer
GUtech
Muscat
Oman

Omer F. Rana
Cardiff University
Cardiff
UK

ISSN 0302-9743   ISSN 1611-3349   (electronic)
Lecture Notes in Computer Science
ISBN 978-3-319-19847-7   ISBN 978-3-319-19848-4   (eBook)
DOI 10.1007/978-3-319-19848-4

Library of Congress Control Number: 2015941112

LNCS Sublibrary: SL3 – Information Systems and Applications, incl. Internet/Web and HCI

Springer Cham Heidelberg New York Dordrecht London

Springer International Publishing AG Switzerland is part of Springer Science+Business Media
(www.springer.com)

Preface

Recent advances in information and communication technologies (ICT) such as computing, storage, and networking have led to the development of a new generation of electronic services and systems that are ubiquitous, available at the touch of a button, and affect all aspects of life and economy. Cloud computing, one of the ICT advances, provides an important integration of many of these aspects — combining both the ability to offer services over distributed, remotely accessed infrastructure, along with the ability to combine off-site, remote infrastructure with local infrastructure available within an institution. It is therefore expected that cloud-based services will revolutionize the way we do business, maintain our health, conduct education, and how we secure, protect, inform, and entertain ourselves.

Increasing integration across multiple types of computing infrastructure and the deployment of services across such infrastructure lead to significant design, development, and management challenges. For instance, how should such remote resources be managed, accessed, and paid for? Or how can cloud computing platforms be used to host and manage large and complex data sets (aka big data) — arising from social media data feeds (e.g., Twitter), open government data, to large-scale scientific simulations? Owing to the significant development effort invested into cloud systems, there is a pressing need to re-visit existing design, development, and management strategies so that dynamic adaptability, rapid delivery, and efficient access to cloud-based services can take place in a seamless manner.

A variety of intelligent mechanisms and techniques may be used to develop advanced cloud systems, solutions, and services that offer new functionalities and more advanced user-centric services. Implementing intelligence in cloud computing systems will make them more adaptive, exible, and autonomic in resource management, in service provisioning, and in running large-scale applications. In addition, it will help organizations build an intelligent network capable of providing security, visibility, and optimization for a better user experience.

The objective of the First International Conference on Intelligent Cloud Computing: Theory and Applications (ICC 2014) was to bring together researchers, practitioners, and developers working with cloud systems and intelligent systems, intending to address some of the challenges identified above. The conference featured invited talks from leading organizations working in cloud computing in Oman (such as Omantel and the Information Technology Authority) and in the region (such as the Qatar Computing Research Institute and Huawei Technologies Middle East). The conference had 131 registered participants, many hailing from ministries and leading research universities in Oman, which demonstrates a significant interest in cloud computing in the region.

The current volume contains all papers presented at the conference, which were subsequently updated based on discussions and comments from the audience, in the areas of "Resource Management and Energy Efficiency" and "Security" — both key research challenges at present. We thank all reviewers for their timely contributions, and the authors and keynote speakers for presenting their work at the conference.

April 2015

Asma Al-Saidi
Rudolf Fleischer
Zakaria Maamar
Omer F. Rana

Organization

ICC 2014 was organized by the Department of Computer Science of the German University of Technology in Oman (GUtech) under the patronage of H.E. Dr. Ali bin Masoud bin Ali Al Sunaidi, Minister of Commerce and Industry, Sultanate of Oman.

Conference Chairs

Asma Al-Saidi	Sultan Qaboos University, Oman
Rudolf Fleischer	GUtech, Oman

Organizing Committee

Huda al-Amri	Sultan Qaboos University, Oman
Ali Al-Badi	Sultan Qaboos University, Oman
Wasila al-Busaidi	Sultan Qaboos University, Oman
Asma Al-Saidi (Co-chair)	Sultan Qaboos University, Oman
Rudolf Fleischer (Co-chair)	GUtech, Oman
Nabil Sahli	GUtech, Oman

Publicity Chair

Manuela Gutberlet	GUtech, Oman

Program Committee Chairs

Zakaria Maamar	Zayed University, UAE
Omer F. Rana	Cardiff University, UK

Program Committee

Imad M. Abbadi	University of Oxford, UK
Sherif Abdelwahed	Mississippi State University, USA
Bader Al-Manthari	Information Technology Authority, Oman
Saqib Ali	Sultan Qaboos University, Oman
Ashiq Anjum	University of Derby, UK
Boualem Benatallah	University of New South Wales, Australia
Kenneth P. Birman	Cornell University, USA
Luiz Fernando Bittencourt	Institute of Computing University of Campinas, Brazil
Raouf Boutaba	University of Waterloo, Canada
Simon Caton	Karlsruhe Institute of Technology, Germany
Kyle Chard	Argonne National Lab/University of Chicago, USA
Jerome Darmont	University of Pierre Lumiere Lyon, France
Karim Djemame	Leeds University, UK

Said Elnaffar	UAE University, UAE
Rudolf Fleischer	GUtech, Oman
Song Fu	University of North Texas, USA
Youssef Iraqi	University of Khalifa, UAE
Omer Khalid	SAP Research, Ireland
Laurent Lefevre	ENS Lyon, France
Bogdan Nicolae	IBM Research, Ireland
Talal H. Noor	University of Adelaide, Australia
Mohammed Odeh	UWE Bristol, UK
Arto Ojala	University of Jyvaskyla, Finland
Claus Pahl	Dublin City University, Ireland
Ivan Rodero	Rutgers University, USA
Bruno Schulze	National Laboratory for Scientific Computing, Brazil
Quan Z. Sheng	University of Adelaide, Australia
Carlos Varela	Rensselaer Polytechnic Institute, New York, USA
Jon Weissman	University of Minnesota, USA
Xiangyang Xue	Fudan University, Shanghai, China
Fan Zhang	Carnegie Mellon University, Qatar
Albert Zomaya	University of Sydney, Australia

Conference Sponsors

Contents

Invited Papers

Cloud Computing: Towards Making Computing a Utility

Mohamed Hefeeda[⊠]

Qatar Computing Research Institute, Doha, Qatar
`mhefeeda@qf.org.qa`

Abstract. Cloud computing strives to achieve the long-standing vision of making computing a utility, similar to electricity, telephone, and water services. This article discusses several research challenges that need to be addressed in order to realize the full potential of cloud computing and get computing closer to being a utility.

Keywords: Cloud computing · Utility computing

1 Cloud Computing Challenges

The cloud computing paradigm has attracted significant attention from academia, industry, governments, and even individual users. This paradigm promises to achieve the long-standing vision of making computing a utility, similar to electricity, telephone, and water services. This means that computer users receive computing services without worrying about the details of creating, managing, and maintaining the infrastructures providing these services. Just as we receive electricity, for example, without paying too much attention to the complex process of power generation and its associated costs.

Cloud computing offers several advantages, such as reduced cost for setting up and managing IT infrastructures, rapid deployment with elastic scaling up and down of services to meet dynamic user demands, and improved reliability and availability of services. While many algorithms and technologies used in building cloud infrastructures existed before, several new research challenges need to be addressed to realize the full potential of the cloud computing paradigm. These research challenges are summarized in the following subsections.

1.1 Cloud Security

Many users perceive more security threats if they were to move their applications and data to a public cloud because of the shared nature of the cloud. While in fact this may not always be the case, since cloud providers typically follow best practices in industry and hire top security experts, way beyond what individual users and organizations can afford. Thus, one of the first tasks in the cloud security area is to clearly identify and document potential security threats resulting

© Springer International Publishing Switzerland 2015
A. Al-Saidi et al. (Eds.): ICC 2014, LNCS 8993, pp. 3–7, 2015.
DOI: 10.1007/978-3-319-19848-4_1

from hosting applications and data on shared cloud infrastructures. To do so, we need to develop a cloud security model that defines standard security metrics, which can be quantified and measured.

A data-centric security model seems to be more appropriate for cloud platforms. In this model, methods for controlling information flow (provenance) within a cloud and across clouds should be developed. Also, end-to-end methods for enforcing security policies should be designed.

In addition, tools to detect and respond to attacks on clouds are needed. These tools should offer multi-level behavior profiling and monitoring, methods for feature selection, data aggregation and correlation, and risk analysis and quantification of various attacks.

Finally, cloud programming models should offer security and privacy-aware APIs, in which users and developers can specify security/privacy requirements of cloud applications.

1.2   Cloud Applications

Cloud applications can range from hosting simple desktop applications in a cloud platform to processing web-scale data for creating web indexes for search engines such as Google and Microsoft, and mining social interactions among users for social networking web sites such as Facebook and Twitter. To accelerate wider adoption of cloud platforms for current and future computing applications, we need to identify and characterize "cloudifiable" applications, i.e., applications that can be moved to cloud platforms. This can be done by developing methods and tools to characterize the requirements of cloud applications and to map these requirements to service level agreements (SLAs) offered by cloud platforms.

Also, aggregating and documenting best-practices and case studies for successful (and failed) cloud applications can provide answers to questions such as how and when to cloudify applications. In addition, we should promote "cloud thinking" among users and application developers. Cloud thinking encourages users and developers to think of the cloud as a computing abstraction, not as a number of machines.

Finally, we need to develop management tools and algorithms to:

1. enable automatic scale-out of applications as resources become available,
2. automatically co-schedule applications with complementary resource requirements on the cloud ("compatible multitenancy", e.g., cache-heavy and frequent blocking),
3. support developers to mitigate frequent failures in the cloud ("design for failure"), and
4. provide provable/auditable security requirements.

1.3   Cloud Programming

Programming models and tools are essential to design, implement, test, and debug cloud applications. For wide cloud adoption, we need to develop tools to assist regular users, e.g., scientists and business analysts, to utilize cloud platforms. For example, tools that enable widely-used software packages such as Excel, Matlab, and R to seamlessly utilize cloud infrastructures are needed. These tools should require minimum or zero programming efforts from users. In addition, we should develop multi-level APIs, which can support various granularities for accessing cloud resources.

For example, high-level APIs should be developed to allow cloud users to describe the requirements of their cloud applications without worrying much about the actual programming models used to develop such applications or the hardware resources that will run these applications.

Medium-level APIs should be designed to assist application developers to rapidly develop cloud applications without getting into details such as data replication, caching, fault tolerance, and process scheduling.

Low-level APIs can be used to control cloud resources, e.g., processors, VMs, network, and disk blocks, in fine-grain manner. These APIs should have primitives for specifying and trading off: elasticity, privacy, security, availability, performance, and energy cost for cloud applications.

Finally, we need to identify a small set of programming models for developing cloud applications with diverse requirements, e.g., batch processing, online stream processing, dependency of computation parts on each other, and distribution of input data sets. These programming models should be mathematically formalized in order to provide assurance on cloud applications correctness and performance.

1.4   QoS in Clouds

In order to accelerate the adoption of cloud infrastructures by diverse users, cloud providers should consider offering different levels of quality of service (QoS). Clearly specified SLAs for cloud services should be defined. These SLAs should be easy to understand by administrators of IT infrastructures of business with different sizes, which will facilitate moving more applications and data to clouds. SLAs should consider environmental issues, e.g., energy consumption and carbon footprint of applications, as well as application performance metrics such as completion time, availability, and response time. Ideally, SLAs should be transferable from one cloud provider to another. Allocation and management algorithms of cloud resources should be enhanced to enforce SLAs.

1.5   Energy-Efficient Clouds

The energy consumption bill makes a sizable portion of the cost of running data centers, and this is portion is increasing relative to other costs including the cost of servers, storage, and networking equipment. We do need to improve the energy efficiency of cloud data centers, not only for reducing costs but also for minimizing the carbon footprint of data centers especially as more of them are being deployed worldwide.

To improve energy efficiency, we first need to define energy consumption metrics for data centers. Current metrics such as PUE (power usage efficiency) are not sufficient as they only give coarse-grain measure for the whole data center. We need more elaborate metrics for the data center as well as for individual applications. Then, we need to design cloud applications that are energy aware, which means that they can adapt their computations based on a given energy budget and they can trade off some performance metrics for energy saving.

In addition, we should consider designing data centers that employ renewable energy sources, such as solar and wind powers. UPS (Uninterruptable Power Supply) units can be utilized to absorb variations and sporadic outages in renewable energy sources. Different organization of UPS units in data centers need to be explored and analyzed. UPS units can be used per server, per rack of servers, per row of racks, or combinations thereof.

Furthermore, research efforts should be targeted to designing servers that approach energy proportionality, as well as data centers that employ low-power processing units such as Graphics Processing Units (GPUs) and asymmetric processors that could have few fast cores and many slower cores.

Finally, we need to develop regulation, taxation, and energy pricing schemes to encourage energy conservation in data centers.

1.6   Cloud + X Architectures

We should encourage developers and users to think of cloud as a part of a bigger computing platform in which all components can efficiently be utilized to contribute to the accomplishment of a computational task. For example, parts of a cloud application could run on local desktops or mobile devices while others could run on the cloud. We need to develop resource management tools for clouds composed of heterogeneous elements. We need to design programming models for "Cloud + X" platforms, where X could be a client device, specialized computing resource, or anything else. The programming models should offer services to partition and manage cloud applications.

1.7   Cloud Storage Systems

Variability in the performance of cloud storage systems is a major concern for cloud applications. The variability comes from the shared nature of the cloud platform. We first should define the appropriate performance metrics and consistency models for various cloud applications.

Then, we need to improve the cloud middleware layer to reduce performance variability of storage systems. Better schedulers need to be designed to route requests within the cloud storage system in order to meet the performance requirements of cloud applications. In addition, new storage media such as FLASH and tapes should be integrated into cloud storage systems, and tools to efficiently utilize them for different cloud applications need to be designed.

Finally, we need to define guidelines for choosing the appropriate logical storage structure(s) based on the requirements of different cloud applications.

1.8   Cloud Legal Frameworks and Standards

Many organizations deal with sensitive data. A clear and legally-binding frame-work for hosting data and applications is needed. The framework should allow fine access control on data and applications. We also need legal processes to handle hosting data and applications on international clouds. Which laws are enforced on cloud providers? Local or international laws? Currently, many organizations prefer local clouds, which are not always available or efficient.

In addition, organizations would like to have the option to move from one cloud provider to another with minimal effort and disruption of services. We need to design well-defined standards for interoperability across different cloud providers.

Semantic Engine and Cloud Agency for Vendor Agnostic Retrieval, Discovery, and Brokering of Cloud Services

Alba Amato, Giuseppina Cretella, Beniamino Di Martino[✉], Luca Tasquier, and Salvatore Venticinque

Department of Industrial and Information Engineering, Second University of Naples, Aversa, Italy
bemiamino.dimartino@unina.it,
{alba.amato,giuseppina.cretella,luca.tasquier,
salvatore.venticinque}@unina2.it

Abstract. Cloud computing is moving from being a testing ground for isolated projects to being a strategic approach of the entire business organization. So the choice among the possible cloud offers, with a strong focus on the choice of services that enable better processes and projects of the business lines, is gaining importance. Nevertheless the heterogeneity of the Cloud services, resources, technology and service levels offered by the several providers make difficult to decide. Besides the inconveniences caused by the "lock-in", give rise to the need for developers to be able to develop an application regardless of where it is released, structuring and building it in a vendor agnostic way so that it is possible to deploy on the provider that best fits them at the moment. The mOSAIC project aims at designing and developing an innovative open-source API and platform that enables applications to be Cloud providers' neutral and to negotiate Cloud services as requested by their users, allowing automatic discovery, matchmaking, and thus supporting selection, brokering, interoperability end even composition of Cloud Services among multiple Clouds. In this paper, we illustrate the interoperation of the two components, the Semantic Engine and the Cloud Agency for the agnostic retrieval, discovery and brokering of cloud services. The focus will be put on the way to support the Cloud Application Developer to express the requirements and services/resources in vendor agnostic way and to translate automatically these requirements into a neutral format in order to compare it with the different offers of providers and to broker the best one according to defined policies.

Keywords: Cloud brokering · Multi-agents systems · Cloud ontology · Semantic discovery · Cloud interoperability

1 Introduction

Cloud computing is moving from being a testing ground for isolated projects to being a strategic approach of the entire business organization. So the choice

© Springer International Publishing Switzerland 2015
A. Al-Saidi et al. (Eds.): ICC 2014, LNCS 8993, pp. 8–25, 2015.
DOI: 10.1007/978-3-319-19848-4_2

among the possible cloud offers, with a strong focus on the choice of services that enable better processes and projects of the business lines, is gaining importance. Nevertheless the heterogeneity of the Cloud services, resources, technology and service levels offered by the several providers make it difficult to decide [1,2]. In fact different vendors have introduced different paradigms and services so leading to clouds that are diverse and vendor-locked, as happened during the early days of the computer hardware industry, when each vendor made and marketed its own version of incompatible computer equipment. Besides the inconveniences caused by the "lock-in", give rise to the need for developers, to be able to develop an application regardless of where it is released structuring and building it in a vendor agnostic way so that it is possible to deploy on the provider that best fits them at the moment. Even if several efforts have been made to standardize clouds' important technical aspects, for example from the US National Institute of Standards and Technology (NIST), standardization is still far from reality.

In this scenario, it would be useful to have a way to express the user's requirements closer to the user logic, translate automatically these requirements into a neutral format in order to compare it with offers of providers and for choosing the best one according to defined policies. A common ontology can help to bridge the gap between application requirements and technical requirements declared by resource providers. In fact semantic can help address clouds key interoperability and portability issues. For example semantic technologies are useful to define an agnostic, machine readable, description of resources to be compared with the vendor offers using a brokering system, that acquire autonomically resources from providers on the basis of SLA evaluation rules.

The mOSAIC project [3] aims at designing and developing an innovative open-source API and platform that enables applications to be Cloud providers' neutral and to negotiate Cloud services as requested by their users, allowing automatic discovery, matchmaking [4], and thus supporting selection, brokering, interoperability end even composition of Cloud Services among multiple Clouds.

In order to support this selection and requirements specification has been developed:

- a Knowledge Base, representing resources and domain concepts and rules by means of Semantic Web Ontologies and inference rules;
- a support tool, the Semantic Engine, that helps the user to abstract the requirements in vendor independent way starting from application requirements or from specific vendor resources;
- a Cloud Agency, that compares the different offers of providers with the user proposal and retrieves the best offer. The user can also delegate to the Agency the monitoring of resource utilization, the necessary checks of the agreement fulfillment and eventually re-negotiations.

In this paper, we illustrate the interoperation of the two components, the Semantic Engine and the Cloud Agency for the agnostic retrieval, discovery and brokering of cloud services. The focus will be put on the way to support the Cloud Application Developer to express the requirements and services/resources in vendor agnostic way and to translate automatically these requirements into a neutral format in order to compare it with the different offers of providers and to broker the best one according to defined policies.

The user can choose the known concepts that describe his application or the required resources, utilizing a knowledge base and inference rules managed by the Semantic Engine, which supports him/her to produce a vendor agnostic template of a Service Level Agreement, to be used for negotiating a concrete offer from the available Cloud vendors. The Cloud Agency interacts with the supported providers for retrieving the available offers and brokers the best one(s). The Semantic Engine can further be useful for filtering many proposals, which are optimal according to different criteria, when the user's knowledge is not helpful.

The paper is organized as follows. In Sect. 2 we present the design architecture, in Sects. 3 and 4 we present an ontology supporting the semantic representation of resources and the engine based on it. In Sect. 5 a description of the Cloud Agency and of the utilization of Broker Agents is provided; In Sect. 6 an example is shown. In Sect. 7 we present an overview of works related to semantic representation of cloud resources and multi-cloud resource brokering and negotiation. Conclusions are drawn in Sect. 8.

2 Approach and Architecture

A Cloud Application Developer, who intends to develop a cloud based application, would like to express his or her requirements according to the application logic, to make a choice based on what he or she knows and based on high level requirements. In order to support this selection and requirements specification, we have developed:

- a Knowledge Base, representing resources and domain concepts and rules by means of Semantic Web Ontologies and inference rules;
- a support tool, the Semantic Engine, that helps the user to abstract the requirements in vendor independent way starting from application requirements or from specific vendor resources;
- a Cloud Agency, that compares the different offers of providers with the user proposal and retrieves the best offer.

In Fig. 1 the integration and interaction of such components is shown.

The Semantic Engine, based on the ontologies and inference rules representing the Knowledge Base, enables the user in defining his or her requirements in a format suitable for comparison among offers and produces an SLA template that is passed to the Cloud Agency. The Cloud Agency adds the brokering rules so composing the *Call for Proposal (CFP)* [5] that describes the list of resources, which are necessary to run cloud applications. It includes also the negotiation rules to select the best offer among those proposed by providers. After that the Cloud Agency compares each proposal with the user's template and retrieves the best offer.

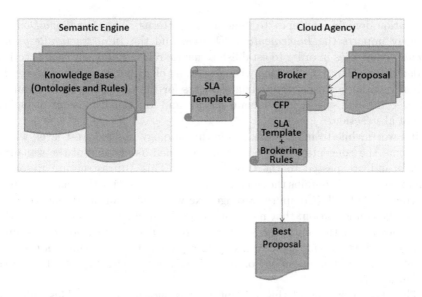

Fig. 1. Integrated view of knowledge base, Semantic Engine and Cloud Agency

3   An Ontology for the Development of Cloud Based Application

The knowledge base developed in order to support the search and discovery of suitable Cloud resources and component is structured into four sub-ontologies and is developed using OWL language [6].

The sub-ontologies have the following purpose.

- The *ApplicationDomain* ontology represents the application and its patterns expressed in the domain terminology of the end user. This level of abstraction contains concepts related to the application domain of applications, as instance data mining, big data application related concepts.
- The *FunctionalDomain* ontology represents functional concepts of both cloud and non cloud domain, such as Cloud functionalities and services but also traditional design and execution patterns for distributed and concurrent application.
- The *InfrastructureResourceDomain* ontology provides concepts and relation useful to describe information related to the resource such as Virtual Machines, storage and network and their composite configurations.
- The *ImplementationDomain* ontology models information related to the concrete APIs of Cloud platforms. In particular this level contains the grounding elements of effective cloud services, that means the elements useful to invoke the implemented functionalities.

The four ontologies are linked together with relationships, for example, the *ApplicationDomain* ontology imports the *FunctionalDomain* in order to relate application-domain concepts to functional patterns. The *FunctionalDomain* ontology imports the *ImplementationDomain* and the *InfrastructureResource-Domain* ontologies in order to establish semantic relationships for each function needed by the Cloud application with grounding elements as specified above. In such a way, the necessary grounding elements for the Cloud application can be retrieved through selection of domain specific and functional concepts at higher level of abstraction.

It's worthwhile to have a look inside the ontology of the lowest level, which represents the concepts that are actually returned as outputs of the semantic module and are passed to the Cloud Agency. This "Infrastructure Resource Domain ontology" contains the semantic structure to describe the basic resources described by OCCI (Compute, Storage, Network) and an additional concept that is the configuration, that means a composition of single resources. For the representation of this ontology we started from OCCI description of resource interface and we provide a uniform way to represent these information through an ontology. For this reason our ontology is compliant with the OCCI resource description [7].

The class hierarchy of this sub-ontology is shown in Fig. 2. This ontology classifies the resources of type compute, storage and network in vendor resources and agnostic resources. In the vendor resources we collect a series of offers by cloud provider like IBM and Amazon, while in agnostic resources we collect resources and their characteristic not linked with the offers of cloud provider. The link between a configuration element and the resources that compose it are represented through owl object property, while the characteristic of the single resource are defined through owl data property according to the attribute defined in OCCI [8] (Fig. 4). To the standard OCCI attributes we added two parameters for the description, *gpu* and *price*. The vendors' offers of several IAAS cloud provider are represented in this ontology through individuals and their characteristics. Figure 3 reports the list of individuals representing resources from the IBM and Amazon Cloud provider offers already represented in the ontology. Of course this list can be easily enriched. A cloud user accustomed to a particular cloud provider may start from the specific customized solution (for instance the IBM Silver Compute) and translate this solution in vendor independent' terms through the Semantic Engine, then pass this neutral representation to the Cloud Agency to find an equivalent solution that fulfill additional requirements.

If instead the user don't know which are the technical requirement of his/her application, he/she can start specifying high level requirements as the complexity of the algorithms used or functional/design requirements. These requirements may be expressed using concepts contained in the knowledge base and then can be translated in infrastructural requirements by the application of heuristic rules. By following the generic structure of an *ApplicationPattern* that is based on a design pattern or a composition of design pattern, it is possible to semantically describe a whole range of engineering applications. This engineering application can be semantically described by instantiating an *ApplicationPattern* class and all the composing concepts including the *AlgorithmicConcept* and the *Patterns* concepts with specific instances. All these concepts are semantically represented in the Application and Functional Domain Ontologies.

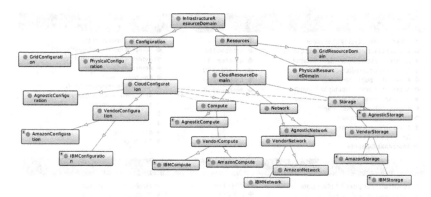

Fig. 2. Infrastructure resource ontology class hierarchy

An important feature of the Semantic Engine is its capability to deduce an appropriate parameterized configuration of the Cloud application and a generic description of needed IaaS resources based on high level requirements. This feature is made possible by the execution of inference rules that extensively use the semantic description of the application, particularly its design pattern and the description of the critical aspects of the application that need elasticity, such as the computational or data complexity of the algorithm. Listing 1.1 shows an example of a rule that provides information on the needed properties of a Virtual Machine that hosts a Web server in a Cloud application. This rule, based on the design logic of the application, in this case a three-tier architectural pattern, and on information about the expected visitors peak, aims to provide information to the developer about the properties of the Virtual Machine that has to be acquired from an IaaS provider.

Listing 1.1. Inference Rules

```
@prefix AP:ApplicationPattern.owl#
@prefix IRD:ResourceDomain.owl#
@prefix FP:FunctionalDomain.owl#

[WebAppRule:
(?x rdf:type AP:WebApplication),
(?x AP:hasDesignLogic  ?dl),
(?dl rdf:type FP:Three-tier),
(?x AP:hasPeakVisitors ?y),
swrlb:divide(?k, 100, ?y),
swrlb:add(?k4, 4, ?k)
(?z rdf:type  IRD:Compute),
(?z IRD:cores ?k ),
greaterThan(?r, ?k),lessThan(?r, ?k4),
-> (?x AD:PatternUseInfrastructure ?z) ]
```

Amazon Compute	Amazon Storage	Amazon Configuration
◆ AmazonClusterEightXLCompute ◆ AmazonClusterGpuQuadrupleXLCompute ◆ AmazonClusterQuadrupleXLCompute ◆ AmazonHiCpuMediumCompute ◆ AmazonHiCpuXLCompute ◆ AmazonHiMemoryDoubleXLCompute ◆ AmazonHiMemoryQuadrupleXLCompute ◆ AmazonHiMemoryXLCompute ◆ AmazonLargeCompute ◆ AmazonMicroCompute ◆ AmazonSmallCompute ◆ AmazonXLCompute	◆ Amazon160 ◆ Amazon1690 ◆ Amazon3370 ◆ Amazon350 ◆ Amazon420 ◆ Amazon850	◆ AmazonClusterEightXL ◆ AmazonClusterGpuQuadrupleXL ◆ AmazonClusterQuadrupleXL ◆ AmazonHiCpuMedium ◆ AmazonHiCpuXL ◆ AmazonHiMemoryDoubleXL ◆ AmazonHiMemoryQuadrupleXL ◆ AmazonHiMemoryXL ◆ AmazonLarge ◆ AmazonMicro ◆ AmazonSmall ◆ AmazonXL

IBM Compute	IBM Storage	IBM Configuration
◆ IBMBronzeCopper32bCompute ◆ IBMBronzeCopper64bCompute ◆ IBMGold32bCompute ◆ IBMGold64bCompute ◆ IBMPlatinum64bCompute ◆ IBMReservationUnitCompute ◆ IBMSilver32bCompute ◆ IBMSilver64bCompute	◆ IBM1024 ◆ IBM175 ◆ IBM2048 ◆ IBM350 ◆ IBM60 ◆ IBM850 ◆ IBM9600	◆ IBMBronzeCopper32b ◆ IBMBronzeCopper64b ◆ IBMGold32b ◆ IBMGold64b ◆ IBMPlatinum64b ◆ IBMReservationUnit ◆ IBMSilver32b ◆ IBMSilver64b

Fig. 3. Amazon and IBM resources list

The execution of inference rules on the knowledge base results in a list of the needed IaaS resources for the application. Listing 1.2 presents a part of such description.

Listing 1.2. Description of a resource necessary for the Cloud application

```
<ws:ServiceDescriptionTerm ws:Name ="Compute" >
    <Compute >
      <cpuSpeed>1.25</cpuSpeed>
          <cpuCores>16</cpuCores>
          <architecture>x86</architecture>
          <memory>16</memory>
    </ Compute >
</ws:ServiceDescriptionTerm >
```

The list of needed resources provided by the Semantic Engine can be used by the Cloud Agency to automatically negotiate resources with a variety of IaaS providers. Once the needed resources are negotiated with the Cloud provider, the application can be deployed by using the list of needed software components and the mOSAIC's deployment tool.

4   Semantic Engine

The Semantic Engine [9] is a prototype tool that supports the user in Cloud Applications' development by discovering cloud APIs functionalities and resources based on semantic technologies. It handles, maintains and exposes to the user in a graphical way the semantic descriptions of application domain

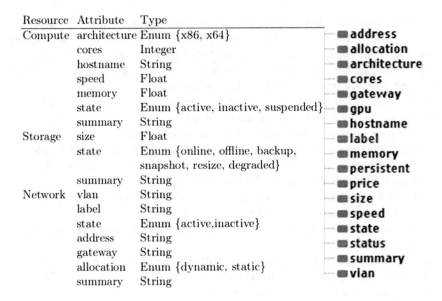

Resource	Attribute	Type
Compute	architecture	Enum {x86, x64}
	cores	Integer
	hostname	String
	speed	Float
	memory	Float
	state	Enum {active, inactive, suspended}
	summary	String
Storage	size	Float
	state	Enum {online, offline, backup, snapshot, resize, degraded}
	summary	String
Network	vlan	String
	label	String
	state	Enum {active,inactive}
	address	String
	gateway	String
	allocation	Enum {dynamic, static}
	summary	String

Fig. 4. List of object property to define resources compliant with OCCI

concepts, application related concepts, general design patterns and programming functionalities, specific API implementations and Cloud resources. In other words it exposes graphically the knowledge base presented in Sect. 3. In order to achieve its mission, the Semantic Engine (based on the ontology levels already described) introduces a high level of abstraction over a range of domain concepts from the engineering discipline [10], generic application patterns as well as details on existing Cloud APIs and IaaS providers. By implementing an additional layer of abstraction, this tool overcomes syntactical differences of existing Cloud APIs, so that it is possible to explore application design patterns independently from the target API. The Semantic Engine fully exploits the expressivity of the OWL DL language specie to relate entities with properties and constraints.

It allows for reuse of the semantic description of the application to be developed, performed by the user during the query phase, by allowing for the definition of application patterns, stored in the knowledge base, and reused in future searches.

In this section we describe how the user can create an agnostic description of resources guided by the Semantic Engine. To produce the CFP part related to resource list the user can use three different options. The first one (the simplest) is to fill the fields suggested by the tool for the particular resource selected. The second one is to select a cloud vendor customized resource configuration and from this obtain an agnostic description. The third one is to specify the user requirements referring to the application he or she intends to develop like information related to the workload or design and functional pattern.

In particular for this third usage mode, the developer, who is a domain specialist may use the Semantic Engine to:

- search for domain concepts related to the application domain, for example the information retrieval, e.g. KWIC (Key Word In Context) index and find the concept of an application for KWIC system based on a specific model;
- investigate the key requirements of the application, e.g. find out that a critical computationally intensive part of the application;
- analyse the Cloud application pattern and eventually associate algorithms or functional patterns to the *ApplicationPattern*;
- identify key software components, such as message queues and storage components, necessary for the Cloud application, as represented in terminology of the appropriate programming model and the associated software platform;
- identify the workflow between the components;
- draw a detailed design of the necessary software components of the application and the information and data flow among them;
- query the Semantic Engine to retrieve the number of needed software components for the task at hand;
- use the Semantic Engine to prepare a list of required resources (i.e. Virtual Machines) for the application, which can be used by the mOSAIC's Cloud Agency for negotiation of optimal offers;
- analyse a list of proposed IaaS providers suitable for the application;
- finally, provide a descriptor of the Cloud application, which can be used by the software platform to start the execution of all the necessary software components i.e. to launch the Cloud application.

In addition to the list of resources and their characteristic, the Semantic engine provides also a way to support the definition of some constraints. The definition of these constraints can be driven by heuristic rules that define the parameters to take into account while developing a certain kind of application and by user constrains. For example the user can express constraints like the maximum price, or the need to have at least a certain value for a resource's parameter.

5   Cloud Agency

Cloud Agency (CA) [11] is a Multi Agent System conceived for provisioning by negotiation, monitoring and reconfiguration of acquired resources (Fig. 5). Using Cloud Agency, the user can negotiate the needed resources in order to run his applications. The user can also delegate to the Agency the monitoring of resource utilization, the necessary checks of the agreement fulfillment and eventually re-negotiations. Cloud Agency will supplement the common management functionalities which are currently provided by IaaS Private and Public infrastructure with new advanced services, by implementing transparent layer to IaaS Private and Public Cloud services. Cloud Agency will support the Cloud user in two different scenarios. In the *Deployment* scenario Cloud Agency supports the discovering and provisioning of the available resources needed to run Cloud applications. In this case the user is negotiating, by the Cloud Agency, the resources it needs to run his/her applications. In order to propose to the user

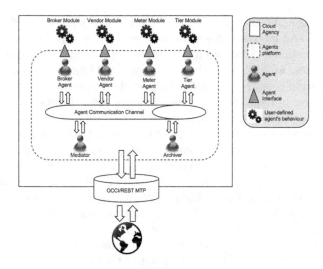

Fig. 5. Cloud Agency architecture

the best offer of resources, that fits his requirements at best, the Cloud Agency will use a Brokering Module that chooses among the available offers the best one. Furthermore for configuration and start of resources it will provide management facilities. In the *Execution* scenario it allows to monitor and eventually to reconfigure Cloud resources according the changed requirements of the Cloud Application. More specifically, during the execution Cloud Agency allows the user for the Monitoring of the infrastructure in terms of resource utilization and for the definition of some strategy of autonomic reconfiguration. Reconfiguration can use management facilities by stopping, starting, moving instances, but it could ask for provisioning of additional resources. By going more in details, Cloud Agency exposes four main services:

- The *Provisioning Service* allows the user to discover, acquire and set up resources for deployment of his/her applications. The result of provisioning is a set of Cloud resources that are described, together with the offered service levels, in a Service Level Agreement (SLA).
- The *Management Service* is used both for deployment and for execution. In fact it is needed to configure and start resources before starting the application, and it is necessary to start/stop/migrate and reconfigure in general the resource dynamically during its utilization.
- The *Monitoring Service* is used to take under control Cloud resources in terms of performance indexes and QoS parameters. This service is implemented by the using of dedicated agents that act as probes on the selected resources.
- The *Reconfiguration Service* is in charge of reconfiguring the Cloud infrastructure when some critical events occur, such as saturation or under-utilization of a resource, SLA violation and so on.

Cloud Agency provides asynchronous APIs in order to access the Cloud Agency services. To address this issue Use Cases are designed in terms of Service

Requests, Events and Callbacks. Access to Cloud Agency services will be enabled by *HTTP RESTful interface*. Asynchronous requests are used to ask the Cloud Agency for something to be executed. For example to start a Negotiation, to accept or to refuse an SLA, to change a Policy, etc. They are not-blocking invocations. Execution is started remotely, but the client can continue to run. Completion or failures of requests are notified at client side. Clients are in charge to handle incoming events. Synchronous requests are available to get information. For example clients can ask for reading an SLA, the status of a negotiation, to get the list of vendors, or the list of resources. Queries are synchronous, they return immediately the response if it is available, an exception otherwise. An OCCI compliant Message Transfer Protocol (OCCI-MTP) allows the communication between the client and the Cloud Agency [12,13]. By using this interface, clients can start new provisioning transactions in order to broker the Cloud resources.

The configuration of the resources that are necessary to execute the user's application produced by Semantic Engine and expressed in terms of SLA template may be complemented by the user with other information. In particular the SLA template can include desired service levels and other terms of service like contract duration, data location and billing frequency. In listing 1.3 an example of SLA template is shown. It contains service description terms and guarantee terms in WS-Agreement. The requested resource is a Virtual Machine configuration with an architecture x86, 2 Cores, 2 Gb of available memory and a price not greater than 0.8 $.

Listing 1.3. Service Description Term and Guarantee Term

```
<ws:ServiceDescriptionTerm ws:Name=''Compute'' >
              <Compute>
                   <cpuCores>2</cpuCores>
                        <architecture>x86</architecture>
                        <memory> 2GB </memory>
              </Compute>
</ws:ServiceDescriptionTerm>
         [..]
<wsag:GuaranteeTerm wsag:Name=''Availability''>
         <wsag:Variables>
            <wsag:Variable wsag:Name="Price"
                           wsag:Metric="price/hour" />
                   <wsag:ServiceLevelObjective> 0.8 </
                           wsag:ServiceLevelObjective>
         </wasg:Variables>
         [..]
</wsag:GuaranteeTerm>
```

The SLA template is part of the Call for Proposal (CfP). The last part of the CfP is a set of brokering rules. Examples of brokering rules are the best price, the greatest number of cores, the best accredited provider or the minimum accepted availability. The provisioning service provided by Cloud Agency implements an extension of the Contract Net Interaction Protocol [14]. The CfP is submitted to Cloud Agency that returns one or a number of different solutions, which can be optimal according to different criteria. The sequence diagram that describes the interaction among agents for resource provisioning is shown in Fig. 6.

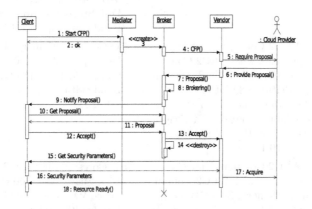

Fig. 6. Interaction among agents for resource provisioning

For each received CFP Cloud Agency creates a broker that searches for vendors that can offer resources with the required QoS (Quality of services). Cloud Vendors neither implement negotiation services, nor provide descriptions of their SLA in machine-readable language. We address these issues by Vendor Agents, which wrap the services of each Cloud provider and return, for each SLA template received from the broker, the available proposal that accomplishes at the best the claimed requirements. The broker collects a number of proposals described in a uniform way and chooses the best one(s) according to the brokering rules. If the user accepts one among the received proposals an SLA is agreed and the offered resources are allocated.

6   A Concrete Use Case

In order to show how the brokering process takes place and the two components (Semantic Engine and Cloud Agency) interact, we present in this section a simple example involving real cloud providers. Please consider that, even if the proposals reported in this example are real, the final result of evaluation may have completely different results with little changes in offerings, that continuously happen in the cloud environment. Let us assume a user (Cloud Application Developer) looking for a Virtual Machine with (i) specific CPU architecture and a fixed amount of memory, (ii) the maximum number of cores, (iii) brokering the best price among the proposals which satisfy (i) and (ii). The user can identify and express in agnostic way her/his requirements with the help of Semantic Engine, by means of the graphical facility shown in Fig. 7, to express the resources' requirements and then to automatically translate them into the SLA template.

Table 1. Available Instance Types And Prices

Offer	Amazon EC2	Windows Azure
xsmall	N/A	CPU Cores: Shared, Memory: 768 MB, Disk Space Web: 20 GB, Disk Space VM Role: 20 GB, Bandwidth: 5, Cost/Hour: $0.04
small	CPU: 1 EC2 Compute Unit (1 virtual core with 1 EC2 Compute Unit), Memory: 1.7 GB, Disk: 160 GB, Platform:32-bit or 64-bit, I/O Performance: Moderate, Cost/Hour Linux/UNIX Usage: $0.09, Cost/Hour Windows Usage $0.115	CPU Cores: 1, Memory: 1.75 GB, Disk Space Web: 230 GB, Disk Space VM Role: 165 GB, Bandwidth: 100, Cost/Hour: $0.12
medium	CPU: 2 EC2 Compute Unit (1 virtual core with 2 EC2 Compute Unit), Memory: 3.75 GB, Disk: 410 GB, Platform:32-bit or 64-bit, I/O Performance: Moderate Cost/Hour Linux/UNIX Usage: $0.180, Cost/Hour Windows Usage $0.230	CPU Cores: 2, Memory: 3.5 GB, Disk Space Web: 500 GB, Disk Space VM Role: 340 GB, Bandwidth: 200, Cost/Hour: $0.24
large	CPU: 4 EC2 Compute Unit (2 virtual core with 2 EC2 Compute Unit), Memory: 7.5 GB, Disk: 850 GB, Platform: 64-bit, I/O Performance: High Cost/Hour Linux/UNIX Usage: $0.360, Cost/Hour Windows Usage $0.460	CPU Cores: 4, Memory: 7 GB, Disk Space Web: 1 TB, Disk Space VM Role: 850 GB, Bandwidth: 400, Cost/Hour: $0.48
xlarge	CPU: 8 EC2 Compute Unit (4 virtual core with 2 EC2 Compute Unit), Memory: 15 GB, Disk: 1690 GB, Platform: 64-bit, I/O Performance: High Cost/Hour Linux/UNIX Usage: $0.720, Cost/Hour Windows Usage $0.920	CPU Cores: 8, Memory: 14 GB, Disk Space Web: 2 TB, Disk Space VM Role: 1890 GB, Bandwidth: 800, Cost/Hour: $0.96

In the example we assume that the user requests a VM with at least 2 GB memory, CPU Intel architecture, the maximum number of cores and that she/he wants to broker a best offer that does not exceed 0.8 $ per hour. The Cloud Agency adds the brokering rules to the SLA template produced by Semantic Engine, asks to vendors for available offers, brokers the best one and allows to close the transaction. Table 1 summarizes some of the available offers of the Amazon EC2 and Microsoft Azure cloud providers. Each cloud provider has an

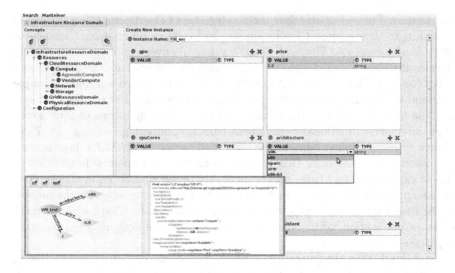

Fig. 7. SLA template graphical composition

offer consisting of several Virtual Machine configurations, which are different in cpu cores, available memory and price.

Vendor Agents of Amazon and Azure have to answer to the broker with their proposal that best fits the user's requirements. In this case Amazon VA will exclude the small offer because of its memory. Three offers remain, but the most powerful machine, compliant with the fixed price is the xlarge. Azure VA will exclude xsmall and small offers because of the memory requirement. Furthermore its xlarge offer is too much expensive. The selected offer eventually is the large one. Finally the broker will select the best price, i.e. Azure's offer. The presented example represents a basic application of a methodology, which is currently been developed, and in which we are considering not only price constraints but also factors like the capacity for each provider, the service levels that providers ensure and the trustworthiness of the provided measured using user's feedback and benchmarking report.

7   Related Works

Semantic and agent technology are being applied to the task of automated resource brokering in many areas, including cloud computing. In this field, the solutions provided are commonly oriented towards standardization.

The cloud service landscape is growing up very rapidly and there are different aspects of this evolution that need to be systematized in a formal way. A good means that can allow overcoming the limits related to heterogeneity of terms used by Cloud vendors are surely ontologies. Indeed for this reason a lot of ontologies related to cloud computing emerged. Darko et al. in [15] try to provide an overview of Cloud Computing ontologies, their types, applications and focuses. They identified four main categories of cloud computing ontologies according to their scopes: Cloud resources and services description, Cloud security, Cloud interoperability and Cloud services discovery and selection. Among the classified ontologies, relevant to our work are ontologies used to discover and select the best Cloud service alternative. In [16] is presented a notable example of Cloud service discovery system based on matchmaking. In the presented system the users can identify the Cloud services required by means of three kinds of requirements: functional requirement (like programming language for PaaS service type), technical requirement (like CPU clock or RAM for IaaS service type) and cost requirement (like max price) as input parameters. In addition to this work, our ontology takes into account additional kind of requirements, such as the application category which is not considered in any other works present in the literature. In particular our approach promotes the Cloud agnostic principles of application development and covers both the design and application deployment part.

SLA@SOI [17] is the main project which aims at offering an open source based SLA management framework that will provide benefits of predictability, transparency and automation in an arbitrary service-oriented infrastructure, being compliant with the OCCI standard. SLA@SOI results are extremely interesting and offer a clear starting basis for the SLA provisioning and management in complex architectures.

In [18] an architecture is presented for a federated Cloud computing environment named InterCloud to support the scaling of applications across multiple vendor Clouds using a Cloud Broker for mediating between service consumers and Cloud coordinators for an allocation of resources that meets QoS needs of users.

Sim [19] proposes an extension of the alternate offers protocol that supports multiple complex negotiation activities in interrelated markets between user agents and broker agents, and between broker agents and provider agents.

In [20] is presented an architectural design of a framework capable of powering the brokerage based cloud services that is currently being developed in the scope of OPTIMIS, an EU FP7 project. In this model a broker is used to serve the needs of several different models. In particular it is used to ensure data confidentiality and integrity to service customers, to match the requirements of cloud consumer with the service provided by the provider, to negotiate with service consumers over SLAs, to maintain performance check on these SLA's and take actions against SLA violation, to effectively deploy services provided by the cloud provider to the customer, to manage the API so that provider does not learn anything about the identity of the service consumer, to securely transfer customer's data to the cloud, to enforce access control decisions uniformly across multiple clouds, to scale resources during load and provide effective staging and pooling services, to securely map identity and access management systems of the cloud provider and consumer, to analyze and take appropriate actions against risks, to handle cloud burst situations effectively. OPTIMIS introduces the problem and the architectural design, but we have not knowledge about an implementation or algorithms to achieve the brokering.

Tordsson [21] explores the heterogeneity of cloud providers, each one with a different infrastructure offer and pricing policy, in a cloud brokering approach that optimizes placement of virtual infrastructures across multiple clouds and also abstracts the deployment and management of infrastructure components in these clouds. Besides he presents a scheduling algorithm for cross-site deployment of applications. However he presents a fine grained interoperability of cloud services by way of a cloud API that do not takes into account the different implementation models for the virtual machine manager (VMM) that are at the base of each of the cloud providers infrastructure.

8   Conclusion

The support for brokering of service level agreement is a weakness in cloud market nowadays. The increasing number of Cloud providers, the lack of interoperability and the heterogeneity in current public Cloud platforms, leads to the need of innovative mechanisms to find the most appropriate Cloud resource configuration as easy and automated as possible. In this paper, which includes results of the mOSAIC project, we have shown how it is possible to build a complex brokering system, that is independent from the cloud provider technologies and allows the user to broker the best cloud service, that is compliant with his requirements. The proposed solution adopts two collaborative modules. The Semantic Engine, whose aim is to create an agnostic description of resource based on users' service requirements and a brokering system, the Cloud Agency, whose aim is to acquire autonomically resources from providers on the basis of SLA evaluation rules finding the most suitable Cloud provider that satisfy users' requirements. Recently we have investigated the chance of using a scalable broker as a service solution. We presented a prototype implementation and provided preliminary performance figures [22]. In future work we aim at improving the proposed solution, investigating mechanisms for dynamic filtering of the proposals.

Acknowledgments. The research leading to these results has received funding from the European Community's Seventh Framework Programme (FP7/2007–2013) under grant agreement n 256910 (mOSAIC Project).

References

1. Amato, A., Venticinque, S.: Multi-objective decision support for brokering of cloud SLA. In: 27th International Conference on Advanced Information Networking and Applications Workshops, WAINA 2013, pp. 1241–1246 (2013)
2. Amato, A., Di Martino, B., Venticinque, S.: Evaluation and brokering of service level agreements for negotiation of cloud infrastructures. In: 7th International Conference for Internet Technology and Secured Transactions, ICITST 2012, London, United Kingdom, pp. 144–149 (2012)
3. mOSAIC. The mOSAIC Project. http://www.mosaic-cloud.eu/

4. Cretella, G., Di Martino, B.: Semantic and matchmaking technologies for discovering, mapping and aligning cloud providerss services. In: Proceedings of the 15th International Conference on Information Integration and Web-based Applications and Services (iiWAS 2013), pp. 380–384 (2013)

5. Venticinque, S.: European research activities in cloud computing. In: Agent Based Services for Negotiation, Monitoring and Reconfiguration of Cloud Resources, pp. 178–202. Cambridge Scholars, January 2012

6. McGuinness, D.L., van Harmelen, F.: Owl web ontology language overview (2004). http://www.w3.org/TR/2004/REC-owl-features-20040210/

7. Open Grid Forum: Open Cloud Computing Interface (OCCI). http://forge.ogf. org/sf/projects/occi-wg

8. Metsch, T., Edmonds, A.: Open Cloud Computing Interface - Infrastructure, GFD-P-R.184, April 2011. http://ogf.org/documents/GFD.184.pdf

9. Di Martino, B., Cretella, G.: Towards a semantic engine for cloud applications development support. In: Proceedings of CISIS-2012: The Sixth International Conference on Complex, Intelligent, and Software Intensive Systems, July 4–6th 2012, Palermo, Italy. IEEE CS Press (2012)

10. Cretella, G., Di Martino, B., Stankovski, V.: Using the mosaics semantic engine to design and develop civil engineering cloud applications. In: Proceedings of 14th International Conference on Information Integration and Web-based Applications and Services (iiWAS 2012), p. 9. ACM (2012)

11. Venticinque, S., Tasquier, L., Di Martino, B.: Agents based cloud computing interface for resource provisioning and management. In: 2012 Sixth International Conference on Complex, Intelligent and Software Intensive Systems (CISIS), pp. 249–256, 4–6 July 2012

12. Amato, A., Tasquier, L., Copie, A.: Vendor agents for iaas cloud interoperability. In: Fortino, G., Badica, C., Malgeri, M., Unland, R. (eds.) IDC 2012. SCI, vol. 446, pp. 271–280. Springer, Heidelberg (2012)

13. Venticinque, S., Amato, A., Di Martino, B.: An OCCI compliant interface for IAAS provisioning and monitoring. In: CLOSER 2012 - Proceedings of the 2nd International Conference on Cloud Computing and Services Science, pp. 163–166 (2012)

14. Fipa, TC Communication. Fipa contract net interaction protocol (2002). http:// www.fipa.org

15. Androcec, D., Vrcek, N., Seva, J.: Cloud computing ontologies: a systematic review. In: MOPAS 2012, The Third International Conference on Models and Ontology-based Design of Protocols, Architectures and Services, pp. 9–14 (2012)

16. Han, T., Sim, K.M.: An ontology-enhanced cloud service discovery system. In: Proceedings of the International MultiConference of Engineers and Computer Scientists, vol. 1, pp. 17–19 (2010)

17. SLA@SOI, sla-at-soi.eu

18. Buyya, Rajkumar, Ranjan, Rajiv, Calheiros, Rodrigo N.: InterCloud: utility-oriented federation of cloud computing environments for scaling of application services. In: Hsu, Ching-Hsien, Yang, Laurence T., Park, Jong Hyuk, Yeo, Sang-Soo (eds.) ICA3PP 2010, Part I. LNCS, vol. 6081, pp. 13–31. Springer, Heidelberg (2010)

19. Sim, K.M.: Towards complex negotiation for cloud economy. In: Bellavista, P., Chang, R.-S., Chao, H.-C., Lin, S.-F., Sloot, P.M.A. (eds.) GPC 2010. LNCS, vol. 6104, pp. 395–406. Springer, Heidelberg (2010)

20. Nair, S.K., Porwal, S., Dimitrakos, T., Ferrer, A.J., Tordsson, J., Sharif, T., Sheridan, C., Rajarajan, M., Khan, A.U.: Towards secure cloud bursting, brokerage and aggregation. In: Proceedings of the 2010 Eighth IEEE European Conference on Web Services, pp. 189–196 (2010)
21. Tordsson, J., Montero, R.S., Moreno-Vozmediano, R., Llorente, I.M.: Cloud brokering mechanisms for optimized placement of virtual machines across multiple providers. Future Gener. Comput. Syst. **28**(2), 358–367 (2012). ISSN: 0167–739X
22. Amato, A., Di Martino, B., Venticinque, S.: Cloud Brokering as a Service. In: 3PGCIC 2013, pp. 9–16 (2013)

A Concurrency Mitigation Proposal for Sharing Environments: An Affinity Approach Based on Applications Classes

Antonio R. Mury[1], Bruno Schulze[1], Fabio L. Licht[2], Luis C.E. de Bona[2], and Mariza Ferro[1]([⊠])

[1] National Laboratory of Scientific Computing, Petrópolis, Brazil
{aroberto,schulze,mariza}@lncc.br
[2] Federal University of Paraná, Curitiba, Brazil
licht@lncc.br,bona@inf.ufpr.br

Abstract. The increased use of virtualized environments has led to numerous research efforts about the possibilities and restrictions of the use of these virtualized environments in cloud computing or for resource consolidation. However, most of these studies are limited to a level of performance analysis, that does not address the effects of concurrency among the various virtual environments, and how to mitigate these effects. The study presented below proposes the concept of affinity, based on the correct combination of certain applications classes, that are able to share the same environment, at the same time, causing less loss of performance. The results show that there are combinations of applications that could share the same environment with minimum loss, but there are combinations that must be avoided. This study also shows the influence of the type of parallel library used for the implementation of these applications.

1 Introduction

The use of virtual environments has increased driven by the adoption of cloud computing solutions, data centers consolidation and legacy systems maintenance. The appeal of cloud computing arises from its use as an additional resource for High-Performance Parallel and Distributed Computing (HPDC), especially concerning its use in support of scientific applications, with many studies devoted to determining the effect of the virtualization layer on the performance.

Those studies were motivated because clouds appear as extra computational resources available on demand, able to satisfy the computational resource need, at any given time, for HPDC applications. However, most of the studies conducted so far, have focused on the performance evaluation comparing one virtualization layer to another or one particular provider or architecture. Little work has been devoted to checking in depth on the effects that the concurrency in these sharing environments has in terms of application' class perspective that would be useful for the development of new cloud schedulers, able to identify the applications that could benefit from the use of cloud computing resources and the applications where the loss in performance would be prohibitive.

© Springer International Publishing Switzerland 2015
A. Al-Saidi et al. (Eds.): ICC 2014, LNCS 8993, pp. 26–45, 2015.
DOI: 10.1007/978-3-319-19848-4_3

Regarding the applications, studies have sought to categorize sets of applications into classes, grouping them based on their characteristics in terms of consumption of computational resources. This type of approach has the advantage of allowing the development of new applications and their association with one of these classes, allowing prediction of its behavior.

What has previously been presented leads immediately to a question about the effects of the concurrency of these classes of applications when running concurrently in virtual environments hosted at the same real resource. Because each application has different system requirements (e.g., memory bound, I/O bound and CPU bound), how would it be possible to predict what would happens when there are many virtual environments with those different classes of applications running on the same real server? What will happen to the performance? A superficial analysis might lead us to think that with the same class of applications competing for the same resources, there will be a performance loss, but is this loss the same for all types of application classes? Which classes of applications can share the same environment to minimize the concurrency and, consequently, the loss of performance? How can the virtualization layer contribute to minimize contention?

Trying to answer these questions and mitigate these problems, this work introduces the concept of *affinity*, defined as the degree of influence that an application has on another applications when running in virtual environments hosted in the same real environment. The study presented here provides a series of tests conducted on three broad classes of applications, whit characteristics present in applications that span the activities related to massively parallel and distributed computing, gaming, business and multimedia. The objective was to analyze the effects in performance for those classes of applications when running in virtualized environments, while competing for the same real resources; and, based on their *affinity*, a proposal of which classes running in virtual environments could be hosted in the same real resource, minimizing the performance loss, and which ones must be avoided in executing the combination at the same resource.

2 Virtual Environment Concurrency and Affinity

In this section, some limitations related to the use of virtualized environments will be presented, especially for HPDC environments and also introduced the concept of affinity among virtual environments (in this case clouds, consolidated data centers or any type of computational environment using virtualization as a tool to encapsulate a particular application or group of applications) will also be introduced.

Regarding the virtualization layer, many studies have been devoted to the examination of the effects of the virtualization layer in the performance of running applications, especially concering the use of cloud computing in support of HPCD. These studies are important for HPDC as the cloud paradigm emerges as an alternative solution for scientific computing, capable of supplying massive on demand computer power, just-in-time, and somehow changing the usage pattern of HPDC environments and the structure, even with some loss of performance [1–4].

The work of Bientinesi, Iakymchuck and Napper [5] deepens the knowledge and points to the diverse demands on the cloud environment facing scientific and commercial applications. Using the cloud to support HPDC, review of the metrics used as a way to evaluate the performance of the environment is necessary. The existing contention problems affect the overall performance, particularly communication. In addition to communication, the results of a series of tests point to aspects that must be considered, such as the variability of the environment, the context exchanges of the cores, the type of processor architecture, the virtual machine and, particularly, the type of application being executed. The same conclusion about the influence of communication, contention and type of application is observed in [6–8]. In [9], there is a detailed analysis of the loss resulting from the contention effects in a virtualized environment and the influence of message-type traffic.

With respect to the concurrency and the contention problem, this is important even for real environments. From the point of view of the HPDC environment, the influence exerted by the system architecture and the contention is well presented in the work of Skinner and Krammer [10], analyzing data obtained over a period of two years and listing the following factors as causes of variability: Symmetric Multiprocessing (SMP) resource contention, communication among and within nodes, kernel process scheduling, cross application contention and system activities. These factors become more critical when looking at an environment, hosting multiple virtualized environments, or running HPCD applications at the same time.

Those effects of the concurrency and the degradation caused by processing in a virtualized environment that consumes all the processor of the real server are presented in [11], which shows the effects over another process in a different virtualized environment, when the other process was allocated on the same real server and had to compete for CPU usage, undermining its processing capacity and performance.

The previous examples show us what can happen with virtual environments when hosted on the same real server. So what would be the best approach to be adopted to minimize this loss when allocating virtualized environments, whether in a cloud, data centers or even on a small scale to optimize the use of real resources?

One of the possible approaches that could be adopted as an example is to analyze the past behavior of combinations of virtualized servers and the actual loss levels recorded in this environment. This analysis would be performed and validated through the use of continuous monitoring of resources and processes, checking the load of network usage, memory and processing. This task, however, is complex and requires a high degree of abstraction, given the amount of totally heterogeneous resources available in a cloud. Goscinski [12] warns that the creation of a mechanism able to control and monitor the impact of an application, finding out if a resource supports such a task execution, is not easy to implement. [13] also consider the effective resource management of a virtualized environments to be a challenging task. They consider that the management systems must rely on analytic models, based on the allocation of resources by running real experiments. However, both approaches incur significant overhead.

Another approach is to use the evaluation of a class of applications as proposed in the work of Colella [14]. The work proposes the use of the Dwarfs, where the applications are divided into classes, and each one of these classes is able to capture all the main characteristics of these applications. The concept of the Dwarfs is presented in more detail in the following section.

So, based on what has been possible to research so far, there is still a gap in evaluating the effects of the concurrency in a virtualized environment and how to minimize these effects. This work proposes an approach based on the Dwarfs classification, evaluating the effects of the concurrency among the classes of Dwarfs, identifying those classes hosted in virtualized environments, that could share the same real environment, with the minimum loss of performance.

This work proposes the use of the term affinity, characterized by the degree of compatibility between classes of applications, whose concurrent execution in the same computing environment would result in a minimum loss for these applications and the environment itself. Although the virtual environments are the focus of the analysis and the mitigation of the performance loss, this concept could also be used for real environments.

The work presented here is ongoing research about the thirteen proposed Dwarf classes. At the current stage of the study, three classes have been evaluated. Of the fourteen areas identified in the study of the Dwarfs, eleven of these areas are covered with a high degree of adherence. The Dwarf approach is presented in more depth in the next section.

3 Applications and Dwarfs

With the aim of categorizing the styles of computation seen in scientific computing, the work of Colella [14] identified seven numerical methods that he believed to be important for science and engineering and introduced the "Seven Dwarfs" of scientific computing. These Dwarfs are defined at a high level of abstraction to explain their behavior across different HPDC applications, and each class of Dwarfs shows similarities in computation and communication. According to his definition, applications of a particular class can be implemented differently with the change in numerical methods over time, but the underlying patterns have remained the same over generations of change and will remain the same in future implementations.

The Berkeley team in parallel computation extended these classifications to thirteen Dwarfs after they examined important applications domains. They were interested in applying Dwarfs to a broader number of computational methods and investigating how well the Dwarfs could capture computation and communication patterns for a large range of applications. Ideally, the Berkeley team would like good performance across the set of Dwarfs to indicate that new manycore architectures and programming models will perform well for a broad range of future applications. Traditionally, applications target existing hardware and programming models but instead, they wanted to design hardware keeping future applications in mind [15]. They compared the Dwarf classes against collections of benchmarks for embedded computing (42 benchmarks EEMBC[1]) and for desktop and server computing (28 benchmarks SPEC2006[2]). Additionally, they examined important application domains: artificial intelligence/machine learning, database software and computer graphics/games. The goal was to delineate applications requirements to draw broader conclusions about hardware requirements. A diverse set of important scientific applications is supported by the current 13 Dwarfs. A more complete discussion about the thirteen Dwarfs can be found in [15–17].

The Dwarf classes that are under investigation at in this present work are Dense Linear Algebra (DLA), Structured Grid (SG) and Graph Traversal (GT). We focus on these classes because there are many scientific applications in many scientific areas classified in these classes, as seen in Fig. 1. Additionally, we focus on these classes because these three classes together offer a diverse set of patterns that comprises a more complete set of experiments. Scientific applications classified in the DLA class are computationally limited while in the GT class, scientific applications are memory latency limited and in SG class are more memory bandwidth limited. However, to investigate whether one single application completely captures the breadth of a Dwarf, our longer term investigations will include more than one application for each class, which could present different aspects of a given Dwarf. Next, Dwarf classes are described with the applications that are being used in this work.

1. Dense Linear Algebra Dwarf class computations involve a set of mathematical operators performed on scalars, vectors or matrices when most of the matrix or vector elements are non-zeros. Dense in this Dwarf refers to the data structure accessed during the computation. The arithmetic intensity of the computation operating upon the data may be low intensity operators (scalar-vector, vector-vector, matrix-vector, matrix-matrix, vector reduction, vector scan and dot product) that carry a constant number of arithmetic operations per data element. This Dwarf has a high ratio of math-to-load operations and a high degree of data interdependency between threads. These set of mathematical operators are the basis of more sophisticated solvers such as LU Decomposition (LUD) or Cholesky and exhibit high arithmetic intensity [16]. Generally, such applications use unit-stride memory accesses to read data from rows and strided access to read data from columns. Applications classified as DLA are relevant across a variety of domains such as in material science to molecular physics and nanoscale science; in energy assurance for combustion, fusion and nuclear energy; in fundamental science

---

[1] http://www.eembc.org/.
[2] http://www.spec.org/cpu2006.

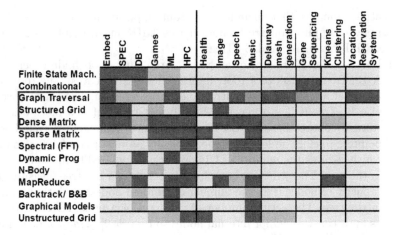

Fig. 1. Some examples of scientific areas that have applications characterized by Dwarf classes (http://stamp.stanford.edu). The colors represent the relevance of the class to domain applications (more relevant - red to blue - less relevant). Emphasis is on classes used in this work (Color figure online).

such as astrophysics and nuclear physics; in engineering design for aero-dynamics. Representative algorithms of this class are LUD, matrix transpose, triangular solver, symmetric eigensolver, clustering algorithms such as Kmeans and Stream Cluster, and many others. We performed experiments with the LUD and Kmeans algorithms.

(a) LUD is an algorithm to calculate the solutions of a set of linear equations that decomposes a matrix as the product of a lower triangular matrix and an upper triangular matrix to achieve a triangular form that can be used to solve a system of linear equations easily. A matrix $A \in \mathbb{R}^{n \times n}$ has a LU factorization *iff* all of its leading principal minors are non-zeros, i.e., $det(A[1:k,1:k]) \neq 0$ for $k = 1:n-1$.

(b) The Kmeans is a well-known clustering algorithm used extensively in data mining that is a method that partitions n points that lie in $d-$dimensional space into k clusters in this way: seeded with k initial cluster centers, Kmeans assigns every data point to its closest center, and then recomputes the new centers as the means of their assigned points. This process of assigning data points and readjusting centers is repeated until it stabilizes.

2. The Graph Traversal Dwarf class applications must traverse a number of objects in a graph and examine characteristics of those objects such as would be used for search. A graph or a network is an intuitive and useful abstraction for analyzing relational data where unique entities are represented as vertices, and the interactions between them are depicted as edges. The vertices and edges can further be assigned attributes based on the information they encapsulate. Such algorithms typically involve a significant amount of random memory access for indirect lookups and little computation [16].

Scientific domains that include important applications in this class and examples of application are bioinformatics (MUMmer), graphs and search (Breadth-First Search and B+Tree).

(a) B+Tree is an n-ary tree often with a large number of children per node. A B+Tree consists of a root, internal nodes and leaves. The root may be either a leaf or a node with two or more children. The primary value of a B+Tree is in storing data for efficient retrieval in a block-oriented storage context because B+Trees have very high fan-out (number of pointers to child nodes in a node, typically on the order of 100 or more), which reduces the number of I/O operations required to find an element in the tree. The order, or branching factor, b of a B+ tree measures the capacity of nodes (i.e., the number of children nodes) for internal nodes in the tree. The actual number of children for a node, referred to here as m, is constrained for internal nodes so that $[b/2] \leq m \leq b$. Leaf nodes have no children, but are constrained so that the number of keys must be at least $[b/2]$ and at most $b - 1$. In the situation where a B+Tree is nearly empty, it contains only one node, which is a leaf node. The root is also the single leaf in this case. This node is permitted to have as little as one key if necessary and at most b.

3. Structured Grid algorithms organize data in a regular multidimensional grid where computation proceeds as a series of grid updates. For each grid update, all points are updated using values from a small neighborhood around each point. The neighborhood is normally implicit in the data and determined by the algorithm. Due to their inherent parallelism and computation intense nature, structured grid applications are typically a good fit for the manycore architectures such as the GPU. Structured grid algorithms appear in many scientific domain, which are cited in the following list with an example of an application for each algorith: medical imaging (Leukocyte, Heart Wall and Particle Filter), physics simulations (HotSpot), image processing (Speckle Reducing Anisotropic Diffusion) and biological simulations (Myocyte) [17].

(a) Speckle Reducing Anisotropic Diffusion (SRAD) is an image processing application for ultrasonic and radar images. SRAD reduces the noise of a given image while maintaining its important features. Each element of the structured grid represents a pixel of the image.

Some evidence for the existence of the equivalence classes proposed by the Dwarfs can also be found in some numerical libraries such as The Fastest Fourier Transform in the West (FFTW) [18], a software library for computing discrete Fourier transforms (equivalent to the Spectral Methods Dwarf class), the LAPACK/ScaLapack [19] software library for numerical linear algebra (equivalent of the DLA Dwarf class) and OSKI [20], a collection of primitives that provide automatically tuned computational kernels on sparse matrices (Sparse Linear Algebra class - SLA). The thirteen Dwarfs are also related to the Intel classification of computation in three categories: Recognition, Mining and Synthesis (RMS). The RMS applications are considered important to guide new architectural research and development that comprises applications in Artificial

Intelligence and Machine Learning, databases, games and computer graphics. These applications are represented by diverse Dwarf classes, such as DLA, SLA, Spectral Methods, Backtrack and Branch Bound, and others [15]. Rodinia [21], Parboil [22], Torch [16] and Parallel Dwarfs Project[3] are open-source benchmark suites that implement applications based on a subset of the 13 Dwarfs. The Rodinia applications are designed for heterogeneous computing infrastructures, and the applications use OpenMP and CUDA to allow comparisons between manycore GPUs vs. multi-core CPUs. The Parboil implementations are on GPU and some basic CPU implementations. The Torch project identified several kernels for benchmarking purposes classified accordingly to the 13 Dwarfs and the authors discuss possible code optimization strategies that can be applied to these kernels. The Parallel Dwarfs project teams also adopt the 13 Dwarfs classification to describe the underlying computation in each of their benchmarks. The classification corresponds to a suite of 13 kernels parallelized using various technologies such as OpenMP, TPL and MPI code.

These examples motivate the Dwarf use as a way of categorizing scientific applications, both for the importance of libraries and application areas mentioned as well as for these recent benchmark suite developments, which cover new architectures and could indicate the relevance and contemporariness of these classes for scientific community.

The experiments conducted in this work using Dwarf classes are presented in next section.

4   Methodology

Two different experiments with different sets of tests were carried out to assess the influence of the concurrency. The first experiment, the most common experiment, aimed to create a baseline for comparison, and consisted of verifying the performance of the Dwarfs in the real and in the virtual environment without the effect of concurrency. The second experiment aimed to verify the effects of concurrency by the two-by-two combination of the three chosen Dwarfs, mixing real and virtual environments.

Both experiments also sought to determine the effect of the type of libraries used in the implementation of the Dwarfs. For testing OpenMP [23] and OpenCL [24] libraries were used because both libraries allow parallel execution on a CPU, and the results obtained showed that the implementation using OpenCL libraries was more stable the implementation using OpenMP.

The first experiment consisted of the following tests for the baseline:

1. Real Environment without concurrency, and
2. Virtual Environment without concurrency.

---

[3] http://paralleldwarfs.codeplex.com/.

The second experiment consisted of the following tests for the concurrency effects:

1. Real Environment versus Virtual Environment,
2. Virtual Environment versus Real Environment
3. Real Environment versus Real Environment, and
4. Virtual Environment versus Virtual Environment.

The values used in the graph represent the percentage increase in the runtime of the algorithms when implemented in a real or virtual environment, using a baseline to calculate this increase in the runtime of the algorithm without concurrency in the real or virtualized environment respectively.

In the graphs the result is closest to the center, and the lowest loss was caused by the concurrency. The graphs also differentially present the performances of the libraries used in the implementation (OpenMP and OpenCL). Although the focus of this work is the analysis of concurrency or virtualized environments sharing the same resources, the analysis of concurrency in real environments is also presented.

4.1 Experimental Infrastructure

The experimental infrastructure used three real servers, each with two Xeon 5520 (2.26 GHz) processor with hyper-threading (HT) technology and virtualization instructions, 24 GB of DDR3 RAM (1333) and Gigabit Ethernet connection. In each server, two virtual machines were implemented, and the set of tests performed in each experiment were made, both in the real environment and in the virtual environment, by the two-by-two combination of the servers and virtual machines. Twenty samples were generated for each test, and the comparison among them was made based on the average, considering the 95 % confidence interval.

4.2 Results Analysis

In this section we will present the results of the tests considering the concurrency among the four chosen algorithms. Although the focus of this work was to assess the effects of the concurrency when consolidating virtualized environments on a real server, we also present the results considering the concurrency in real environments. The term baseline means the loss of performance of the running application when the environment in which it is being executed is shared by another application.

Evaluation of the Concurrency with the LUD Algorithm as the Baseline. Figure 2 shows the results with the LUD algorithm, as baseline, running in a real environment under concurrency from other virtual or real environments hosting the LUD or Kmeans or B+Tree or SRAD algorithm. In the figure, with the exception of the concurrency of the real or virtual B+Tree, when running all other algorithms implemented with OpenCL libraries, the results are better (less loss) than when run with OpenMP, but the best results were obtained with the B+Tree algorithm running concurrently in a virtual environment (20 % loss) and the B+Tree algorithm running concurrently in a real environment (40 % loss). The worst combination was the Real LUD with the virtual SRAD environment (143 % loss), the virtual LUD environment (140 % loss) and the virtual Kmeans (138 % loss) running with an algorithm implemented with OpenMP libraries. With respect to the implementations using OpenCL, the loss varied from 64 % with virtual B+Tree to 97 % with virtual Kmeans.

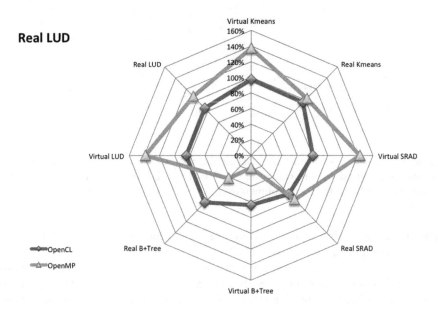

Fig. 2. Performance loss value of the LUD application algorithm executed in a real environment, caused by the concurrency of LUD or B+Tree or Kmeans or SRAD running in a real or virtual environment.

Figure 3 shows the results with the LUD algorithm, as baseline, running in a virtual environment under concurrency from other virtual or real environments hosting the LUD or Kmeans or B+Tree or SRAD algorithm. In the figure, with the exception of the concurrency of the real or virtual B+Tree, running all others algorithms implemented with OpenCL libraries, the results are better than with OpenMP, and the best results were obtained with SRAD running concurrently in a real environment (11 % loss) and SRAD running concurrently in a virtual environment (21 % loss).

The worst combination was the virtual LUD with the virtual Kmeans environment (211 % loss), the virtual LUD environment (176 % loss) and the real LUD (147 % loss) implemented with OpenMP libraries. With respect to the

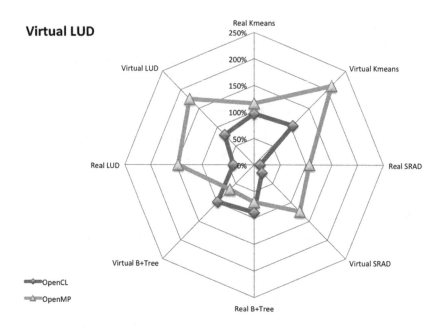

Fig. 3. Performance loss value of LUD application algorithm executed in a virtual environment, caused by the concurrency of LUD or B+Tree or Kmeans or SRAD running in a real or virtual environment.

implementations using OpenCL, they are worse than using OpenMP libraries only for virtual B+Tree and Real B+Tree.

The results above show that if a real server runs a LUD algorithm, and there is the need to share this server with another application, the best choice is to allocate an application running the B+Tree algorithm (preferably encapsulated in a virtual environment), with both the LUD and the B+Tree implemented with OpenMP.

For LUD running in a virtual environment, the best choice is to share with another application running the SRAD algorithm (preferably in the same real environment), with both LUD and SRAD implemented with OpenCL libraries.

The final conclusion is that for applications with the LUD algorithm, the best choice is to have this application encapsulated in a virtual environment and sharing the real environment with an SRAD application in a real or virtual environment respectively, implementing both with OpenCL libraries.

Evaluation of the Concurrency with the B+Tree Algorithm as the Baseline. Figure 4 shows the results with the B+Tree algorithm, as baseline, running in a real environment under concurrency with other virtual or real environments hosting the LUD or the Kmeans or the B+Tree or the SRAD algorithm. In the figure, for a B+Tree algorithm running in a real environment, with respect to all possible combinations of algorithms and environments, the best results were obtained with the implementation using OpenMP libraries (just for real B+Tree concurrent with another real B+tree or with SRAD; the loss of performance was similar). The best result was obtained sharing the same environment with a real or virtual environment, running a Kmeans algorithm application.

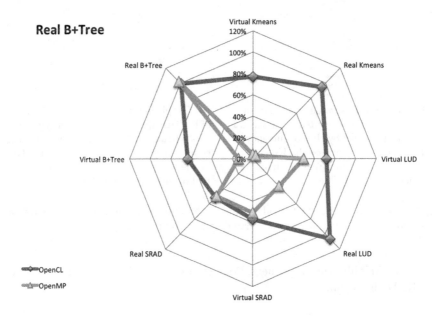

Fig. 4. Performance loss value of the B+Tree application algorithm executed in a real environment, caused by the concurrency of LUD or B+Tree or Kmeans or SRAD running in a real or virtual environment.

Figure 5(a) shows the results with the B+Tree algorithm, as baseline, running in a virtual environment under concurrency with other virtual or real environment hosting the LUD or the Kmeans or the B+Tree or the SRAD algorithm. The figure shows that for all types of algorithms implemented with OpenCL libraries, the results were worse than for the OpenMP, except for the SRAD algorithm. Figure 5(b) shows a details of a loss between 0 % to 20 %. The best result for the implementation with OpenCL was obtained sharing the processing with the real SRAD (5 % loss) and after the virtual SRAD (15 % loss).

For all the algorithms implemented with the OpenMP libraries, the loss ranges from 4 % for the concurrency with a virtual environment hosting the Kmeans algorithm to 16 % for a virtual environment with the B+Tree and the SRAD algorithms. So the best choice to share a server running a real or virtual environment running a B+Tree algorithm application is to share it with the LUD or the Kmeans or the B+Tree or the SRAD with the implementation

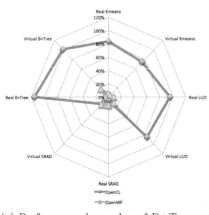 

(a) Performance loss value of B+Tree application algorithm executed in a virtual environment, caused by the concurrency of the LUD or the B+Tree or the Kmeans or the SRAD running in a real or virtual environment.

(b) Graph detail performance loss value of B+Tree application algorithm executed in a virtual environment, caused by the concurrency of the LUD or the B+Tree or the Kmeans or the SRAD running in a real or virtual environment.

Fig. 5. Results with the B+Tree algorithm, as baseline, running in a virtual environment under concurrency with other virtual or real environment.

using OpenMP libraries implementations with OpenCL should be used only for the SRAD algorithm.

Evaluation of the Concurrency with the Kmeans Algorithm as the Baseline. Figure 6 shows the results with the Kmeans algorithm, as baseline, running in a real environment with concurrency from other virtual or real environments hosting the LUD or the Kmeans or the B+Tree or the SRAD algorithm. In the figure, for a Kmeans algorithm running in a real environment, with respect to all possible combinations of algorithms and environments, the best results were obtained with the implementation using OpenMP libraries, except for the SRAD running concurrently in real or virtual environments or for LUD running in a virtual environment. For these three cases, the best results were obtained with the algorithms implemented using OpenCL. The best result was obtained with a 4 % loss for the sharing with the B+Tree virtual environment and 8 % loss for the sharing with the B+Tree running in the real environment (both with OpenMP implementation).

Figure 7 shows the results with the Kmeans algorithm, as baseline, running in a virtual environment with concurrency from other virtual or real environments hosting the LUD or the Kmeans or the B+Tree or the SRAD algorithm. In the figure, for a Kmeans algorithm running in a virtual environment, with respect to all possible combinations of algorithms and environments, the best results were obtained with the implementation using OpenMP libraries, except for the SRAD

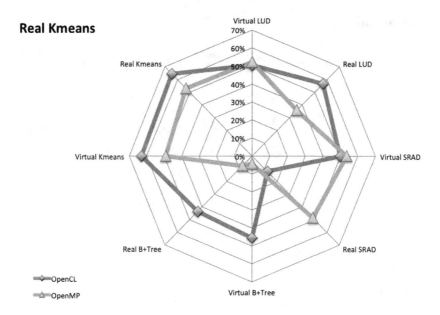

Fig. 6. Performance loss value of Kmeans application algorithm executed in a real environment, caused by the concurrency of LUD or B+Tree or Kmeans or SRAD running in a real or virtual environment.

running concurrently in real or virtual environments or for Kmeans running in a real environment. For these three cases, the best results were obtained with the algorithms implemented using OpenCL. Comparing the real Kmeans as a baseline with the virtual Kmeans as a baseline, the difference in performance between the two approaches concurring with itself (virtual Kmeans and real Kmeans, respectively), the reason was the load of the data already completed before the execution of the concurrent algorithm.

The best result was obtained with a 4 % loss for the sharing with the B+Tree virtual environment and 8 % loss for the sharing with the B+Tree running in the real environment (both with OpenMP implementation). The conclusion is that for the real or virtual Kmeans as baseline the best combination is to run Kmeans concurrently with the B+Tree using OpenMP libraries.

Evaluation of the Concurrency with the SRAD Algorithm as the Baseline. Figure 8(a) shows the results with the SRAD algorithm, as baseline, running in a real environment under concurrency with other virtual or real environment hosting the LUD or the kmeans or the B+Tree or the SRAD algorithm. In the figure, for an SRAD algorithm running in a real environment, with respect to all possible combinations of algorithms and environments, the best results were obtained with the implementation using OpenMP libraries, except for the SRAD

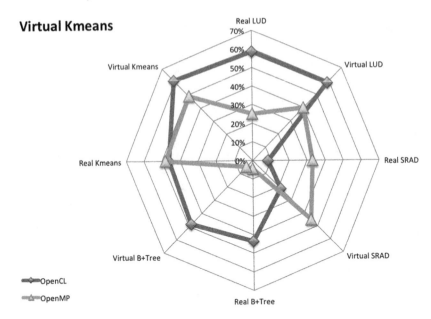

Fig. 7. Performance loss value of the Kmeans application algorithm executed in a virtual environment, caused by the concurrency of LUD or B+Tree or Kmeans or SRAD running in a real or virtual environment.

running concurrently in a real or virtual environment or for LUD running in a real environment. For these three cases, the best results were obtained with the algorithms implemented using OpenCL. The best result was obtained with 61 % loss for the sharing with the B+Tree virtual environment implemented with OpenMP libraries, as detailed in Fig. 8(b). In this test, the worst combination: real SRAD with virtual LUD with a loss of 758 %.

Figure 9 shows the results with the SRAD algorithm, as baseline, running in a virtual environment with concurrency from other virtual or real environments hosting the LUD or the Kmeans or the B+Tree or the SRAD algorithm.

In the figure, for an SRAD algorithm running in a virtual environment, with respect to all possible combinations of algorithms and environments, the best results were obtained with the implementation using OpenCL libraries, except for the LUD running concurrently in a virtual environment or the Kmeans running concurrently in a virtual environment or the B+Tree running concurrently in a virtual environment. For these three cases, the best results were obtained with the algorithms implemented using OpenCL.

The best result was obtained with 14 % loss for the sharing with the SRAD running in a real environment implemented with OpenCL libraries. The conclusion is that for the real or virtual SRAD as the baseline, the best combination is to run SRAD concurrently with SRAD (virtual or real) using OpenCL libraries.

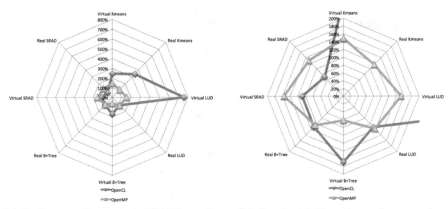

(a) Performance loss value of SRAD application algorithm executed in a real environment, caused by the concurrency of the LUD or the B+Tree or the Kmeans or the SRAD running in a real or virtual environment.

(b) Graph detailing the performance loss value of the SRAD application algorithm executed in a real environment, caused by the concurrency of the LUD or the B+Tree or the Kmeans or the SRAD running in a real or virtual environment.

Fig. 8. Results with the SRAD algorithm, as baseline, running in a real environment under concurrency with other virtual or real environment.

4.3   Results and Conclusions

Table 1 shows the best combinations among the four chosen algorithms and the implementation libraries. The analysis of the concurrency shown in this work just presents the results of the pairwise comparison between the four types of algorithms based on Dwarf classifications running concurrently, but ongoing research shows that the performance loss when adding more than one of these four types

Table 1. Comparison table showing the best combination in concurrent environments. R and V indicate that algorithms were executed in a real or virtual environment, respectively.

	R Kmeans	V Kmeans	R SRAD	V SRAD	R B+Tree	V B+Tree
R LUD						OpenMP
V LUD			OpenCL	OpenCL		
R Kmeans			OpenCL			OpenMP
V Kmeans			OpenCL		OpenMP	OpenMP
R SRAD			OpenCL			OpenMP
V SRAD			OpenCL			
R B+Tree	OpenMP	OpenMP				
V B+Tree	OpenMP	OpenMP	OpenCL		OpenMP	

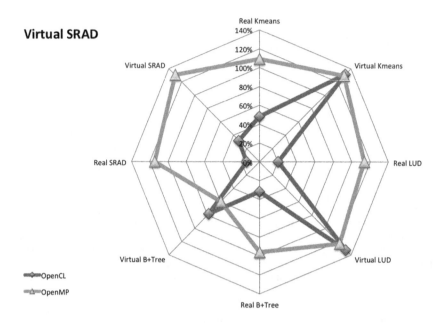

Fig. 9. Performance loss value of the SRAD application algorithm executed in a virtual environment, caused by the concurrency of the LUD or the B+Tree or the Kmeans or the SRAD running in a real or virtual environment.

of algorithms has a constant pattern. Table 1 shows the baseline algorithms in the columns.

5   Final Considerations

The presented study sought to evaluate the effects of application concurrency. The importance of this study increases as the use of virtual environments has become increasingly common as a means of optimizing the use of real resources (consolidation) or the extent that cloud computing is presented as a solution to obtain additional resources on demand. The results obtained so far tend to provide subsidies for the best combinations among the various applications sharing these resources. The results of the experiments showed that if there is a real need for resource sharing and there is, consequently, a concurrency in usage, i.e., some types of applications can coexist without significant degradation of the environment, enabling this sharing, while other combinations of applications should be avoided.

As an extension of this work, the results and conclusions presented here can be used to develop application schedulers for these environments to minimize the loss resulting from concurrency, as well as the estimated value of the performance loss. To evaluate the applications, the approach adopted here was the concept of classes of Dwarfs. The four classes of applications used for the tests in this study were chosen because these four cover most of the types of existing applications.

The results presented, in addition to measuring the amount of performance loss during the sharing of resources, also allowed us to verify that the order in which the scheduling of execution of the applications directly influences the performance. For example, in the case of the LUD application implemented in OpenMP, when running in a real environment, with the concurrent instantiation of a virtual environment with the same algorithm, the average loss was 136 % for the application in the real environment and 144 % for the virtual environment, but in the case of a running virtual environment with the same application, when another application was instantiated in the real environment, the loss was 147 % (144 %, case before) and 139 % (136 %, case before), respectively.

Another important aspect was the influence of the type of the parallel library used to implement the algorithms. This study evaluated OpenMP and OpenCL libraries. This study proved important, as in the case of the tests that assessed the SRAD algorithm in a real environment, running concurrently with the LUD algorithm encapsulated in a virtualized environment using OpenCL libraries, where the performance loss was 758 % for the SRAD algorithm, whereas the same test, now with the use of OpenMP libraries caused a loss of 153 % for SRAD.

Table 1 presents a synthesis of the results showing the types of applications that could be running concurrently with less performance loss and the best type of parallel library. The results obtained allow us to propose the concept of affinity, which is characterized by the degree of compatibility between classes of applications, where concurrent execution in the same computing environment would result in a minimum loss for these applications and the environment itself, and its use in support of virtual or real resource sharing.

References

1. Lee, C.A.: A perspective on scientific cloud computing. In: Proceedings of the 19th ACM International Symposium on High Performance Distributed Computing, HPDC 2010, pp. 451–459. ACM, New York (2010)
2. Tudoran, R., Costan, A., Antoniu, G., Bougé, L.: A performance evaluation of azure and nimbus clouds for scientific applications. In: Proceedings of the 2nd International Workshop on Cloud Computing Platforms, CloudCP 2012, pp. 4:1–4:6. ACM, New York (2012)
3. U.S., E.D.: The magellan report on cloud computing for science (2011). http://magellan.alcf.anl.gov/
4. CERN: Helix nebula the science cloud: A catalyst for change in europe (2013). http://cds.cern.ch/record/1537032/files/HelixNebula-2013-002.pdf
5. Bientinesi, P., Iakymchuk, R., Napper, J.: HPC on competitive cloud resources. In: Furht, B., Escalante, A. (eds.) Handbook of Cloud Computing, pp. 493–516. Springer, US (2010)
6. Cholia, S., Shalf, J., Wasserman, H.J., Wright, N.J.: Performance analysis of high performance computing applications on the amazon web services cloud. In: Proceedings of the 2010 IEEE Second International Conference on Cloud Computing Technology and Science, CLOUDCOM 2010, pp. 159–168. IEEE Computer Society, Washington, DC (2010)

7. He, Q., Zhou, S., Kobler, B., Duffy, D., McGlynn, T.: Case study for running HPC applications in public clouds. In: Proceedings of the 19th ACM International Symposium on High Performance Distributed Computing, HPDC 2010, pp. 395–401. ACM, New York (2010)

8. El-Khamra, Y., Kim, H., Jha, S., Parashar, M.: Exploring the performance fluctuations of HPC workloads on clouds. In: Proceedings of the 2010 IEEE Second International Conference on Cloud Computing Technology and Science, CLOUD-COM 2010, pp. 383–387. IEEE Computer Society, Washington, DC (2010)

9. Ekanayake, J., Fox, G.: High performance parallel computing with clouds and cloud technologies. In: Avresky, D.R., Diaz, M., Bode, A., Ciciani, B., Dekel, E. (eds.) CloudComp 2009. LNICST, vol. 34, pp. 20–38. Springer, Heidelberg (2009)

10. Skinner, D., Kramer, W.: Understanding the causes of performance variability in HPC workloads. In: 2013 IEEE International Symposium on Workload Characterization (IISWC), pp. 137–149 (2005)

11. Technologies, C.: The complete guide to monitoring virtualized environments (2013). http://cai.com/co/media/Files/eBooks/the-complete-guide-to-monitoring-virtualized-environments.PDF

12. Goscinski, W., Abramson, D.: Motor: A virtual machine for high performance computing. In: International Symposium on High-Performance Distributed Computing, pp. 171–182 (2006)

13. Vasić, N., Novaković, D., Miučin, S., Kostić, D., Bianchini, R.: Dejavu: accelerating resource allocation in virtualized environments. SIGARCH Comput. Archit. News **40**(1), 423–436 (2012)

14. Colella, P.: Defining software requirements for scientific computing. DARPA HPCS Presentation (2004)

15. Asanovic, K., Bodik, R., Catanzaro, B.C., Gebis, J.J., Husbands, P., Keutzer, K., Patterson, D.A., Plishker, W.L., Shalf, J., Williams, S.W., Yelick, K.A.: The landscape of parallel computing research: a view from berkeley. Technical report UCB/EECS-2006-183, EECS Department, University of California, Berkeley, December 2006

16. Kaiser, A., Williams, S., Madduri, K., Ibrahim, K., Bailey, D., Demmel, J., Strohmaier, E.: TORCH computational reference kernels: a testbed for computer science research. Technical report UCB/EECS-2010-144, EECS Department, University of California, Berkeley, December 2010

17. Springer, P.: Berkeley's Dwarfs on CUDA. Technical report, RWTH Aachen University, Seminar Project (2011)

18. Frigo, M., Johnson, G.S.: The design and implementation of FFTW3. In: Proceedings of the IEEE, pp. 216–231 (2005)

19. Blackford, L.S., Choi, J., Cleary, A.J., Demmel, J., Dhillon, I.S., Dongarra, J., Hammarling, S., Henry, G., Petitet, A., Stanley, K., Walker, D.W., Whaley, R.C.: ScaLAPACK: a portable linear algebra library for distributed memory computers - design issues and performance. In: Proceedings of the 1996 ACM/IEEE conference on Supercomputing, p. 5. IEEE (1996)

20. Williams, S., Oliker, L., Vuduc, R., Shalf, J., Yelick, K., Demmel, J.: Optimization of sparse matrix-vector multiplication on emerging multicore platforms. In: Proceedings of the 2007 ACM/IEEE Conference on Supercomputing, SC 2007, pp. 38:1–38:12. ACM, New York (2007)

21. Che, S., Boyer, M., Meng, J., Tarjan, D., Sheaffer, J.W., Lee, S.H., Skadron, K.: Rodinia: A benchmark suite for heterogeneous computing. In: IISWC, pp. 44–54. IEEE (2009)

22. Stratton, J.A., Rodrigrues, C., Sung, I.J., Obeid, N., Chang, L., Liu, G., Hwu, W.M.W.: Parboil: a revised benchmark suite for scientific and commercial throughput computing. Technical report IMPACT-12-01, University of Illinois at Urbana-Champaign, Urbana, March 2012
23. Chapman, B., Jost, G.: Pas, Rvd: Using OpenMP: Portable Shared Memory Parallel Programming (Scientific and Engineering Computation). The MIT Press, Cambridge (2007)
24. Stone, J.E., Gohara, D., Shi, G.: Opencl: a parallel programming standard for heterogeneous computing systems. IEEE Des. Test **12**(3), 66–73 (2010)

On Cloud Spot Market:
An Overview of the Research

Zheng Li[1,2]([⊠]), Liam O'Brien[3], Rajiv Ranjan[2,4], Shayne Flint[2],
and Albert Y. Zomaya[5]

[1] CRL Lab, National Information and Communications Technology Australia
(NICTA), 7 London Circuit, Canberra, ACT 2601, Australia
zheng.li@nicta.com.au
[2] School of Computer Science, Australian National University (ANU), Canberra,
ACT 0200, Australia
shayne.flint@anu.edu.au
[3] ICT Innovation and Services, Geoscience Australia, Cnr Jerrabomberra Avenue
and Hindmarsh Drive, Symonston, ACT 2609, Australia
liamob99@hotmail.com
[4] CSIRO Computational Informatics, CS & IT Building, Building 108, North Rd,
ANU Campus, Acton, ACT 2601, Australia
raj.ranjan@csiro.au
[5] School of Information Technologies, The University of Sydney,
Sydney, NSW 2006, Australia
albert.zomaya@sydney.edu.au

Abstract. In Cloud computing, Infrastructure-as-a-Service (IaaS) can
be purchased with three pricing schemes, namely reserved pricing, on-
demand pricing and spot pricing. Within the spot pricing model, the
spot Cloud resources usually refer to the spare compute capacity that
can be auctioned in a spot market. A commercial spot market has been
established since Amazon launched its spot instance service. Unlike the
straightforward fixed-price schemes, the market-driven mechanism
behind spot pricing is inevitably sophisticated for both Cloud consumers
and providers. In addition, the de facto vendor Amazon does not disclose
any backend detail except for its recent spot price history. To help practitioners better understand the spot market and help researchers identify
research opportunities, we focused on Amazon's spot service and investigated the relevant studies of the Cloud spot market. The result of our
investigation has been organized and summarized into an overview of the
current research, as described in this chapter.

Keywords: Amazon EC2 · Cloud computing · Market-driven mechanism · Spot market · Spot pricing

1 Introduction

With the boom in Cloud computing, compute capacity as a utility has been
widely recognized and accepted. To help fully utilize compute resources, providing spot resources in the Cloud market is supposed to be a promising way

© Springer International Publishing Switzerland 2015
A. Al-Saidi et al. (Eds.): ICC 2014, LNCS 8993, pp. 46–61, 2015.
DOI: 10.1007/978-3-319-19848-4_4

from the perspective of market economy [22,23]. In fact, a commercial spot market has been established when Amazon's spot instance service was launched in December 2009. Amazon uses a continuous market-driven mechanism to sell spare EC2 instance resources [2]. Through varying prices in real-time based on supply and demand, the pricing model of spot instances is supposed to complement Amazon's On-Demand and Reserved Instance pricing models. On the one hand, the spot prices are generally far below the on-demand prices. On the other hand, although the spot instances could be slightly more expensive than the same type of reserved instances, the spot service consumers do not need to pay any reservation fee in advance. As such, by potentially incurring less cost, the spot instances could be the most cost-effective service among the three options for obtaining compute capacity.

Nevertheless, unlike the static and straightforward pricing models of on-demand and reserved instances, the market-driven mechanism for pricing spot instance service is dynamic and sophisticated. Furthermore, as the only provider offering spot instance service in the market, Amazon does not disclose any back-end detail of the market-driven mechanism. Consequently, since the overall supply and demand of spot resources are both uncertain during runtime, spot service consumers would have to suffer from the irregular fluctuations in service price and availability. In fact, the prices of a particular Amazon instance type could fluctuate significantly and variously across different zones even within a day, as shown in Fig. 1. Note that us-east-1a, us-east-1b, and us-east-1c indicate three available zones where the spot instances are located.

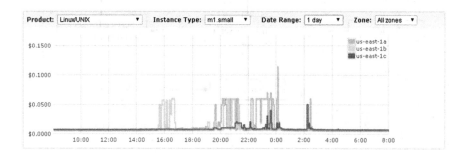

Fig. 1. An example of 24-h price history of a spot instance.

Given the significantly distinctive characteristics of spot resources, the spot market for Cloud computing has attracted increasing interests from various research directions in academia. To help practitioners better understand the spot market and help researchers identify opportunities for future work, we deliver an overview of the current investigations into the Cloud spot market. In particular, since Amazon is currently the only provider in the Cloud spot market, most of the reviewed studies have taken Amazon's spot instance service as an industrial case.

This chapter aims to build a straightforward tutorial to briefly introduce the results of our work. Section 2 outlines a consumption chain of the spot instance service, and categorizes the current research works according to four roles located in the chain. Section 3 distinguishes between five implications of spot prices, and accordingly summarizes and indexes sample technical investigations respectively. Conclusions are drawn in Sect. 4. In particular, four open questions are highlighted for future attention by the research community.

2   Consumption Chain of the Spot Instance Service: A Role-Based Categorization of the Current Research

Given different research objectives, the existing studies have taken perspectives of four roles respectively around Amazon's spot instance service, such as service provider, service consumer, typical applications and service broker (or secondary provider). Considering their relationships, these four roles can compose a consumption chain of the spot instance service, as shown in Fig. 2. Note that this consumption chain is drawn according to the reviewed research works only. Here we briefly describe and categorize the reviewed research works into the following subsections, while leaving the technical discussions to Sect. 3.

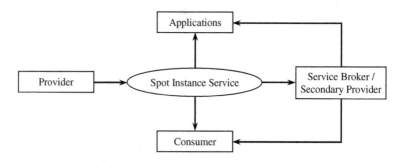

Fig. 2. The consumption chain of the spot instance service.

2.1   Studies Related to Service Provider

It has been claimed that providers would gain various benefits from offering spot instance services. Firstly, the spot prices may attract more consumers to utilize the spare compute capacity, and generate more revenue for the service provider. Secondly, economic theory suggests that auctions (dynamic pricing) could be more efficient over the fixed-price mechanisms [28]. Thirdly, when needing to reclaim the compute capacity, providers have the privilege to terminate service by automatically/intentionally raising the price and decreasing the demands [25]. Thus, this class of research would naturally be beneficial for service providers.

We further distinguish the relevant studies between two research directions. The first direction is taking Amazon as a real case to reveal the current pricing mechanism, while the second is to propose new mechanisms to optimize pricing and provisioning of spot resources.

Revealing the Current Spot Mechanism. The investigations into the current spot mechanism mainly emphasize service pricing. As mentioned previously, the de facto provider Amazon is not open about the underlying pricing policies of its spot instance service. By profiling and statistically analyzing Amazon's spot price history, Wee [24] summarize a set of regular patterns of the observations. For example, the price of spot instances is likely to change hourly; spot instances are averaging 52.3 % cheaper than their equivalent instance types at standard price; and the price intervals are too narrow for further shifting workloads. A reverse engineering study [4] was conducted to reveal how the spot prices are set by Amazon, which raises doubts about the officially claimed market-driven pricing mechanism. Such a viewpoint is supported by several later studies [21,25] with independent analysis.

Proposing New Spot Mechanisms. The proposed spot mechanisms focus not only on service pricing but also on resource provisioning. For example, optimal strategies have been presented with consideration of both pricing and provisioning for Cloud systems based on game theoretical approaches [9]. However, in most cases, one individual study may incline toward paying attention to one side only, i.e. either service pricing or resource provisioning.

- *Mechanisms toward service pricing.* These types of mechanisms are proposed usually from the perspective of adjusting service prices. For example, several works investigate how a provider can set spot prices to maximize its revenue, while formulating the revenue maximization problem into different models [23,25]; Sharma et al. [17] try to handle pricing spot resources at a required QoS through portraying the lower and upper price bounds; and the profit-reliability trade-off is supposed to be effectively tuned online by adapting spot price and inter-price time [18]. In particular, a proposed mechanism is to scale down the Quality of Service (QoS) instead of terminating out-of-bid spot instances by increasing prices [8].

- *Mechanisms toward resource provisioning.* These types of mechanisms are proposed usually from the perspective of allocating spot resources. Most studies here are also aimed at maximizing the service providers' revenue, although they have considered different provisioning scenarios. For example, a frequent scenario is that the available compute resources are viewed as a "liquid" resource pool and configured into different numbers and types of spot instances depending on the requests of consumers [28,29]; and a particular study investigates the runtime management of spot compute capacity for multiple competing secondary service providers [3].

2.2 Studies Related to Service Consumer

The spot instance service provides an economic alternative to consumers to utilize Cloud resources, and this alternative option would be particularly cost-effective for suitable computing tasks. Given the unknown demand statistics and the dynamic adjustment in prices [25], however, spot service consumers may have to suffer from uncertain service interruptions. As such, the trade-off between availability and cost of consuming the spot service has become an intensive research topic, and two typical research directions can be further distinguished: one is to optimize bidding strategies (e.g., [20]), and the other is to investigate fault tolerance strategies (e.g., [26]). More sophisticatedly, some studies try to model consumers' behavior to help them make bidding decisions [12,15], while some other studies consider balancing service cost with goal achievement under a mixed pricing scheme [5,15].

2.3 Studies Related to Typical Applications

Essentially, the Cloud applications are concrete consumers of the Spot instance service. As suggested by Amazon, spot instances would be suitable for some distributed fault-tolerant tasks like web-crawling or Monte Carlo applications [2]. A few other examples of divisible workloads well-suited to spot instances are: Data analytics, Financial modeling and analysis, Scientific research data processing, and Image/Video processing, conversion and rendering [19,20,26, 27]. In particular, an empirical study shows that spot instances can be used as accelerators and well fitted into the MapReduce paradigm [7]; Jangjaimon and Tzeng aim to employ the spot instance service for multithreaded applications to reduce the cost as well as boosting the overall execution performance through an incremental checkpointing technique [10].

2.4 Studies Related to Service Broker (or Secondary Provider)

As the name suggests, there could exist a service broker or a secondary service provider acting as the middle layer between the spot service and its end consumer/application. Given the aforementioned complexity in employing spot instance service, a service broker is supposed to relieve the management burdens on end consumers [19] and facilitate running suitable applications [22]. The secondary providers discussed in the literature usually refer to Software-as-a-Service (SaaS) providers who use spot instances to deliver their business services within a three-tier business model [6]. The research in both service broker and secondary provider would face more complex challenges. On the one hand, service broker and secondary provider are essentially consumers of spot instance service, and therefore they have to deal with the same issues as the normal service consumers, such as bidding strategies [9,19] and fault tolerance [16,22]. On the other hand, service broker and secondary provider also act as service providers to the end consumers, and thus they have to consider their profits and customer satisfaction [6,19] while avoiding the "Cloud ripple effect" [13].

3 Underlying Meaning of Spot Prices: An Exploration of the Technical Investigations

Since the only open information about the spot instance service is its temporal prices [4], various technical investigations have been unfolded to reveal the underlying meaning of spot prices. The intensive research efforts are mainly on five fields, such as the service pricing, resource supplying, consumer requesting, service availability, and service fault tolerance. Their relationships with the spot instance price can be illustrated as shown in Fig. 3, and the investigated technical details are summarized in the following subsections respectively.

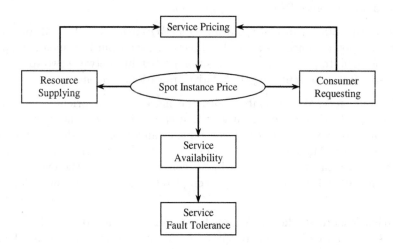

Fig. 3. The technical investigations behind the spot instance prices.

3.1 Service Pricing

Naturally, the spot prices are delivered by the backend pricing mechanism. To understand the backend mechanism, different researchers have developed numerous models and algorithms based on statistics and economics, as specified below.

Statistics-Based Frontend Models are generally concerned with spot price variations. Thus the modeling work is normally based on the observations on, and the statistical analysis of the spot price history.

- *Markovian model.* This is essentially a particular type of random model. By viewing the price change as state transition, a simple Markov model is used to mathematically represent the spot price evolution over time [27]; while a more complicated case is to use a semi-Markovian process to model the spot price variation [19]. Moreover, the spot market has been viewed as a *faulty machine* with up and down states regulated by the semi-Markovian process model.

- *Mixture of Gaussians (MoG) distribution model.* Through a set of statistical analyses of the spot price trace and the inter-price time, Javadi, Thulasiram, and Buyya have developed a model with MoG distribution with 3 or 4 components to reveal the price patterns and characterization of spot instances [11]. Compared to other distributions like Weibull, Normal, Lognormal and Gamma distributions, the MoG distribution is claimed to be a better match with the trace simulation.

- *Normal distribution model.* Given the proposition that the price variation in Amazon's spot service does not follow any particular law, Mazzucco and Dumas assume that the spot prices are normally distributed with the same mean and variance [16].

- *Price Transition Probability Matrix (PTPM) model.* The PTPM for a particular spot instance type can be directly learnt from the open spot price history [20]. In particular, the transition probability between two spot prices is estimated by calculating the relative transition frequency.

- *Random model.* With doubt about the market-driven pricing claimed by Amazon, Ben-Yehuda et al. suggest that spot prices are usually drawn from a tight and fixed price interval, reflecting a random and hidden reserve price [4]. Similarly, Ma and Huang consider that the fluctuation of spot price has a random mean that is known by all consumers [15]. In the extreme case, the spot price is even treated as a completely uncertain parameter [5].

Statistics-Based Backend Algorithms can be designed according to the previous frontend models. Due to space limitation, here we only specify the key techniques instead of elaborating the detailed algorithms.

- *Auto-Regressive (AR(1)) reserve price algorithm.* By matching Amazon's spot price traces with an auto-regressive process, this algorithm dynamically adjusts the reserve price within a particular floor-ceiling range to keep a linear relation between availability and prices [4].

- *Order-Statistic-Based Online Pricing (OSOP) algorithm.* OSOP calculates the current spot price by adapting and learning from bids received in a certain number of previous time slots [18]. Although the authors treat the spot market as an economics-inspired model (modified repeated single-price auction), this algorithm essentially relies on statistics without considering any consumer behavior.

Economics-Inspired Frontend Models employ concepts and ideas of economic processes to represent the variables involved in the pricing-related activities and the logical/quantitative relationships between them. Recall Amazon's market-driven spot mechanism [2], in this case, the relationships between activities of service pricing, resource supplying and consumer requesting are usually modeled all at once. As such, for the convenience and conciseness of reporting, we also put the supplying-oriented (e.g., [3]) and requesting-oriented (e.g., [12]) economics-inspired models all together here.

- *Black-Scholes-Merton (BSM) model.* By treating Cloud resources as assets, the study [17] formulates the spot service pricing function as an option pricing problem.

- *Combinational auction model.* Considering the nature of diverse demands of different numbers and types of Cloud resource, the combinational auction is claimed to be best suited for representing resource allocation in Clouds [28].

- *Continuous sealed-bid uniform price auction model.* According to Amazon's description about how spot instances work [2], the spot mechanism has been directly translated into a continuous sealed-bid uniform price action model [21,29]. "Sealed bid" refers to that the bidders' bids are unknown to each other. "Uniform price" indicates that the identical goods are sold at an identical price.

- *Demand curve model.* In Economics, a demand curve represents the relationship between price and quantity demanded. The study [23] considers the number of supplied spot instances as a function of the current spot price, and utilizes a demand curve to model such a function. A similar function is described in [29], while a simple auto-regression (AR) method is further used to model demand quantity independently of the price.

- *Generalized Nash Equilibrium (GNE) game model.* This model is proposed with particular respect to the resource provisioning between an IaaS provider and its consumers (SaaS providers in this case) [3]. The GNE is an extension of the classic Nash Equilibrium. In GNE problems, the objective functions of each player not only depend upon all the other players' strategies, but may also depend on the rival players? strategies.

- *Modified repeated single-price auction model.* Since only losers may submit new bids repetitively (winners have to remain with their bids until an out-of-bid event occurs), the spot service market can be modeled as a modified version of the repeated single-price auction [18].

- *Prisoner Dilemma game model.* This can be viewed as a secondary model based on the auction mechanism model. By treating the spot market as a uniform price auction of multiple units of a homogeneous good, the interactions of spot service bidders are modeled as a Prisoner Dilemma game [12].

- *Stackelberg game model.* The situation that a set of SaaS providers bid and compete for an IaaS provider's compute capacity can be modeled as a Stackelberg game [9]. Stackelberg game is a particular type of non-cooperative game whereby the leader player takes its decision before the follower players, which is commonly in the attacker-defender scenarios.

Economics-Inspired Backend Algorithms usually do not need to be designed from scratch. Given the economics-inspired models, suitable economic solutions can be employed and adapted to pricing algorithms by mapping necessary parameters between these two fields. Similarly, we only index the relevant algorithms without explaining their details.

- *BSM model-based algorithm.* Sharma et al. have identified five parameters related to pricing Cloud services. After mapping these parameters to the BSM model, the BSM equation can be used to price the Cloud resources [17].

- *Lyapunov optimization algorithm.* Based on the aforementioned demand curve model, optimal pricing for (single-type) spot instances has been formulated as a Lyapunov optimization problem towards maximizing the time-average revenue for providers [23]. The basic idea of Lyapunov optimization is to minimize a bound on the drift-plus-penalty term.

- *Market clearing algorithm.* Given the AR-based demand curve and the non-linear objective function, the problem of dynamic revenue maximization with variable price is suggested being solved by adapting the similar work on market clearing algorithms for piecewise linear objective revenue function [29].

- *Mathematical Programs with Equilibrium Constraint (MPEC) based algorithm.* The Stackelberg-game-modeled pricing/provisioning tasks can be solved by dealing with suitable MPEC problems [9]. An MPEC is an optimization problem with constraints including variational inequalities.

3.2 Resource Supplying

Different spot prices may attract/constrain different amounts of consumption and then influence the amount of spare resources that can be supplied, while the supply of spot resources is one of the weights of pricing from the provider's perspective [2]. We remark that the resource supplying is not independent of service pricing. The identification of resource supplying solutions here are only according to the orientations of the original research works.

- *CA-PROVISION.* Based on the combinational auction model, a dynamic resource provisioning and allocation mechanism CA-PROVISION is proposed in [28]. CA-PROVISION is supposed to be truthful and works in three phases: (1) all the consumers' bids are collected; (2) the winning bidders and the VM configurations to be provisioned by the provider are determined; and (3) all the consumers' payments are calculated.

- *GNE identification algorithms.* By proving the existence of at least one social equilibrium in the spot resource provisioning problem targeting revenue maximization, two different algorithms are developed for finding a GNE [17]: one is based on the best-reply dynamics, which has to be executed at the IaaS provider side; and the other is based on optimal Karush-Kuhn-Tucker multipliers, which can be implemented fully distributed.

3.3   Consumer Requesting

Consumers may adjust their demand and bidding strategies according to the current and/or historical spot prices, while the demand of spot resources is also one of the weights of pricing from the provider's perspective [2]. The technical investigations into consumer requesting mainly focus on the strategies for bidding spot resources.

- *Autocorrelation Function (ACF) based algorithm.* ACF measures the correlation of a random variable with itself at different points in time, and this algorithm assumes a normal distribution model of prices to realize spot price prediction for bidding [16].

- *Constrained Markov Decision Process (CMDP) based algorithm.* Benefitting from a price transition probability matrix (PTPM) that accomodates the historical price transition frequents, the bid decision making has been formulated as a CMDP problem that can be solved by the corresponding Linear Programming [20].

- *Discrete-time stochastic Dynamic Programming.* Based on the Markov model for spot price evolution, Zafer, Song, and Lee define the cost minimization problem in the field of discrete-time stochastic Dynamic Programming, and utilize the relevant mathematical tools to achive optimal bids from the consumer's perspective [27].

- *Naive strategies.* Five simple bidding strategies are proposed and compared with each other in [22], such as (1) Current: using the current spot price plus the minimum bid granularity 0.001; (2) High: using a value much higher than any price observed in the history; (3) Mean: using the mean of all values in the price history; (4) Minimum: using the minimum price observed in the history plus the minimum bid granularity 0.001; (5) On-demand: using the price of the equivalent on-demand instance type.

- *Portfolio algorithms.* With consideration of the trade-off between customer satisfaction and expected profit, two portfolio strategy-based bidding algorithms are developed from the secondary provider's perspective [6]: the FirstFit-profit algorithm is to maximize profit while maintaining a certain level of customer satisfaction, and the FirstFit-satisfaction algorithm is to maximize customer satisfaction while keeping a particular target of profit. The basic idea of portfolio strategies (borrowed from the financial investment domain) is allowing different types of spot instances to satisfy the consumers' requests at different bidding sessions.

- *Prisoner Dilemma game-based solution.* By determining the band of control limits and establishing propositions to make bids meet the Prisoner Dilemma condition, bidders can estimate the ratio of co-operators vs. defectors to make decisions [12]. Essentially, rational and self-interested consumers would converge on the Nash Equilibrium solution for spot resource bidding.

- *Profit-Aware Dynamic Bidding (PADB) algorithm.* Given the semi-Markovian process price model, this algorithm is designed to make sequential bidding decisions for a job queue, and each decision only requires the current job size and the current spot price [19]. PADB is supposed to achieve a near-optimal bidding solution to the profit maximization problem from the service broker's perspective.

3.4 Service Availability

According to the characteristics of Amazon spot instances [26], the service stops immediately without any notice if the current price is out of the previous bid. Such service interruptions can be comprehended from the angle of either Reliability (failure number) or Availability (time lost) [14]. In this chapter, we interpret that the relevant descriptions in the reviewed studies are all with regard to service availability. To the best of our knowledge, there are three different ways of defining the availability of spot instance service.

- *Up time/ratio at a declared price.* Being compatible with the clarified definition [14], the availability of spot instance service at a declared price during a period of time can be directly reflected through counting the hours in which the spot price was equal to or lower than the declared price [4,24]. In particular, the up-time fraction of the total time interval is used to measure service availability in [4].

- *Spot instance revocation (unavailability) model.* The service unavailability is investigated for estimating the expected turnaround time of a running application in [10]. In detail, the revocation of spot instances is modeled as a modified exponential distribution for the purpose of low complexity of $O(1)$ in time and space, which comprises three main parameters: the revocation rate, an adjusting factor, and the average time duration between two revocations.

- *Markov chain based spot instance lifetime.* The spot instance lifetimes have been formulated by building a Markov chain, and the edges of the Markov chain refer to the probabilities of hourly price transitions [7]. Given such a Markov chain, the probability of a spot instance running for n hours (i.e. a particular n-step probability) can be calculated using a variant of the Chapman-Kolmogorov equation.

3.5 Service Fault Tolerance

Given the uncertain availability of individual spot instances over time, suitable fault-tolerance mechanisms would be clearly crucial for consumers when pursuing the cost effectiveness of spot instance service. Interestingly, different mechanisms have been proposed from the perspectives of not only consumer side but also provider side.

- *Checkpointing.* According to the literature, checkpointing seems to be the most promising fault-tolerance mechanism for spot resources in order to boost overall computing performance and productivity. Four checkpointing schemes (i.e. Hourly, Rising edge-driven, Basic adaptive, and Current-price based adaptive checkpointing) are developed and compared with two baseline policies in [26], and the Hourly checkpointing technique is particularly highlighted in [22]. Based on an adjusted Markov model (AMM) that takes into account both revocation events and hardware failures of spot instances, Jangjaimon and Tzeng have designed and implemented an enhanced adaptive incremental checkpointing (EAIC) mechanism that enables fast prediction with high accuracy on when a checkpoint should be taken [10].

- *Duplication of long jobs.* A relatively simple fault-tolerance technique, namely duplication, is proposed to increase the chance of satisfying longer jobs' deadline constraints [22]. This technique creates one replica of each job that could run for more than one hour, and the replicas are supposed to be deployed with different instance type/datacenter combinations.

- *Dynamic Scalability.* Differing from the other fault-tolerance mechanisms, Dawoud, Takouna, and Meinel suggest using dynamic scalability to improve spot instances' availability from the provider's perspective [8]. In other words, when necessary to free some compute capacity, the provider may sacrifice some QoS of its service instead of terminating the relevant spot instances.

- *Migration.* Unlike waiting until re-acquiring the same spot resources in the checkpointing mechanism, the migration-based mechanism suggests rebidding at a comparable per-core price for different types of instances even from a different datacenter [22,26]. Although it is impossible to determine an optimal spot instance for migration, three different heuristics (i.e. Lowest price, Lowest failure rate, and Highest failure rate) can be used to facilitate selecting the next instance type [26].

4   Conclusions

As a significant step towards fitting Cloud computing into a full-fledged market economy [22], Amazon launched a spot market to sell its spare compute capacity. Given such an emerging market with distinctive characteristics, various academic studies have taken Amazon's spot service as an example to investigate the Cloud's spot market from diverse angles. By reviewing the relevant publications, we portray a landscape of the current research into the spot market for Cloud computing in this chapter. On the one hand, the relevant works are classified according to different roles in the spot market, and these roles are essentially joined together by a consumption chain of the spot service. On the other hand, different directions of revealing the underlying meaning of spot prices are distinguished, and typical samples of technical investigations are demonstrated along those directions.

When collecting and sorting the research outcomes about Cloud spot market, we find that there is still a lack of consensuses on several topics. Some investigation results and conclusions even conflict with each other. Here we particularly summarize the identified gaps into four open questions that may indicate potential research opportunities in the future, as listed below.

(1) Is Amazon's spot mechanism truthful?

A truthful mechanism requires incentive-compatible players [18,28]. It is known that a single round of sealed-bid uniform price auction is truthful if the provider can adjust its supply. By arguing that under this auction style there is an incentive for consumers to submit true value-based bids, Amazon's spot mechanism is claimed to be truthful [22,29]. On the contrary, by formulating the losers-rebid-while-winners-remain situation as a modified version of the repeated single-price auction, Amazon's spot mechanism is considered as being untruthful [18]. Thus, the truthfulness of the de facto spot mechanism should be further investigated before working on Amazon's spot market.

(2) Are consumer biddings rational?

As a continuation of the previous question, the research based on a truthful market assumes rational biddings with consumers' true valuation of the spot service. It is sensible that, according to the studies of applying game theory to investigating the spot market [3,9,12], the self-interested consumers have to be rational to reach equilibria for spot resource bidding. However, given the observations that spot prices frequently surpassed on-demand prices in the price history across different instance types and datacenters, the consumers may have issued irrational biddings unless they tried to bid as high as possible to decrease the chance of service interruptions [12,22]. Therefore, the rationality of consumers' bidding activities and the corresponding impacts on the Cloud spot market would be a potential research opportunity.

(3) Is Amazon's market-driven mechanism real?

In fact, most of the reviewed studies have been conducted based on a real market-driven mechanism as claimed by Amazon. Recall that the economics-inspired studies have employed various economic concepts and processes to formulate Amazon's spot market (cf. Sect. 3.1). Nevertheless, from some statistical perspectives, Amazon's spot prices are unlikely to be set with regard to market supply and demand. Instead, it is believed that some artificial algorithm with predetermined reserve price must have been adopted by Amazon behind its so-called spot market [4,21,25]. In other words, there may exist a gap between industrial practice (Amazon) and academic research. It would be necessary to develop practical mechanisms for the Cloud spot market rather than directly borrowing economic models.

(4) Is spot pricing more profitable than fixed pricing for Cloud providers?

It is clear that unsold compute resources are wasted capacity from the perspective of Cloud providers [4]. As mentioned previously, offering spot resources has been viewed as an effective approach to attracting more consumers so as to fully utilize the Cloud resources and generate more revenue [23]. Furthermore, from the economic point of view, the auction-based spot pricing would be more efficient over the fixed-pricing scheme by targeting the consumers who have high valuations [28]. According to theoretical analyses and simulations, in an opposite opinion, using fixed prices can generate higher expected revenues for providers than using a hybrid (fixed + spot) pricing mechanism [1]. Such a fierce debate indicates that an evidence-based comparison study is needed through rigorously and systematically reviewing the relevant publications.

Acknowledgments. NICTA is funded by the Australian Government through the Department of Communications and the Australian Research Council through the ICT Centre of Excellence Program. NICTA is also funded and supported by the Australian Capital Territory, the New South Wales, Queensland and Victorian Governments, the Australian National University, the University of New South Wales, the University of Melbourne, the University of Queensland, the University of Sydney, Griffith University, Queensland University of Technology, Monash University and other university partners.

References

1. Abhishek, V., Kash, I.A., Key, P.: Fixed and market pricing for Cloud services. In: Proceedings of the 7th Workshop Economics of Networks System Computer (NetEcon 2012), pp. 157–162. IEEE Computer Society, Orlando, 20 March 2012
2. Amazon: Amazon EC2 spot instances, March 2014. https://aws.amazon.com/ec2/purchasing-options/spot-instances/
3. Ardagna, D., Panicucci, B., Passacantando, M.: Generalized Nash Equilibria for the service provisioning problem in Cloud systems. IEEE Trans. Serv. Comput. **6**(4), 429–442 (2013)
4. Ben-Yehuda, O.A., Ben-Yehuda, M., Schuster, A., Tsafrir, D.: Deconstructing Amazon EC2 spot instance pricing. In: Proceedings of the 3rd IEEE International Conference on Cloud Computing Technology and Science (CloudCom 2011), pp. 304–311. IEEE Computer Society, Athens, 29 November–1 December 2011
5. Chaisiri, S., Kaewpuang, R., Lee, B.S., Niyato, D.: Cost minimization for provisioning virtual servers in Amazon elastic compute Cloud. In: Proceedings of the 19th Annual IEEE International Symposium Modeling Analysis and Simulation of Computer Telecommunication System (MASCOTS 2011), pp. 85–95. IEEE Computer Society, Singapore, 25–27 July 2011
6. Chen, J., Wang, C., Zhou, B.B., Sun, L., Lee, Y.C., Zomaya, A.Y.: Tradeoffs between profit and customer satisfaction for service provisioning in the Cloud. In: Proceedings of the 20th International Symposium High Performance Distributed Computing (HPDC 2011), pp. 229–238. ACM Press, San Jose, 8–11 June 2011
7. Chohan, N., Castillo, C., Spreitzer, M., Steinder, M., Tantawi, A., Krintz, C.: See spot run: using spot instances for MapReduce workflows. In: Proceedings of the 2nd USENIX Conference on Hot Topics Cloud Computing (HotCloud 2010), pp. 1–7. USENIX Association, Boston, 22 June 2010
8. Dawoud, W., Takouna, I., Meinel, C.: Increasing spot instances reliability using dynamic scalability. In: Proceedings of the 5th IEEE International Conference on Cloud Computing (CLOUD 2012), pp. 91–98. IEEE Computer Society, Honolulu, 24–29 June 2012

9. Di Valerio, V., Cardellini, V., Lo Presti, F.: Optimal pricing and service provisioning strategies in Cloud systems: A Stackelberg game approach. In: Proceedings of the 6th IEEE International Conference on Cloud Computing (CLOUD 2013), pp. 115–122. IEEE Computer Society, Santa Clara, 28 June - 3 July 2013

10. Jangjaimon, I., Tzeng, N.F.: Effective cost reduction for elastic Clouds under spot instance pricing through adaptive checkpointing. IEEE Trans. Comput. (2013) (in press)

11. Javadi, B., Thulasiram, R.K., Buyya, R.: Statistical modeling of spot instance prices in public Cloud environments. In: Proceedings of the 4th IEEE/ACM International Conference on Utility Cloud Computing (UCC 2011), pp. 219–228. IEEE Computer Society, Melbourne, 5–7 December 2011

12. Karunakaran, S., Sundarraj, R.P.: On using prisoner dilemma model to explain bidding decision for computing resources on the Cloud. In: Proceedings of the 13th International Conference Group Decision Negotiation (GDN 2013), Stockholm, Sweden, pp. 206–215, 17–20 June 2013

13. Li, Z., Liang, M., O'Brien, L., Zhang, H.: The cloud's cloudy moment: a systematic survey of public cloud service outage. Int. J. Cloud Comput. Serv. Sci. 2(5), 321–330 (2013)

14. Li, Z., O'Brien, L., Cai, R., Zhang, H.: Towards a taxonomy of performance evaluation of commercial Cloud services. In: Proceedings od the 5th IEEE International Conference on Cloud Computing (CLOUD 2012), pp. 344–351. IEEE Computer Society, Honolulu, 24–29 June 2012

15. Ma, D., Huang, J.: The pricing model of Cloud computing services. In: Proceedings of the 14th Annual International Conference on Electronic Commerce (ICEC 2012), pp. 263–269. ACM Press, Singapore, 6 August 2012

16. Mazzucco, M., Dumas, M.: Achieving performance and availability guarantees with spot instances. In: Proceedings of the 13th IEEE International Conference on High Performance Computing and Communications (HPCC 2011), pp. 296–303. IEEE Computer Society, Banff, 2–4 September 2011

17. Sharma, B., Thulasiram, R.K., Thulasiraman, P., Garg, S.K., Buyya, R.: Pricing Cloud compute commodities: A novel financial economic model. In: Proceedings of the 12th IEEE/ACM International Symposium Cluster Cloud Grid Computing (CCGrid 2012), pp. 451–457. IEEE Computer Society, Ottawa, 13–16 May 2012

18. Song, K., Yao, Y., Golubchik, L.: Exploring the profit-reliability trade-off in Amazons spot instance market: A better pricing mechanism. In: Proceedings of the 21st International Symposium on Quality of Service (IWQoS 2013), pp. 1–10. IEEE Press, Montreal, 3–4 June 2013

19. Song, Y., Zafer, M., Lee, K.W.: Optimal bidding in spot instance market. In: Proceedings of the 31st Annual IEEE International Conference on Computer Communications (INFOCOM 2012), pp. 190–198. IEEE Press, Orlando, 25–30 March 2012

20. Tang, S., Yuan, J., Li, X.Y.: Decision model for provisioning virtual resources in Amazon EC2. In: Proceedings of the 5th IEEE International Conference on Cloud Computing (CLOUD 2012), pp. 91–98. IEEE Computer Society, Honolulu, 24–29 June 2012

21. Tian, C., Wang, Y., Qi, F., Yin, B.: Decision model for provisioning virtual resources in Amazon EC2. In: Proceedings of the 8th International Conference on Network Service Management (CNSM 2012), pp. 159–163. International Federation for Information Processing, Las Vegas, 2–26 October 2012

22. Voorsluys, W., Buyya, R.: Reliable provisioning of spot instances for compute-intensive applications. In: Proceedings of the 26th IEEE International Conference on Advanced Information Networking (AINA 2012), pp. 542–549. IEEE Computer Society, Fukuoka, 26–29 March 2012

23. Wang, P., Qi, Y., Hui, D., Rao, L., Lin, X.: Present or future: Optimal pricing for spot instances. In: Proceedings 33rd IEEE nternational Conference on Distributed Computing Systems (ICDCS 2013), pp. 410–419. IEEE Computer Society, Philadelphia, 8–11 July 2013

24. Wee, S.: Debunking real-time pricing in Cloud computing. In: Proceedings of the 11th IEEE/ACM International Symposium on Cluster Cloud Grid Computing (CCGrid 2011), pp. 585–590. IEEE Computer Society, Newport Beach, 23–26 May 2011

25. Xu, H., Li, B.: Dynamic Cloud pricing for revenue maximization. IEEE Trans. Cloud Comput. **1**(2), 158–171 (2013)

26. Yi, S., Andrzejak, A., Kondo, D.: Monetary cost-aware checkpointing and migration on Amazon Cloud spot instances. IEEE Trans. Serv. Comput. **5**(4), 512–524 (2012)

27. Zafer, M., Song, Y., Lee, K.W.: Optimal bids for spot vms in a cloud for deadline constrained jobs. In: Proceedings of the 5th IEEE International Conference on Cloud Computing (CLOUD 2012), pp. 75–82. IEEE Computer Society, Honolulu, 24–29 June 2012

28. Zaman, S., Grosu, D.: A combinatorial auction-based mechanism for dynamic VM provisioning and allocation in Clouds. IEEE Trans. Cloud Comput. **1**(2), 129–141 (2013)

29. Zhang, Q., Gürses, E., Boutaba, R., Xiao, J.: Dynamic resource allocation for spot markets in Clouds. In: Proceedings of the 11th USENIX Conference Hot Topics Management Internet Cloud Enterprise Networks Service (Hot-ICE 2011), pp. 1–6. USENIX Association, Boston, 29 March 2011

Resource Management & Energy

Analysis and Optimization on FlexDPDP: A Practical Solution for Dynamic Provable Data Possession

Ertem Esiner[(⊠)], Alptekin Küpçü, and Öznur Özkasap

Department of Computer Engineering, Koç University, İstanbul, Turkey
{eesiner,akupcu,oozkasap}@ku.edu.tr

Abstract. Security measures, such as proving data integrity, became more important with the increase in popularity of cloud data storage services. Dynamic Provable Data Possession (DPDP) was proposed in the literature to enable the cloud server to prove to the client that her data is kept intact, even in a dynamic setting where the client may update her files. Realizing that variable-sized updates are very inefficient in DPDP (in the worst case leading to uploading the whole file again), Flexible DPDP (FlexDPDP) was proposed.

In this paper, we analyze FlexDPDP scheme and propose optimized algorithms. We show that the initial pre-processing phase at the client and server sides during the file upload (generally the most time-consuming operation) can be efficiently performed by parallelization techniques that result in a speed up of 6 with 8 cores. We propose a way of handling multiple updates at once both at the server and the client side, achieving an efficiency gain of 60 % at the server side and 90 % in terms of the client's update verification time.

We deployed the optimized FlexDPDP on the large-scale network testbed PlanetLab and demonstrate the efficiency of our proposed optimizations on multi-client scenarios according to real workloads based on version control system traces.

1 Introduction

Data outsourcing to the cloud has become popular with the availability of affordable and more satisfying services (e.g. Dropbox, box.net, Google Drive, Amazon S3, iCloud, Skydrive) as well as with several studies in academia [2–4,11,15,16,18,25,30,31]. The most important impediment in public adoption of cloud systems is the lack of some security guarantees in data storage services [19,24,33]. The schemes providing security guarantees should incur minimal overhead on top of the already available systems in order to promote wide adoption by the service providers.

In this work, we address the integrity of the client's data stored on the cloud storage servers. In a cloud storage system, there are two main parties, namely a server and a client, where the client transmits her files to the cloud storage server and the server stores the files on behalf of the client. For the client to be

© Springer International Publishing Switzerland 2015
A. Al-Saidi et al. (Eds.): ICC 2014, LNCS 8993, pp. 65–83, 2015.
DOI: 10.1007/978-3-319-19848-4_5

able to trust the service provider, she should be able to verify the integrity of the data. A trustworthy brand is not sufficient for the client, since hardware/software failures or malicious third parties may also cause data loss or corruption [9].

Solutions for the static cases (i.e., logging or archival storage) such as Provable Data Possession (PDP) [2] were proposed [2,3,15,25,30]. For the dynamic cases where the client keeps interacting (updating, manipulating) with her data, Scalable PDP was proposed by Ateniese et al. [4], which allows a limited number of operations before a full re-calculation of the redundant data is required to continue providing provable data possession. Extensions of the PDP, using some data structures for dynamic cases, were first studied in Dynamic Provable Data Possession (DPDP) [16] that allows data updates while still providing integrity guarantees. Implementation of DPDP needs rank-based authenticated skip list as the underlying data structure. It is shown that DPDP is not applicable to variable block sized settings (due to the data structure used), hence resulting in unacceptable performance in the dynamic secure cloud storage systems [17]. To solve this issue, a flexible length-based authenticated skip list, called FlexList, and its application to a DPDP scheme allowing variable block-sized updates, called FlexDPDP, were proposed [17]. In this study, we ameliorate the efficiency of the FlexDPDP system by proposing optimized algorithms on FlexList.

Our Contributions are as follows:

- We optimize the first pre-processing phase of the FlexDPDP provable cloud storage protocol by showing that the algorithm to build a FlexList in $O(n)$ time is well parallelizable even though FlexList is an authenticated data structure that generates dependencies over the file blocks. We propose a parallelization algorithm and our experimental results show a speed up of 6 and 7.7, with 8 and 12 cores respectively.
- We provide a multi-block update algorithm for FlexDPDP. Our experiments show 60 % efficiency gain at the server side compared to updating blocks independently, when the updates are on consecutive data blocks.
- We provide an algorithm to verify update operations for FlexDPDP. Our new algorithm is applicable to not only modify, insert, and remove operations but also a mixed series of multiple update operations. The experimental results show an efficiency gain of nearly 90 % in terms of verification time of consecutive updates.
- We deployed the FlexDPDP implementation on the network testbed Planet-Lab and also tested its applicability on a real SVN deployment. The results show that our improved scheme is practically usable in real life scenarios after optimization, namely 4 times faster proof generation for consecutive updates.

2   Related Work

Ateniese et al. proposed the first provable storage service named PDP [2] that can only be applied to the static cases. To overcome this problem, Scalable PDP was proposed which allows limited updates [4]. When it consumes its precomputed tokens, Scalable PDP requires a setup phase from scratch. Wang et al. [32] proposed using Merkle tree and Zheng and Zu [34] proposed 2-3 trees as the data structure on top of PDP. Yet, these are also applicable to the static scenarios since there is no efficient algorithm, which keeps the authentication information maintained, is shown for re-balancing neither of these data structures. The authenticated skip lists that are probabilistically balanced in case of any updates were first proposed by [29].

For improving data integrity on the cloud, protocols [10,12,21,22,26,27] provide Byzantium fault-tolerant storage services based on some server labor. There also exist protocols using quorum techniques, which do not consider the server-client scenarios but works on local systems such as hard disk drives or local storage [1,13,20,23]. A recent protocol using quorum techniques [5] replicates the data on several storage providers to improve integrity of the data stored on the cloud; yet it also considers static data.

Within provable data possession techniques, Erway et al. proposed a skip-list-like data structure called rank based skip list [16] that allows dynamic operations. Yet Esiner et al. [17] showed that updates in DPDP needs to be of fixed block size, and proposed the FlexList data structure that allows variable length dynamic operations with DPDP scheme. Detailed comparison and extended descriptions of these two data structures are provided in [16,17]. Some distributed versions of the idea have been studied as well [14,18]. There are also studies showing that a client's file is kept intact in the sense that client can retrieve (recover) it fully whenever she wishes [7,11,15,25,30].

FlexDPDP, using FlexList, can perform modify, insert, and remove operations one block at a time on the cloud, without any limit on the number of updates and block sizes, while maintaining data possession guarantees. It also provides verification algorithms for update queries on single blocks. In this work, we show that the functions in FlexDPDP are open to optimization, and propose optimized efficient algorithms by evaluating them on the PlanetLab network testbed and with real data update scenarios.

3   Preliminaries

FlexDPDP approach provides variable block sized dynamic provable data possession and uses FlexList as the underlying data structure. We first introduce the intuition behind FlexList and definitions of FlexDPDP to form the basis for describing the proposed optimizations.

FlexList is a skip-list-like **authenticated** data structure (Fig. 1). Each node keeps a *hash* value calculated according to its rank, level, the hash value of below neighbor, and the hash value of the after neighbor, where *rank* indicates the number of bytes that can be reached from the node, and *level* is the height of a node in the FlexList. Note that the hash of the root node is dependent on all leaf level nodes' hashes. Each leaf level node keeps a link to the **data** (the associated block of the file stored) to which it refers, the length of the data, and a **tag** value

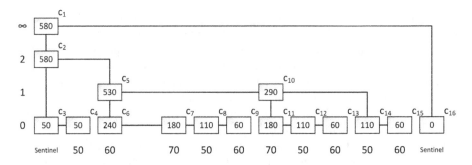

Fig. 1. A FlexList example.

calculated for the data. **Rank** values are calculated by adding the below and after neighbors' ranks. If a node is at the leaf level, we use the length of its data as below neighbor's rank. FlexList has *sentinel* nodes as the first and the last nodes, which have no data and hence their length value is 0, as shown in Fig. 1. These nodes generate no new dependencies but are useful to make algorithms easier and more understandable.

A node's below neighbor's rank shows how many bytes can be reached following the below link. The **search** operation uses this information to find a searched index. We check if the searched index is less than the rank of the below neighbor, if so we follow the below link, otherwise we follow the after link. When we follow an after link, the index we look for is diminished by the amount of bytes passed (rank of the below node). We repeat this procedure to reach the node that includes the search index. A **search path** is the ordered set of nodes visited on the way to reach a searched index by following the above rule starting from the root.

Insert/Remove operations perform addition/removal of a leaf node by keeping the necessary non-leaf nodes and removing the unnecessary ones, thus preserving the optimality of the structure (definitions and details are provided in [17]). Figure 2 illustrates an example of both **insert and remove** operations. First we insert a data of length 50 to index 110 at level 2. Dashed lines show the nodes and links which are removed, and bold lines show the newly added ones. Node c_5 is removed to keep the FlexList optimal [17]. The old rank values are marked and new values written below them. For the removal of the node at index 110, read the figure in the reverse order, where dashed nodes and lines are newly added ones and strong nodes and lines are to be removed, and the initial rank values are valid again.

Besides search, modify, insert, and remove algorithms, a **build skip list** algorithm was introduced in [17] that generates a FlexList on top of an ordered data using $O(n)$ time. The algorithm takes all data blocks, their corresponding tag values, and levels of prospective nodes as input, and generates the FlexList attaching nodes from right to left, instead of a series of insert method calls (which would cost $O(n \log n)$ in total). In Fig. 1, the order of node generation is: $c_{16}, c_{15}, c_{14}, c_{13}, c_{12}, c_{11}, c_{10}, c_9$, and so on.

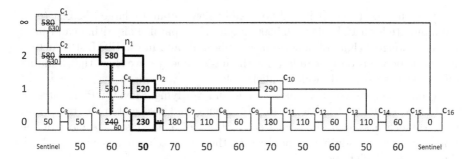

Fig. 2. Insert and remove examples on FlexList.

FlexDPDP [17] is a FlexList-based secure cloud storage scheme built on DPDP [16]. The scheme starts with the client pre-processing and uploading her data to the server. While pre-processing, both the client and the server build a FlexList over the data blocks. The client keeps the root of the FlexList as her meta data and the server keeps the FlexList as a whole. The server later uses the FlexList to generate proofs of data possession.

For **proof of possession**, Esiner et al. proposed an algorithm named **gen-MultiProof** [17], which collects all necessary values through search paths of the challenged nodes without any repetition. A multi proof is a response to a challenge of multiple nodes. For instance, a challenge to indices 50, 180, 230 in Fig. 1 is replied by a proof vector as in Fig. 4, together with a vector of tags of the challenged nodes and the block sum of the corresponding blocks. This proof vector is used to verify the integrity of these specific blocks. We use, in Sect. 4.3, this proof vector to verify the multiple updates on the server as well.

The client **verifies** the proof by calling **verifyMultiProof** which calculates the hash values from the proof vector one by one until the root's hash value. If the hash value of the root is equal to the meta data that the client keeps, and hashes and tags are verified, the client is satisfied. If the client is not satisfied with the proof received, she can use the it to prove that her data is not kept intact. We use the *verifyMultiProof* method to verify the proof of the nodes on which we perform updates. **Update information** consists of the index of the update, the new data and the corresponding tag.

4   Optimizations on FlexDPDP

In this section, we describe our optimizations on FlexDPDP and FlexList for achieving an efficient and secure cloud storage system. We then demonstrate the efficiency of our optimizations in the next section.

First, we observe that a major time consuming operation in the FlexDPDP scheme is the pre-process operation, where a *build FlexList* function is employed. Previous $O(n)$ time algorithm [17] is an asymptotic improvement, but in terms of actual running times, it is still noticeably slow to build a large FlexList (e.g., half a minute for a 1GB file with 500000 blocks). A parallel algorithm can run as fast as its longest chain of dependent calculations, and in the FlexList structure each node depends on its children for the hash value; yet we show that building a FlexList is surprisingly well parallelizable.

Second, we observe that performing and verifying FlexDPDP updates in batches yield great performance improvements, and also match the real world usage of such a system. The hash calculations of a FlexList take most of the time spent for an update, and performing them in batches may save many hash unnecessary calculations.

Therefore, in this section, we provide a **parallel algorithm for building FlexList**, a **multi-block update algorithm** for the server to perform updates faster, and a **multi-block verification algorithm** for the client to verify the update proofs sent by the server. Notation used in our algorithms is presented in Table 1.

4.1 Parallel Build FlexList

We propose a parallel algorithm to generate a FlexList over the file blocks, resulting in the same FlexList as a sequentially generated one. The algorithm has three steps. Figure 3 shows the parallel construction of the same FlexList as in Fig. 1 on three cores. We first distribute tasks to threads and generate small FlexLists. Second, to unify them, we connect all roots together with links (c_1 to r_1 and r_1 to r_2, thus eliminate l_1 and l_2) and calculate new rank values of the roots (r_1 and c_1). Third, we use basic remove function to remove the left sentinels, which remain in between each part (to indices 360 and 180: 360 = c_1.rank - r_2.rank and 180 = c_1.rank - r_1.rank). In the example, the remove operation generates c_5 and c_{10} of Fig. 1 and connects the remaining nodes to them, and rank values on the search paths of c_2, c_6, c_7, c_{11} are recalculated after the removal of sentinel nodes. As a result, all the nodes of the small FlexLists are connected to their level on the FlexList. After the unify operation, we obtain the same FlexList of Fig. 1 generated efficiently in a parallel manner.

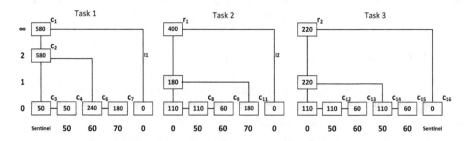

Fig. 3. A build skip list distributed to 3 cores.

Table 1. Symbols and helper methods used in our algorithms.

Symbol	Description
cn / nn	current node / new node
$after$ / $below$	node reached by following the after link / by following the below link
C	contains the indices that are challenged (ascending order)
i / $first$ / $last$	index / C's current index / C's end index
rs	The amount of bytes passed with each follow of an $after$ link
$state$	state contains a node, rank state, and $last$ index. These values are used to set the current node cn to the point where the algorithm will continue
P / T / M	proof vector / tag vector / block sum
$\sqcup_s$	intersection stack, stores states at intersections
$\sqcup_l$	stores nodes for which a hash calculation is to be done
Method	Description
canGoBelow [17]	returns true if the searched index can be reached by following the below link
isIntersection [17]	returns true when the first index can be found following the below link and the second index is found by following the after link. If there are more than one intersection, decrements $last$ for each until finds the closest one
generateIndices	generates an array of indices of the nodes that have been affected. Say the update index is i, the algorithm adds i for an insert or modify, adds i and i-1 for a remove

4.2   Handling Multiple Updates at Once

We investigated the verifiable updates and inferred that the majority of the time spent is for the hash calculations in each update. We discuss this in detail in Sect. 5. The client first downloads the part of the data she is interested in, then when she alters the data and sends it to the server, she generates a vector of updates (U) out of a diff algorithm, which is used to show the changes between the last and the former versions of a file.

Algorithm 4.1. multiUpdate Algorithm

Input: FlexList, U
Output: P, T, M, $newRootHash$

Let $U = (u_0, \ldots, u_k)$ where u_j is the jth update information
1   C = generateIndices(U) //According to the nature of the update for each $u \in U$, we add an index to the vector ($u_j.i$ for insert and modify, $u_j.i$ and $u_j.i - 1$ for remove as it is for a single update proof)
2   P, T, M= genMultiProof(C) //Generates the multiProof using the FlexList
3   **for** $i = 0$ to k **do**
4   apply u_i to FlexList without any hash calculations
5   update C to all affected nodes using U
6   calculateMultiHash(C) // Calculates hash values of the changed nodes
7   $newRootHash$ = FlexList.root.hash

An update information $u \in U$, includes an index i, and (if insert or modify) a block and a tag value. Furthermore, the updates on a FlexList consist of a series of *modify* operations followed by either *insert* or *remove* operations, all to adjacent nodes. This nature of the update operations makes single updates inefficient since they keep calculating the hash values of the same nodes over and over again. To overcome this problem, we propose dividing the task into two: doing a series of **updates without the hash calculations**, and then calculating all **affected nodes' hash values at once**, where affected means that at least an input of the hash calculation of that node has changed. The **multi-Update** (Algorithm 4.1) gets a FlexList and vector of updates U, and produces proof vector P, tag vector T, block sum M, and new hash value $newRootHash$ of the root after the updates.

hashMulti (Algorithm 4.2), employed in *calculateMultiHash* algorithm, collects nodes on a search path of a searched node. In the meantime, it is collecting the intersection points (which is the lowest common ancestor (lca) of the node the collecting is done for and the next node of which the hash calculation is needed). The repetitive calls from *calculateMultiHash* algorithm for each searched node collects all nodes which may need a hash recalculation. Note that each time, a new call starts from the last intersecting (lca) node.

Algorithm 4.2. hashMulti Algorithm

Input: cn, C, $first$, $last$, rs, $\sqcup_l$, $\sqcup_s$
Output: cn, $\sqcup_l$, $\sqcup_s$

// Index of the challenged block (key) is calculated according to the current sub skip list root
1    $i = C_{first} - rs$
2   **while** *Until challenged node is included* **do**
3   cn is added to $\sqcup_l$
         //When an intersection is found with another branch of the proof path, it is saved to be continued again, this is crucial for the outer loop of ``multi'' algorithms
4   **if** *isIntersection*$(cn, C, i, last_k, rs)$ **then**
             //note that $last_k$ becomes $last_{k+1}$ in *isIntersection* method
5            $state(cn.after, last_{k+1}, rs + cn.below.r)$ is added to $\sqcup_s$
6   **if** $(CanGoBelow(cn, i))$ **then**
7            $cn = cn.below$ //unless at the leaf level
8   **else**
             // Set index and rank state values according to how many bytes at leaf nodes are passed while following the $after$ link
9            $i -= cn.below.r;$ $rs += cn.below.r;$ $cn = cn.after$

---

calculateMultiHash (Algorithm 4.3) first goes through all changed nodes and collects their pointers, then calculates all their hash values from the largest index value to the smallest, until the root. This order of hash calculation respects all hash dependencies.

We illustrate handling multiple updates with an example. Consider a *multi-Update* called on the FlexList of Fig. 1 and a consecutive modify and insert happen to indices 50 and 110 respectively (insert level is 2). When the updates are done without hash calculations, the resulting FlexList looks like in Fig. 2. Since the tag value of c_6 has changed and a new node added between c_6 and c_7, all the nodes getting affected should have a hash recalculation. If we first perform the insert, we need to calculate hashes of n_3, n_2, c_6, n_1, c_2 and c_1. Later, when we do the modification to c_6 we need to recalculate hashes of nodes c_6, n_1, c_2 and c_1. There are 6 nodes to recalculate hashes but we do 10 hash calculations. Instead, we propose performing the insert and modify operations and call *calculateMultiHash* to indices 50 and 110. The first call of *hashMulti* goes through c_1, c_2, n_1, and c_6. On its way, it pushes n_2 to a stack since the next iteration of *hashMulti* starts from n_2. Then, with the second iteration of *calculateMultiHash*, n_2 and n_3 are added to the stack. At the end, we call the nodes from the stack one by one and calculate their hash values. Note that the order preserves the hash dependencies.

Algorithm 4.3. calculateMultiHash Algorithm

Input: C
Output:

Let C= $(i_0, \ldots, i_k)$ where i_j is the $(j+1)^{th}$ altered index;
$state_m = (node_m, lastIndex_m, rs_m)$
1    $cn = root$; $rs = 0$; $\sqcup_s$, $\sqcup_l$ are empty; $state=$ (root, k, rs)
       // Call *hashMulti* method for each index to fill the changed nodes stack $\sqcup_l$
2   **for** $x = 0$ **to** k **do**
3       $hashMulti(state.node, C, x, state.end, state.rs, \sqcup_l, \sqcup_s)$
4   **if** $\sqcup_s$ not empty **then**
5          $state = \sqcup_s$.pop(); $cn = state.node$; $state.rs += cn.below.r$
6   **for** $k = \sqcup_l.size$ **to** 0 **do**
7   calculate hash of kth node in $\sqcup_l$

4.3   Verifying Multiple Updates at Once

When the *multiUpdate* algorithm is used at the server side of the FlexDPDP protocol, it produces a proof vector, in which all affected nodes are included, and a hash value, which corresponds to the root of the FlexList after all of the update operations are performed.

The solution we present to verify such an update is constructed in four parts. First, we **verify the multi proof** both by FlexList verification and tag verification.

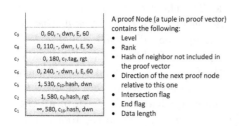

Fig. 4. An output of a multiProof algorithm.

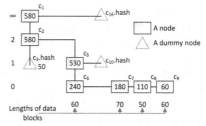

Fig. 5. The temporary FlexList generated out of the proof vector in Fig. 4. Note that node names are the same with Fig. 1.

Second, we **construct a temporary FlexList**, which is constituted of the parts necessary for the updates. Third, we **do the updates** as they are, at the client side. The resulting temporary FlexList has the root of the original FlexList at the server side after performing all updates correctly. Fourth and last, we **check** if the **new root** we calculated is the same as the one sent by the server. If they are the same return accept and update the meta data that is kept by the client.

Constructing a Temporary FlexList out of a Multi Proof: Building a temporary FlexList is giving the client the opportunity to use the regular FlexList methods to do the necessary changes to calculate the new root. **Dummy nodes** that we use below are the nodes that have some values set and are **never subject to recalculation**.

We explain the Algorithm 7.1 (see Appendix) using the proof vector presented in Fig. 4. The output of the algorithm given the proof vector is the temporary FlexList in Fig. 5. First, the algorithm takes the proof node for c_1, generates the root using its values and adds the dummy after, with the hash value (of c_{16}) stored in it. And the nodes are connected to each other depending on their attributes. The proof node for c_2 is used to add node c_2 to the below of c_1 and the c_2's dummy node is connected to its below with rank value of 50, calculated as rank of c_2 minus rank of c_5. Note that the rank values of below nodes are used in regular algorithms so we calculate and set them. The next iteration sets c_5 as c_2's after and c_5's dummy node c_10 is added to c_5's after. The next step is to add c_6 to the below of c_5. c_6 is both an end node and an intersection node, therefore we set its tag (from the tag vector) and its length values. Then we attach c_7 and calculate its length value since it is not in the proof vector generated by *genMultiProof* (but we have the necessary information: the rank of c_7 and the rank of c_8). Next, we add the node for c_8, and set its length value from the proof node and its tag value from the tag vector. Last, we do the same to c_9 as c_8. The algorithm outputs the root of the new temporary FlexList.

Verification: Recall that U is the list of updates generated by the client. An update information $u \in U$, includes an index i, and if the update is an insertion or modification, a block and a tag value. The client calls *verifyMultiUpdate* (Algorithm 7.2) with its meta data and the outputs P, T, M of *multiUpdate* from the server. If *verifyMultiProof* returns accept, we call *buildDummyFlexList* with the proof vector P. The resulting temporary FlexList is ready to handle updates. Again we perform the updates without the hash calculations and then call the *calculateMultiHash* algorithm. But, we do not need to track changes to call a *calculateMultiHash* at the end, but instead calculate the hash of all the nodes present in the list. Last, we check if the resulting hash of the root of our temporary FlexList is equal to the one sent by the server. If they are the same, we accept and update the client's meta data.

5   Experimental Evaluation

We used our implementations of the FlexList data structure and the FlexDPDP protocol, that are in C++ with the aid of the *Cashlib* library [8,28] for cryptography and the *Boost Asio* library [6] for network programming. Our local experiments are run on a 64-bit computer possessing 4 Intel(R) Xeon(R) CPU E5-2640 @ 2.50 GHz CPU, 16 GB of memory and 16 MB of L2 level cache, running Ubuntu 12.04 LTS. The security parameters are as follows: 1024 bit RSA modulus, 80 bit random numbers, SHA1 as hash function resulting with an expected security of 80 bits. Mostly, FlexList operations run on RAM, but we keep each block of a file separately on the hard disk drive and **include the I/O times in our experimental analysis**.

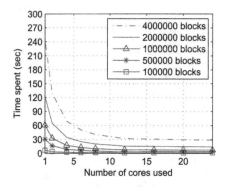
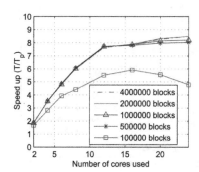

Fig. 6. Time spent while building a FlexList from scratch.

Fig. 7. Speedup values of buildFlexList function with multiple cores.

5.1   Parallel Build FlexList Performance

Figure 6 shows the build FlexList function's time as a function of the number of cores used in parallel. The case of one core corresponds to the buildFlexList function proposed in [17]. From 2 cores to 24 cores, we measure the time spent by our parallel build FlexList function. Notice the speed up where parallel build reduces the time to build a FlexList of 4 million blocks from 240 s to 30 s on 12 cores The speedup values are reported in Fig. 7 where T stands for time for a single core used and T_p stands for time with p number of cores used. The more sub-tasks created, the more time is required to divide the big task into parts and to combine them. We see that a FlexList of 100000 blocks does not get improved as much, since the sub tasks are getting smaller and the overhead of thread generation starts to surpass the gain of parallel operations. Starting from 12 cores, we observe this side effect for all sizes. For 500000 blocks (i.e., 1 GB file) and larger FlexLists, **speed ups of 6 and 7.7** are observed on 8 and 12 cores respectively.

5.2   Server-Side Multi Update Operations

Results for the core FlexList methods (insert, remove, modify) with and without the hash calculations for various sizes of FlexList are shown in Fig. 8. Even with the I/O time, the operations with the hash calculations take 10 times more time than the simple operations in a 4 GB file (i.e., 2000000 nodes). The hash calculations in an update take 90 % of the time spent for an update operation. Therefore, this finding indicates the benefit of doing hash calculations only once for multiple updates in the *performMultiUpdate* algorithm.

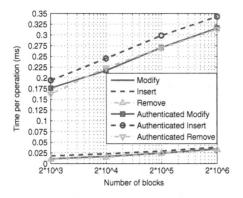

Fig. 8. Time spent for an update operation in FlexList with and without hash calculations.

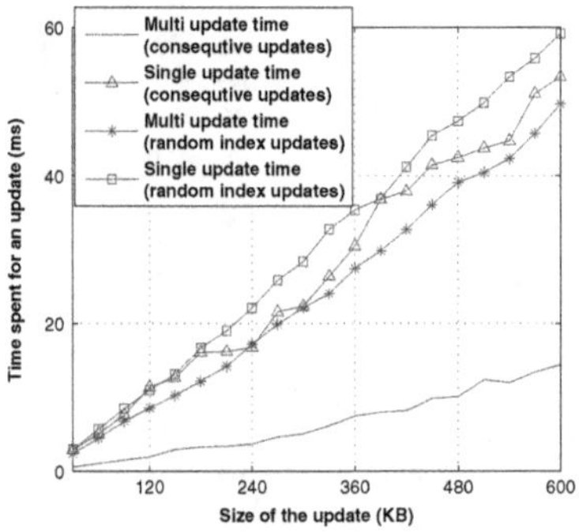

Fig. 9. Time spent on performing multi updates against series of single updates.

performMultiUpdate allows using multi proofs as discussed in Sect. 4. This provides ∼25 % time and space efficiency on the verifiable update operations when the update is ∼20KB, and this gain increases up to ∼35 % with 200 KB updates. The time spent for an update at the server side for various size of updates is shown in Fig. 9 with each data point reflecting the average of 10 experiments. Each update is an even mix of modify, insert, and remove operations. If the update locality is high, meaning the updates are on consecutive blocks (a diff operation generates several modifies to consecutive blocks followed by a series of remove if the added data is shorter than the deleted data, or a series of inserts otherwise [17]), using our *calculateMultiHash* algorithm after the updates without hash calculation on a FlexList for a 1 GB file, the server time for **300 consecutive update operations** (a 600 KB update) decreased **from 53 ms to 13 ms.**

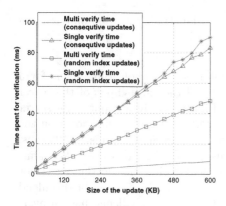

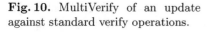

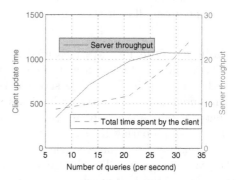

Fig. 10. MultiVerify of an update against standard verify operations.

Fig. 11. Clients challenging their data. Two lines present: first, server throughput in count per second and second, whole time for a challenge query of FlexDPDP, in ms.

5.3 Client-Side Multi Update Operations

For the server to be able to use *multiUpdate* algorithm, the client could be able to verify multiple updates at once. Otherwise, as each single verify update requires a root hash value after that specific update, all hash values on the search path of the update should be calculated each time. Also, each update proof should include a FlexList proof alongside them. Verifying multiple updates at once not only diminishes the proof size but also provides time improvements at the client side. Figure 10 shows that a multi verify operation is faster at the client side when compared to verifying all the proofs one by one. We tested two scenarios: One is for the updates randomly distributed along the FlexList, and the other is for the updates with high locality. The client verification time is highly improved. For instance, with a 1 GB file and a 300 KB update, verification at the client side was reduced from 45 ms to less than 5 ms. With random updates, the multi verification is still 2 times faster.

5.4 Real Usage Performance Analysis via PlanetLab

We deployed the FlexDPDP model on the world-wide network testbed Planet-Lab. We chose a node in Wuerzburg, Germany[1] on PlanetLab as the server which has two Intel(R) Core(TM)2 CPU 6600 @ 2.40 GHz (IC2) and 48 MBit upload and 80 MBit download speed. Our protocol runs on a 1 GB file, which is divided into blocks of 2 KB, having 500000 nodes (for each client). The throughput is defined as the maximum number of queries the server can reply in a second.

---

[1] planetlab1.informatik.uni-wuerzburg.de.

Our results are the average of 50 runs on the PlanetLab with randomly chosen 50 clients from all over the Europe.

Challenge Queries: We measured two metrics, the whole time spent for a challenge proof interaction at the client side and the throughput of the server (both illustrated in Fig. 11). As shown in the Figure, the throughput of the server is around 21. When the server limit is reached, we observe a slowdown on the client side where the response time increases from around 500 ms to 1250 ms. Given that preparing a proof of size 460 using the IC2 processor takes 40ms using *genMultiProof* on a single core, we conclude that the bottleneck is not the processing power. The challenge queries are solely a seed, thus the download speed is not the bottleneck neither. A proof of a multi challenge has an average size of 280 KB (~215 KB FlexList proof, ~58 KB tags, ~2 KB blocksum), therefore to serve 21 clients in a second a server needs 47 MBit upload speed which seems to be the bottleneck in this experiment. The more we increase the upload speed, the more clients we can serve with such a low end server.

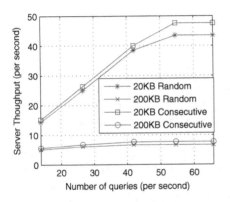

Fig. 12. Server throughput versus the frequency of the client queries.

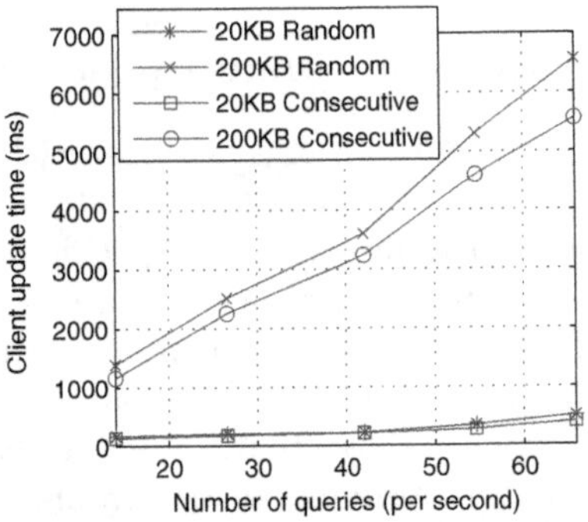

Fig. 13. A client's total time spent for an update query (sending the update, receiving a proof and verifying the proof).

Update Queries:
Real Life Usage Analysis Over Real Version Control System Traces: We have conducted analysis on the SVN server where we have 350 MB of data that we have been using for the past 2 years. We examined a sequence of 627 commit calls and provide results for an average usage of a commit function by means of the **update locality**, the **update size** being sent through the network, and the updated **number of blocks**.

We consider the directory hierarchy proposed in [16]. The idea presented is to set root of each file's FlexList (of the single file scheme presented) in the leaf nodes of a dictionary used to organize files. The update locality of the commits is very high. More than 99 % of the updates in a single commit occur in the same folder, thus do not affect most parts of the directory, thus FlexList but a small portion of them. Moreover, 27 % of the updates are consecutive block updates on a single field of a single file.

With each commit an average of size 77 KB is sent, where we have 2.7 % commits of size greater than 200 KB and 85 % commits has size less than 20KB. These sizes are the amounts sent through the network. Erway et al. show analysis on 3 public SVN repositories. They indicate that the average update size is 28 KB [16]. Therefore in our experiments on PlanetLab we choose 20KB (to show general usage) and 200KB (to show big commits) as the size sent for a commit call. The average number of blocks affected per commit provided by Erway et al. is 13 [16] and is 57.7 in our SVN repository. They both show the necessity of efficient multiple update operations.

We observe the size variation of the commits and see that the greatest common divisor of the size of all commits is 1, as expected. Thus we conclude that fixed block sized rank-based authenticated skip lists is not applicable to the cloud storage scenario.

Table 2. Proof time and size table for various type of updates.

Update size and type	Server proof generation time	Corresponding proof size
200 KB (100 blocks) randomly dist	30 ms	70 KB
20 KB (10 blocks) randomly dist	10 ms	11 KB
200 KB (100 blocks) consecutive	7 ms	17 KB
20 KB (10 blocks) consecutive	6 ms	4 KB

Update Queries on the PlanetLab: We perform analysis using the same metrics as a challenge query. The first one is the whole time spent at the client side (Fig. 13) and the second one is the throughput of the server (Fig. 12), for updates of size ~20 KB and ~200 KB. We test the behavior of the system by varying the query frequency, the update size, and the update type (updates to consecutive blocks or randomly selected blocks). Table 2 shows the measurements for each update type.

Figure 12 shows that a server can reply to ~45 many updates of size 20 KB and ~8 many updates of size 200 KB per second. Figure 13 also approves, that the server is loaded, by the increase in time of a client getting served. Comparing update proofs with the proof size of only challenges (shown in Fig. 11), we conclude that the bottleneck for replying update queries is not the upload speed of the server, since a randomly distributed update of size 200 KB needs 70 KB proof and 8 proof per second is using just 4.5 Mbit of the upload bandwidth or a randomly distributed updates of size 20 KB needs a proof of size 11 KB and 45 proof per second uses only 4MBit of upload bandwidth. Table 2 shows the proof generation times at the server side. 30 ms per 200 KB random operation is required so a server may answer up to 110-120 queries per second with IC2 processor and 10 ms per 20 KB random operation is required, thus a server can reply up to 300 queries per second. Therefore, the bottleneck is not the processing power either. Eventually the amount of queries of a size a server can accept per second is limited, even though the download bandwidth does not seem to be loaded up. But, note that the download speed is checked with a single source and a continuous connection. When a server keeps accepting new connections, the end result is different. This was not a limiting issue in answering challenge queries since a challenge is barely a seed to show the server which blocks are challenged. In our setting, there is one thread at the server side which accepts a query and creates a thread to reply it. We conclude that the bottleneck is the server query acceptance rate of our implementation. These results indicate that with a distributed and replicated server system, a server using FlexDPDP scheme may reply to more queries.

6   Conclusion and Future Work

In this study, we have extended the FlexDPDP scheme with optimized and efficient algorithms, and tested their performance on real workloads in network realistic settings. We obtained a speed up of 6 using 8 cores on the pre-processing step, 60 % improvement on the server-side updates, and 90 % improvement while verifying them at the client side.

We deployed the scheme on the PlanetLab testbed and provided detailed analysis using real version control system workload traces. We measured the throughput of the server and the time spent at the client side after our optimizations and show that even with a low-end server, the bottleneck is the upload speed of the server. And we show that at the client side, the latencies are not perceptible.

After the optimizations, with the experiments, we show that the implemented FlexDPDP scheme is practically usable in real life scenarios. As future work, we plan to extend FlexDPDP to distributed and replicated servers.

Acknowledgement. We would like to thank Ozan Okumuşoğlu at Koç University, Istanbul, Turkey for his contribution on testing and debugging, working on implementation of server-client side of the project and verification algorithms. We also acknowledge the support of TÜBİTAK (the Scientific and Technological Research Council of Turkey) under project numbers 111E019 and 112E115, Türk Telekom, Inc. under grant 11315-06, the European Union COST Actions IC1206 and IC1306, and Koç Sistem, Inc.

7 Appendix: Optimization Algorithms

Algorithm 7.1. constructTemporaryFlexList Algorithm

Input: P, T
Output: root (temporary FlexList)

Let $P = (A_0, \ldots, A_k)$, where $A_j = (\ level_j,\ r_j,\ \text{hash}_j,\ rgtOrDwn_j,\ isInter_j,\ isEnd_j,\ length_j)$ for $j = 0, \ldots, k$; $T = (tag_0, \ldots, tag_t)$, where tag_t is tag for challenged $block_t$ and dummy nodes are nodes including only hash and rank values set on them and they are final once they are created; //

1	$root$ = new Node(r_0, $length_0$) // This node is the root and we keep this as a pointer to return at the end//
2	$\sqcup_s$ = new empty stack
3	$cn = root$
4	dumN = new dummy node is created with hash$_j$
5	cn.after = dumN
6	**for** $i = 0$ *to* k **do**
7	$\quad nn$ = new node is created with Level$_{i+1}$ and r_{i+1}
8	$\quad$ **if** $isEnd_i$ *and* $isInter_i$ **then**
9	$\quad\quad cn$.tag = next tag in T; cn.length = $length_i$; cn.after = nn; $cn = cn$.after
10	$\quad$ **else if** $isEnd_i$ **then**
11	$\quad\quad cn$.tag = next tag in T; cn.length = $length_i$; **if** r_i != $length_i$ **then**
12	$\quad\quad\quad$ dumN = new dummy node is created with hash$_i$ as hash and r_i - $length_i$ as rank
13	$\quad\quad cn$.after = dumN
14	$\quad\quad$ **if** $\sqcup_s$ *is not empty* **then**
15	$\quad\quad\quad cn = \sqcup_s$.pop() ; cn.after = nn; $cn = cn$.after
16	$\quad$ **else if** $level_i = 0$ **then**
17	$\quad\quad cn$.tag = hash$_i$; cn.length = r_i - r_{i+1} ; cn.after = nn ; $cn = cn$.after
18	$\quad$ **else if** $isInter_i$ **then**
19	$\quad\quad cn$ is added to $\sqcup_s$; cn.below = nn; $cn = cn$.below
20	$\quad$ **else if** $rgtOrDwn_i = rgt$ **then**
21	$\quad\quad cn$.after = nn
22	$\quad\quad$ dumN = new dummy node is created with hash$_i$ as hash and r_i - r_{i+1} as rank
23	$\quad\quad cn$.below = dumN ; $cn = cn$.after
24	$\quad$ **else**
25	$\quad\quad cn$.below = nn
26	$\quad\quad$ dumN = new dummy node is created with hash$_i$ as hash and r_i - r_{i+1} as rank
27	$\quad\quad cn$.after = dumN ; $cn = cn$.below
28	**return** $root$

Algorithm 7.2. verifyMultiUpdate Algorithm

Input: P, T, $MetaData$, U, $MetaData_{byServer}$
Output: accept or reject

Let U= $(u_0, \ldots, u_k)$ where u_j is the jth update information

1	**if** !*verifyMultiProof(P, T, MetaData)* **then**
2	$\quad$ **return** reject
3	FlexList = buildTemporaryFlexList(P)
4	**for** $i = 0$ *to* k **do**
5	$\quad$ apply u_i to FlexList without any hash calculations
6	calculate hash values of all nodes in the temporary FlexList. //A recursive call from the root
7	**if** $root.hash$!= $MetaData_{byServer}$ **then**
8	$\quad$ **return** reject
9	**return** accept

References

1. Abraham, I., Chockler, G., Keidar, I., Malkhi, D.: Byzantine disk paxos: optimal resilience with byzantine shared memory. Distrib. Comput. **18**(5), 387–408 (2006)
2. Ateniese, G., Burns, R., Curtmola, R., Herring, J., Kissner, L., Peterson, Z., Song, D.: Provable data possession at untrusted stores. In: ACM CCS (2007)

3. Ateniese, G., Kamara, S., Katz, J.: Proofs of storage from homomorphic identification protocols. In: Matsui, M. (ed.) ASIACRYPT 2009. LNCS, vol. 5912, pp. 319–333. Springer, Heidelberg (2009)
4. Ateniese, G., Di Pietro, R., Mancini, L.V., Tsudik, G.: Scalable and efficient provable data possession. In: SecureComm (2008)
5. Bessani, A., Correia, M., Quaresma, B., André, F., Sousa, P.: Depsky: dependable and secure storage in a cloud-of-clouds. In: EuroSys 2011. ACM (2011)
6. Boost asio library. http://www.boost.org/doc/libs
7. Bowers, K.D., Juels, A., Oprea, A.: Hail: a high-availability and integrity layer for cloud storage. In: ACM CCS (2009)
8. Brownie cashlib cryptographic library. http://github.com/brownie/cashlib
9. Cachin, C., Keidar, I., Shraer, A.: Trusting the Cloud. SIGACT News, New York (2009)
10. Cachin, C.,Tessaro, S.: Optimal resilience for erasure-coded byzantine distributed storage. In: DSN 2006. IEEE Computer Society, Washington (2006)
11. Cash, D., Küpçü, A., Wichs, D.: Dynamic proofs of retrievability via oblivious ram. In: Johansson, T., Nguyen, P.Q. (eds.) EUROCRYPT 2013. LNCS, vol. 7881, pp. 279–295. Springer, Heidelberg (2013)
12. Chockler, G., Guerraoui, R., Keidar, I., Vukolic, M.: Reliable distributed storage. IEEE Comput. **42**(4), 60–67 (2009)
13. Chockler, G., Malkhi, D.: Active disk paxos with infinitely many processes. In: Proceedings of PODC 2002. ACM Press (2002)
14. Curtmola, R.: Khan, O., Burns, R., Ateniese, G.: Multiple-replica provable data possession. In: ICDCS (2008)
15. Dodis, Y., Vadhan, S., Wichs, D.: Proofs of retrievability via hardness amplification. In: Reingold, O. (ed.) TCC 2009. LNCS, vol. 5444, pp. 109–127. Springer, Heidelberg (2009)
16. Erway, C., Küpçü, A., Papamanthou, C., Tamassia, R.: Dynamic provable data possession. In: ACM CCS (2009)
17. Esiner, E., Kachkeev, A., Braunfeld, S., Küpçü, A., Özkasap, Ö.: Flexdpdp: Flexlist-based optimized dynamic provable data possession. Cryptology ePrint Archive, Report 2013/645 (2013)
18. Etemad, M., Küpçü, A.: Transparent, distributed, and replicated dynamic provable data possession. In: Jacobson, M., Locasto, M., Mohassel, P., Safavi-Naini, R. (eds.) ACNS 2013. LNCS, vol. 7954, pp. 1–18. Springer, Heidelberg (2013)
19. Furht, B., Escalante, A.: Handbook of Cloud Computing. Computer Science. Springer, Heidelberg (2010)
20. Gafni, E., Lamport, L.: Disk paxos. Distrib. Comput. **16**(1), 1–20 (2003)
21. Goodson, G., Wylie, J., Ganger, G., Reiter, M.: Efficient byzantine-tolerant erasure-coded storage. In: DSN 2004 (2004)
22. Hendricks, J., Ganger, G.R., Reiter, M.k.: Low-overhead byzantine fault-tolerant storage. In: SOSP 2007. ACM (2007)
23. Jayanti, P., Chandra, T.D., Toueg, S.: Fault-tolerant wait-free shared objects. J. ACM. **45**(3), 451–500 (1998)
24. Jensen, M., Schwenk, J., Gruschka, N., Iacono, L.L.: On technical security issues in cloud computing. In: Cloud Computing CLOUD 2009. IEEE (2009)
25. Juels, A., Kaliski, B.S.: PORs: Proofs of retrievability for large files. In: ACM CCS (2007)
26. Liskov, B., Rodrigues, R.: Tolerating byzantine faulty clients in a quorum system. In: IEEE 32nd International Conference on Distributed Computing Systems (2006)

27. Malkhi, D., Reiter, M.: Byzantine quorum systems. Distrib. Comput. **11**(4), 203–213 (1998)

28. Meiklejohn, S., Erway, C., Küpçü, A., Hinkle, T., Lysyanskaya, A.: Zkpdl: Enabling efficient implementation of zero-knowledge proofs and e-cash. In: USENIX Security (2010)

29. Papamanthou, C., Tamassia, R.: Time and space efficient algorithms for two-party authenticated data structures. In: Qing, S., Imai, H., Wang, G. (eds.) ICICS 2007. LNCS, vol. 4861, pp. 1–15. Springer, Heidelberg (2007)

30. Shacham, H., Waters, B.: Compact proofs of retrievability. In: Pieprzyk, J. (ed.) ASIACRYPT 2008. LNCS, vol. 5350, pp. 90–107. Springer, Heidelberg (2008)

31. Stanton, P.T., McKeown, B., Burns, R.C., Ateniese, G.: Fastad: an authenticated directory for billions of objects. SIGOPS Oper. Syst. Rev. **44**(1), 45–49 (2010)

32. Wang, Q., Wang, C., Li, J., Ren, K., Lou, W.: Enabling public verifiability and data dynamics for storage security in cloud computing. In: Backes, M., Ning, P. (eds.) ESORICS 2009. LNCS, vol. 5789, pp. 355–370. Springer, Heidelberg (2009)

33. Wooley, P.S.: Identifying cloud computing security risks. Technical report, 7 University of Oregon Eugene (2011)

34. Zheng, Q., Xu, S.: Fair and dynamic proofs of retrievability. In: CODASPY (2011)

Leveraging Ad-hoc Networking and Mobile Cloud Computing to Exploit Short-Lived Relationships Among Users on the Move

Jack Fernando Bravo-Torres[1], Martín López-Nores[2]([✉]),
Yolanda Blanco-Fernández[2], José Juan Pazos-Arias[2],
and Esteban Fernando Ordióñez-Morales[1]

[1] Área de Ciencias Exactas, Universidad Politécnica Salesiana,
Calle Vieja 12-30 y Elia Liut, Cuenca, Ecuador
{jbravo,eordonez}@ups.edu.ec
[2] AtlantTIC Research Center for Information
and Communication Technologies, Departamento de Ingeniería
Telemática, Universidade de Vigo, EE Telecomunicación,
Campus Universitario s/n, 36310 Vigo, Spain
{mlnores,yolanda,jose}@det.uvigo.es

Abstract. The interactions enabled by the popular sites of the Web 2.0 are largely confined to the virtual world of the Internet, thus failing to engage people in relevant interactions with people, contents or resources in their physical environment. In this paper, we motivate the potential of automatically establishing sporadic social networks among people (acquaintances or strangers) who happen to be physically close to one another at a certain moment. We present the design of one platform intended to provide solutions from the lowest level of establishing ad-hoc connections among nearby mobile devices, up to the highest level of automatically identifying the most relevant pieces of information to deliver at any time. A number of application scenarios are presented, along with technical details of a solution to empower ad-hoc communications by means of a virtualization layer.

Keywords: Sporadic social networks · Ad-hoc networking · Mobile cloud computing · Knowledge management

1 Introduction

In recent years, research in the field of information services has made significant progress in exploiting the knowledge contained (explicitly or implicitly) on social networks like Facebook, Twitter, Instagram, Foursquare and LinkedIn. Despite having radically different approaches and objectives, these Web 2.0 sites are always based on semi-permanent relationships among people. These relations (bidirectional, as friends, or unidirectional, as followers/followees) serve to gradually build knowledge bases in the form of graphs, with elements representing the pieces of information shared by the individuals: comments, documents,

© Springer International Publishing Switzerland 2015
A. Al-Saidi et al. (Eds.): ICC 2014, LNCS 8993, pp. 84–102, 2015.
DOI: 10.1007/978-3-319-19848-4_6

images etc. The analysis of such meshes of contents enables additional features like recommending potentially interesting contents for each individual, launching of advertising campaigns aimed at specific groups or segments of the population, identifying affinities among people or synergies between different areas of activity, etc.

Despite the penetration of many of the aforementioned social networks, it is noticeable that the interactions they enable are largely confined to the virtual world of the Internet. These are not accompanied by actual interactions (i.e. face-to-face) except in cases in which people communicate to arrange physical meetings for entertainment or work. Moreover, it is noticeable that the individuals' interactions are increasingly focused on the set of people included in their social graphs, which are now accessible at any time. This causes a side effect of de-socialization, in which the individual is isolated from his/her environment and voluntarily (though perhaps not quite consciously) gets trapped in a bubble of communication with his/her contacts. This social phenomenon is being widely studied [14], but its effects in the medium-to-long term are still unknown. Notwithstanding, the current state of technology, together with the ever-growing popularity of smartphones, has led many authors to envisage a new era of information services tailored to the people's physical and social context [7,33]: the era of *pervasive social computing*.

This paper is about applying technology to enable new forms of social interaction outside the aforementioned bubble. Specifically, we are building a platform called SPORANGIUM (*"SPORAdic social networks in the Next-Generation Information services for Users on the Move"*) that aims at facilitating the creation and exploitation of sporadic (short-lived) social networks, communicating each individual with the people that surround him/her at a given moment (both acquaintances and strangers) and considering the information that may be relevant to them in different contexts and at different levels (room, building, street, city, province, etc.). The goal is to allow each individual to make the most of the people and the resources present in the environment at all times. The proposal is applicable in various areas, from the formation of groups and the orchestration of activities around events or venues that attract people with potentially-related interests (e.g. museums, concert halls or campsites) to opportunities for enhanced communications and access to relevant information on the road (advanced information services to vehicular networks) or advances in the vision of the smart cities (related to the planning of personal mobility or the celebration of location-based urban games) [23].

The paper is organized as follows. We present the architecture of the SPORANGIUM platform in Sect. 2, followed by a description of some of the functionalities we aim to support in different areas in Sect. 3. Some technical details about the platform are included in Sect. 4. Conclusions are finally given in Sect. 5.

2   The SPORANGIUM Platform

We are developing the SPORANGIUM platform as an extension of the technology that is already available to people, aiming to incorporate sporadic social networks (henceforth, SSNs) and the mechanisms that make them possible into the technological landscape of the well-known Web 2.0. Conceptually, its architecture has four levels, as shown in Fig. 1.

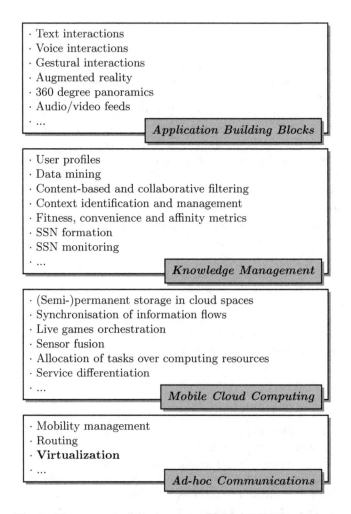

Fig. 1. The conceptual layers of the SPORANGIUM platform.

The sporadic social networks rely firstly on ad-hoc networks laid dynamically among the mobile devices of the people who happen to be close to one another at a given moment. With proper foundations, ad-hoc networks are arguably the most natural and efficient way to exchange information among people who are very close to each other, instead of proceeding *"the Whatsapp way"*, i.e. sending data packets out to servers that may be very far away, only to have the server echo the same packets downlink [6,27]. In this regard, SPORANGIUM provides mechanisms to establish connections proactively and transparently to the users whenever deemed appropriate by the information from higher levels of the architecture. It incorporates virtualization constructs introduced in [31] and refined in [3] to use the ad-hoc networks as reliable channels and repositories of the information available to the members of an SSN. Virtualization provides scalable mechanisms by which the mobile devices can collaborate to support communications from, to and through them, directly or in a multihop fashion, even with the ability to differentiate a range of QoS demands [18].

Whenever the ad-hoc networks are not stable or reliable enough, the "*Mobile Cloud Computing*" (MCC) layer can use the infrastructure accessible through 2G/3G/4G connections or Wi-Fi access points to maintain connectivity as far as possible and to store information temporarily during periods of disconnection. Unlike the classical vision of mobile cloud computing, focused on individuals that would do practically nothing without access to the Internet (see [8]), the goal of MCC in SPORANGIUM is to enable value-added services for groups of people already in the level of ad-hoc communications, harnessing the resources available to each one of them through their mobile devices. There are plenty of things to be done without access to the Internet, which can nonetheless be exploited (and shared) whenever possible to offer more advanced functionalities and more abundant contents. Following this philosophy (which is explicit in the diagram of Fig. 2) the MCC layer in SPORANGIUM provides the following services, with only the last and the last-but-one depending on connectivity out of the ad-hoc networks:

- Storing information in spaces in the cloud, linked to source/target devices, creating/consuming users, location, etc.
- Accessing and serving information of high-level user profiles during the formation of ad-hoc networks.
- Synchronizing multiple flows of information coming from the connected devices.
- Supervising and enforcing interaction patterns to support live games.
- Pooling data from various sensors on multiple devices to achieve greater precision in geolocation.
- Delegating complex tasks on remote machines, to overcome the limitations of the mobile devices in terms of battery, memory and/or computing power.
- Providing access to cloud services on the Internet: maps, databases, semantic repositories, etc.

Upper in the architecture, the "*Knowledge Management*" layer is the place to put solutions from the areas of data mining, recommender systems and the Semantic Web to automatically drive the selection of pieces of information for the greatest benefit of the members of an SSN, while personalizing the contents delivered by each device either to a single person (as typically happens with mobile phones) or several people using the same device (as might be the occupants of a vehicle). In this regard, we are doing our early experiments by reusing semantic reasoning and personalisation mechanisms from previous works of our own, out of the realm of mobile devices and social networking [15,16].

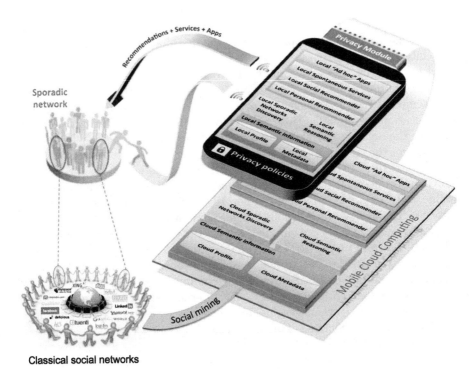

Fig. 2. The combined vision of ad-hoc networks and mobile cloud computing.

The top level of the architecture, *"Application Building Blocks"*, conceptually contains the software components that provide value-added services to the members of an SSN, plus the interfaces that help make the most of those new features: augmented reality, 360 degree panoramic pictures, gestural interactions, etc.

3   Sample Application Scenarios

In the following subsections, we describe some of the features that may be enabled by the vision of the sporadic social networks in different areas of application.

3.1   SPORANGIUM Features for Venues

The use of the SPORANGIUM platform in venues has to do with the formation of groups, the orchestration of activities, the synchronization of multiple flows of information and the collective use of the devices in the hands of the different individuals. Museums, concert halls, campsites, kindergartens, stadiums, ... they are all places where many people get close together and, even though they may not know each other, it is likely that they have common interests (e.g. in History or Science, in a certain kind of music, in nature, in children stuff, in sports, etc.). Hereafter, we will focus on features enabled by SSNs in museums, which put forward ideas that could be easily extrapolated to other venues.

People go to museums during their spare time purposefully to learn about a specific subject, which makes them propitious places to go beyond the individual use of mobile devices promoted by the many previous pieces of work that provided personalized itineraries within the buildings, continuity of experiences from one visit to another, etc [9,12,26,29]. With the corresponding SSN application, a museum visitor would be ready to start interacting with people out of the everyday contacts upon entering the building. To begin with, the user could browse a virtual bulletin board containing a selection of messages posted on Twitter by other current visitors with similar profiles. Short reviews and photos of areas to visit, ratings of activities and exhibitions, ... could be a very good starting point for newcomers to get to know the place and to meet new people, with no need to ever have browsed their Twitter profiles and, of course, with no need to have previously established follower-followee relationships.

The platform could also take the lead in gathering groups of visitors to engage in guided tours inside the museum, considering such parameters as language, country/province of origin, gender and age. Having identified a number of visitors for the task, their mobile devices could be used to agree on the hour, the duration and the topic of the tour in close interaction with the museum staff. Then, when the tour is running, the mobiles devices of the visitors and the guide would be contributing contents (textual comments, pictures, recorded audio, etc.) to one space in the cloud, to be shared accessed by others to the criteria decided by the owner of each device: *"this comment is open for all the others to read"*, *"this annotation is only for me"*, *"this picture can be only seen by the people who appear on it"*.

Contents coming from multiple devices in an SSN are automatically aggregated, annotated and synchronized at the MCC layer to allow accessing them in different ways. For example, they can be displayed on a virtual timeline that the user could scroll to remember what the guide had said minutes before, to compare a picture in display with another one in the preceding room, etc. They can also be displayed on a scrollable map or as augmented-reality items overlaid on the live output of a camera.

3.2 SPORANGIUM Features for Vehicular Social Networking

The application of the SPORANGIUM platform to vehicular environments was motivated by some of the visions put forward in [13] about the future of the mobile Internet, which are largely shared by researchers, car manufacturers and transport authorities. It was proved in [32] that, due to the length and the regularity of people's trips on private cars and/or public transport, vehicle encounters exhibit inherent social structure and behavior. These facts can be exploited at the communications level to improve the performance of protocols like 802.11j [21], but we are more interested in the concept —first introduced in [25]— of vehicular social networks as groups of individuals who may have common interests, preferences or needs in a context of temporal and spatial proximity on the roads. Our first goal in the development of SPORANGIUM is to provide a common framework to support features already tested in previous works [10,28]. To this aim, we want to provide reliable mechanisms to establish direct voice communications among nearby vehicles, with the ability to filter incoming calls based on distance, caller profile, etc. Such communications will flow primarily on wireless ad-hoc networks, typically hop-by-hop, but using mobile telephony networks only in cases where the ad-hoc mechanisms cannot guarantee the required quality. We can envisage various motivations for calls, from unicast messages/questions (e.g. *"it looks like you are driving on a low air wheel"*) to multicast ones (*"can anyone tell me the way to the bullfighting arena?"*) or comments that can lead to conversations and new relationships in a classical social network (e.g. *"that's a JRS spoiler, isn't it?"*).

Additionally, the features provided by the *"Mobile Cloud Computing"* and *"Knowledge Management"* layers of SPORANGIUM are aimed at enabling new features related with a smarter management of information in a collaborative fashion. For example, by managing profiles that include a characterization of the users and their mobility patterns, the platform can assist in the detection of ride-sharing opportunities, as promoted by web sites like carpooling.com.uk as a way to reduce costs, decongest roads and parking lots, reduce pollution, etc. Especially in the vicinity of large cities, many people commute over routes that often overlap significantly, except for a few kilometers to the beginning and the end. It is particularly interesting to exploit situations of traffic congestion during rush hours to automatically detect matches on journeys planned for the next few days, notifying drivers properly and letting them agree on the details through the aforementioned direct communication mechanisms.

An ad-hoc network set up among a number of vehicles can support the downloading and sharing or dissemination of pieces of content relevant to the drivers' location, ranging from notices of accidents and consequent diversion suggestions to advertising material about nearby shops or attractions. The latter point opens up multiple possibilities for customization according to the profiles of each driver and the passengers accompanying him/her, taking into account that the material may cease to be relevant (because the place in question is no longer reachable) after any crossroads or junction.

In line with the previous point, monitoring traffic flows and driver profiles can help create dynamic advertising systems, capable of adapting the content displayed on billboards, signs or other channels to improve the efficiency of the campaigns. The SSN mechanisms make it possible to deploy strategies aimed at bringing together groups of customers, e.g. by offering discounts provided that a minimum number of people show up at a service station for lunch with the same coupon code. There can be previous input from the potential customers, like when the underlying networks are used to transmit on-board diagnostics information (e.g. fuel/oil levels or wheels pressure) to establishments that could perform the appropriate maintenance tasks.

3.3   SPORANGIUM Features for the Smart City

Many institutions are promoting the concept of the smart city as a strategic move to improve the efficiency of the public services, to boost the activity of the local businesses and to improve the quality of life of the citizens. In this line, the sporadic social networks enabled by the SPORANGIUM platform could enable new forms of communication and collaboration among acquaintances or strangers for several purposes.

To begin with, SSNs could support time banking initiatives as a means to forge stronger inter-community connections. Time banking is a pattern of reciprocal service exchange that uses units of time as currency: basically, the time one spends providing these types of community services earns time that one can spend to receive services. This has been primarily used to provide incentives and rewards for work such as mentoring children or caring for the elderly, which a pure market system devalues. However, it also works with otherwise paid jobs like doing haircuts or gardening. Despite their growing interest in the context of global economic crisis [22], time banks usually fail to involve more than a few dozens of people, often from relatively close circles. This is where SSNs may bring benefits, inasmuch as the ability to trigger communications among strangers in close vicinity can greatly facilitate the discovery of potentially interesting offerings and people who might be interesting in what each one can contribute.

Just like it happened with vehicular networks, SSNs can provide means to deliver publicity of local shops and stores more effectively. For example, one user's positive valuation of a restaurant could be made visible not only to his/her contacts in some of the Web 2.0 sites, but also to other people with similar profiles in the surroundings. The valuation could become a coupon that, when redeemed by a new client, would yield free coffee/dessert to the former. Likewise, SSNs could be used to dynamically identify opportunities to trade batches of products in advantageous conditions (e.g. to offer 20 % discount for one smartphone if at least 20 people come within the next 20 min to buy one unit each). Businesses could join the SSNs to tailor their offerings, and even collaborate to offer packs, e.g. dinner + disco tickets + private taxi for the break of dawn.

The SSNs could also become a basic element to improve the classical navigation/guidance systems based on GPS. Most of those systems work only with street names, which forces the user who receives instructions to look for signposts that may be hard to locate or even missing. One would certainly expect more useful and natural indications from the smart city, for example, to advance *"towards the red building at the bottom"*, *"to the roundabout with a Botero statue"* or *"straight ahead towards the sea until finding a newsstand on the left"*. These indications —that should be tailored to each individual (not everyone can recognize a Botero statue)— could be derived from the activity of the citizens in Web 2.0 sites enhanced with the mechanisms of the SSNs, geolocation features, the possibility of making and sharing pictures, etc. For instance, it usually happens that one person (A) asks another (B, probably a stranger) for indications to go to a given place. Beyond a certain distance, the explanations become longer and more complicated, to the point that it is often necessary to ask a third person.

The SPORANGIUM mechanisms could simplify the process by establishing a short-lived connection between the mobile phones of A and B. Thereby, A could follow the first indications given by B up to a certain point, and then send a 360° panorama to B asking where to go on... and thus proceed in three or four rounds, already in the distance.

Finally, the SSNs could provide suitable foundations for running urban games (aka location-based games) that involve groups of people —again, acquaintances or strangers— in entertainment or educational activities in the context of the smart city. Participants in flashmobs could be recruited on the fly, too. The experiences run up to now in several cities worldwide [11,24] reveal great possibilities for community building in the exploitation of new tools for communication, interaction and personalization of contents.

4   The Key to It All: Virtualization

As noticed in Sect. 2, the concept of virtualization is of utmost importance in the SPORANGIUM platform, as long as it provides scalable mechanisms by which the mobile devices can collaborate to support communications from, to and through them, either directly, in a multihop fashion or through 2G/3G/4G connections shared by nodes on the move within ad-hoc networks. The SPORANGIUM solution in this regard is based on an evolution of the virtualization layer presented in [5] (called the *Virtual Node Layer*, VNLayer) which put forward procedures for mobile devices to collaboratively emulate an infrastructure of stationary *virtual nodes*, that could be addressed as static server devices.

The VNLayer divided the geographical area of an ad-hoc network into square regions, whose size was chosen so that every physical node (PN) in a region could send and receive data, at least, from every other physical node in that region and in the neighbouring ones. The virtual nodes (VNs) can be thought of as lying in the center of the corresponding regions (one VN per region), being able to send messages directly to the 8 neighbouring VNs (see Fig. 3). Each VN is emulated by PNs in the corresponding region, who determine their positions by GPS. One PN in each region is chosen as *leader* and takes charge of packet reception, buffering and forwarding in the communication with other VNs. Meanwhile, a subset of non-leaders work as *backups* to maintain replicas of the state information from the upper layers. Thus, the VNs can maintain persistent state and be fault-tolerant even when individual PNs fail or leave the region, as long as there remains at least one PN.

Brown et al. [5] discussed the advantages of the programming abstraction enabled by the VNLayer, noting that it makes it easier for application developers to work at the mobile nodes' upper layers. In turn, Wu et al. [31] and Patil and Shah [19] proved (separately) that a virtualised version of the AODV routing algorithm [20] (called VNAODV) can outperform AODV itself in terms of route stability and packet delivery ratios. Later on, Wu proved the advantages of virtualization for another routing algorithm (RIP [17]) and ancillary protocols like DHCP [30].

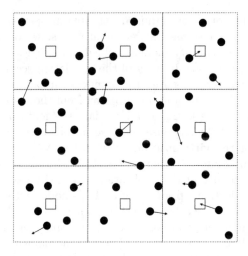

Fig. 3. Static virtual nodes (white squares) overlaying the mobile physical nodes (black circles) in a MANET.

Our goal is to make the virtual node infrastructure flexible enough to embrace communications in/between indoor, pedestrian and vehicular contexts, defining different profiles and configurations for the virtualization layer to choose from. To this aim, we have modified some of the VNLayer procedures and introduced new ones in order to deal with the following shortcomings (revealed by simulation experiments):

- The static layout of equally-shaped, equally-sized VNs neglected the presence of obstacles and adverse propagation conditions for the communications within one region and between neighbouring ones.
- The leader election procedure reacted very slowly to leader withdrawals, so the VNs were down during a non-negligible portion of the time that the PNs would remain in the respective regions.
- Duplicate leaderships (resulting from packet losses during leader elections) were dealt with in a simplistic way, allowing for a newly-arrived node with no state information from the upper layers to drive out a long-standing leader.
- The backup designation process was a probabilistic one, implying that there might be no backup nodes in a region. To make matters worse, there were no mechanisms to replace outgoing backups by other non-leader nodes in the region; only newcomers could take up their place.
- The leader election procedure could designate as new leader either a node that was not acting as a backup node, or a backup node containing data inconsistent with the leader's state (i.e. a non-synchronised backup).
- Finally, we found it critical that the VNLayer does not make any attempts to preserve the state of the VNs when their regions become void of supporting PNs, no matter how long the situation lasts.

These features might not cause significant trouble in open-space MANET scenarios in which the PN movements were relatively slow compared to the size of the regions, and the mobility models yielded more or less uniform counts of PNs over the different regions. In most of the simulation scenarios we have considered for SSNs, however, we noticed a significant impact on the resilience of the VNs, resulting in losses of state information from the upper layers, inconsistent routing tables, routing loops, amplified data traffic, incorrect packet drops and increased overhead. In response to these problems, we have implemented a refined version of the virtualization layer, called VNLayer+, that includes (i) a modified upwards interface that allows the positions, sizes and neighbours of each region to be defined at the applications layer; (ii) a simpler procedure to speed up the leader elections, prioritising backups nodes with up-to-date copies of the leader's state over any other nodes; (iii) a new backup designation process to ensure that the number of backup nodes in a region remains within certain minimum and maximum values; and (iv) a new mechanism to allow handling snapshots of the state information of neighbouring regions to maintain their state during periods of emptiness. The details can be found in [4]; next, we include the results of simulation experiments to show the advantages of VNLayer+ in comparison with the VNLayer.

4.1 Simulation Results

The simulation experiments reported here aimed to compare the performance achieved by the reference implementation of the VNLayer (described in [30]) and our VNLayer+ in supporting the same implementation of the VNAODV routing algorithm (also following the description of [30]) in a scenario of vehicular communications, which is most demanding due to the comparatively faster movements of the nodes, the more abundant losses due to reflection and noise, the presence of obstacles, etc. As indicated by the protocol stacks drawn in Fig. 4, the communications involved constant bitrate (CBR) sessions between pairs of cars chosen at random for each scenario, while the transport protocol chosen was UDP (*User Datagram Protocol*), which implies no acknowledgements and no retries at the transport layer. Each CBR session was set to transmit 500 KB per second and to last throughout the simulation time. Each simulation lasted 450 s, but the traces for the first 50 s in each simulation were skipped to allow the VNAODV routing to stabilize before measurements were started. We repeated each simulation 10 times for each data point collected.

The simulation environment (previously presented in [3]) combines the well-known network simulator *ns-2* [1] and the SUMO simulator of urban mobility [2]. On the one hand, SUMO provided realistic mobility traces for every single vehicle on the streets of an urban area of 476 × 476 m from downtown Cuenca (Ecuador), previously captured in OpenStreetMap (freely available). On the other hand, *ns-2* (version 2.34) was used to simulate communications based on the IEEE 802.11b standard, with wireless signals propagating according to the *shadowing radio* propagation model and a maximum transmission range of 250 m.

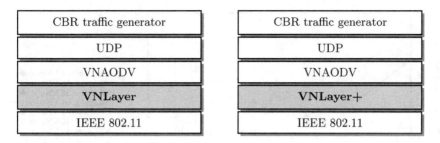

Fig. 4. The protocol stacks of our simulations.

Within these settings, we looked at the following metrics:

- **Average duration of VN downtimes**, directly related to the time spent in recovering from leader withdrawals.
- **Virtualization overhead**, related to the number of VNLayer/VNLayer+ messages exchanged among the vehicles.
- **Packet delivery fraction**, that is, the ratio between the number of packets delivered to the destinations and the number of packets sent by the sources.
- **Number of duplicate leaderships**, i.e. situations in which two vehicles wrongly act simultaneously as leaders of the same virtual node.
- **Overall capacity**, meaning the amount of traffic that can be handled by the ad hoc networks.

The average duration of VN downtimes with the VNLayer and the VNLayer+ is represented in Fig. 5 against varying numbers of physical nodes (60 to 160 vehicles) and varying numbers of virtual nodes (resulting from dividing the square region of downtown Cuenca into 2×2, 4×4, 6×6 and 8×8 grids).[1] The number of CBR communication sessions was initially set to 10. It can be seen that the VNLayer+ consistently reduced the duration of the downtimes by more than 30 % in comparison with the VNLayer, thus ensuring much greater availability of the virtual nodes.

Figure 6 represents the variation of the virtualization overhead caused by the VNLayer and the VNLayer+, again with 10 communication sessions. It can be seen in Fig. 6 that the VNLayer+ achieves substantial savings and accommodates greater numbers of PNs in a more scalable manner.

Probably the best news for the VNLayer+ come from measuring packet delivery fractions, which (as shown in Fig. 7) got very close to 100 % except when there were only 4 VNs (2×2 regions). In that case, the ratio was around 80 %, due to the fact that the big size of the regions (238×238 m) in comparison with the transmission range of the nodes (250 m) made the links between neighboring VNs rather unstable —it was possible to have leader nodes almost out of the reach of their counterparts in neighboring regions. The packet delivery fractions achieved by the VNLayer were always 10 % to 30 % lower, entailing that many

---

[1] The greater the number of VNs, the smaller their corresponding regions.

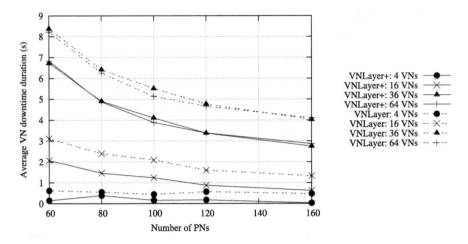

Fig. 5. Average duration of VN downtimes.

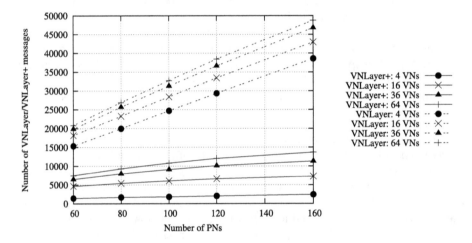

Fig. 6. Virtualization overhead.

packets did not make it to their intended destinations. The losses were due to the fact that UDP protocol does not manage acknowledgements and retries, so that any failure of the virtualization layer to preserve the state information of the VNs (in this case, containing the routing tables handled by VNAODV) leads the PNs to forward packets into dead-ends. These results prove the effectiveness of the backup management policies of the VNLayer+ in combination with the new leader election procedure.[2] The VNLayer might get close to 100 %

---

[2] Note that the numbers of vehicles in the simulations were chosen to ensure sufficiently high densities and, therefore, a certain level of connectedness among the VNs. Otherwise, additional losses would occur for both the VNLayer and the VNLayer+, but there would be nothing to do about them with ad-hoc communications only.

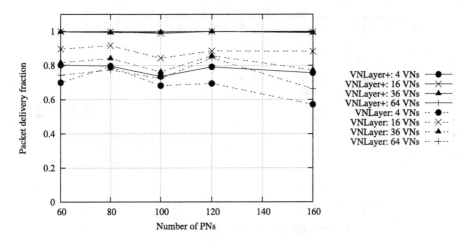

Fig. 7. Variation of packet delivery fraction.

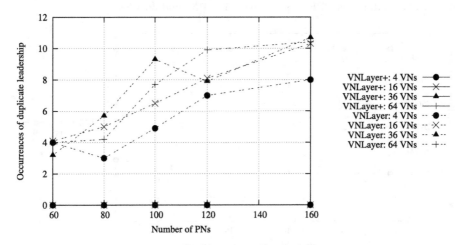

Fig. 8. Duplicate leaderships.

delivery using TCP (*Transmission Control Protocol*) instead of UDP, but the acknowledgements and the retransmitted packets would bring about a significant extra load of traffic and the average delivery delay would increase considerably.

We also found that duplicate leaderships did not occur at all in the VNLayer+ simulations, whereas the VNLayer had to deal with them from time to time. Intuitively, the graph of Fig. 8 suggests that the likelihood of having conflicting leaders increased with the number of PNs around. The faster reactions of the VNLayer+ seemed to consistently avoid the problem of duplicate leaderships until we ran simulations with abnormally-high levels of noise (e.g. with packet loss ratios of 1 % and greater). In such conditions, the VNLayer would deal with

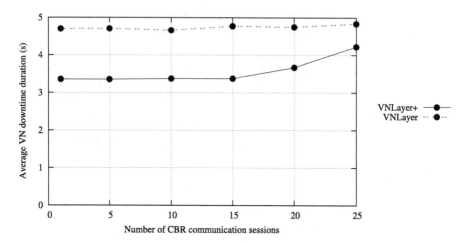

Fig. 9. Average VN downtimes with the VNLayer and the VNLayer+ against a varying number of simultaneous CBR sessions, with 120 PNs and 36 VNs.

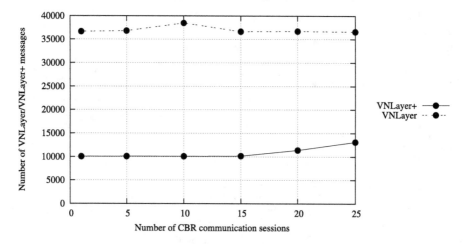

Fig. 10. Virtualization overhead with the VNLayer and the VNLayer+ against a varying number of simultaneous CBR sessions, with 120 PNs and 36 VNs.

fewer duplicates, but that would hardly be considered an advantage given that the global packet delivery fractions would be just too low.

Finally, we made simulations with varying number of communication sessions between pairs of vehicles but fixed numbers of PNs and VNs (120 and 36, respectively, mimicking the experiments reported in [30]). The graphs of Figs. 9, 10, 11 and 12 show that the VNLayer+ can accommodate greater traffic loads than the VNLayer. The VNLayer+ figures are consistently better than those of the VNLayer in terms of VN availability, virtualization overhead, packet delivery fractions and duplicate leaderships (still absent with the VNLayer+). It is particularly interesting to note that the packet delivery fraction achieved by the

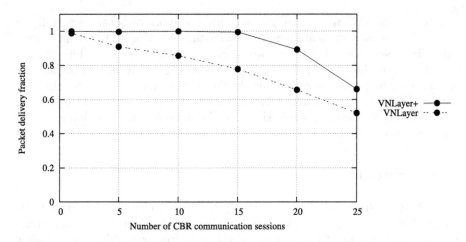

Fig. 11. Packet delivery fraction with the VNLayer and the VNLayer+ against a varying number of simultaneous CBR sessions, with 120 PNs and 36 VNs.

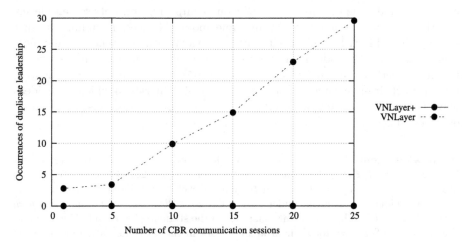

Fig. 12. Duplicate leaderships with the VNLayer and the VNLayer+ against a varying number of simultaneous CBR sessions, with 120 PNs and 36 VNs.

VNLayer+ is not affected by the increase in traffic load until a certain threshold (nearing 15 CBR sessions in the specific scenario of Figs. 9, 10, 11 and 12) has been surpassed, whereas the performance of the VNLayer degrades steadily from the beginning.

4.2   Discussion

Judging from the simulation results, we can confirm that the changes we have made to the VNLayer do serve to increase the benefits of a virtualization layer to support communications in a vehicular ad-hoc network. The new procedures we have put in the VNLayer+ turn the network into more responsive and reliable communication environments than possible with the VNLayer, which ultimately results in greater packet delivery ratios and lower latencies —at this point, it is worth reminding that the VNLayer had been previously proved to improve significantly the performance of plain AODV in MANET settings (see [19,31]). With such performance figures, it is possible to efficiently support TCP sessions on top of the VNLayer+, which should make it even easier for developers to write SSN applications.

5   Conclusions

The SPORANGIUM platform aims at providing mechanisms to exploit the potential of the short-lived social networks that may be built around an individual to make the most of the people and the resources around him/her. Ad-hoc networking provides natural foundations for communications among people who happen to be close to each other, and the concept of virtualization makes it possible to make the most of it. Mobile cloud computing concepts serve to leverage the resources contributed by multiple mobile devices, including Internet access to provide richer services than those available with ad-hoc communications only. Finally, modern knowledge management techniques are the key to bringing together the right groups of people to make the most of the resources present in their environment. There are plenty of scenarios in which SSNs ideas may enable new service opportunities, e.g. for communication, resource sharing or advertising.

Acknowledgment. Research funded by the European Union 7th Framework Programme (FP7/2007–2013) under grant agreement no. 287966 (EXPERIMEDIA project), as well as by the European Regional Development Fund (ERDF) and the Galician Regional Government under project CN 2012/260 *"Consolidation of Research Units: AtlantTIC"*. The authors are thankful to the students Juan Pablo Hurtado and Edgar Patricio Siguenza for their invaluable work in the implementation of the reference VNLayer and VNAODV following the algorithmic details and the results found in the literature.

References

1. Network Simulator (ns-2). http://isi.edu/nsnam/ns/
2. Simulation of Urban MObility (SUMO). http://sumo.sourceforge.net/
3. Bravo-Torres, J., López-Nores, M., Blanco-Fernández, Y.: Virtualization support for complex communications in vehicular ad hoc networks. MTA Rev. **23**(2), 121–140 (2013)
4. Bravo-Torres, J., López-Nores, M., Blanco-Fernández, Y.: VNlayer+: evolution of the virtual node layer to support ad-hoc communications in indoor, pedestrian and vehicular contexts. Department of Telematics Engineering, University of Vigo, Technical report (2013)

5. Brown, M., Gilbert, S., Lynch, N., Newport, C., Nolte, T., Spindel, M.: The virtual node layer: a programming abstraction for wireless sensor networks. ACM SIGBED Rev. **4**(3), 121–140 (2007)

6. Conti, M., Giordano, S. (eds.): Mobile Ad Hoc Networking: The Cutting Edge Directions. Wiley, Hoboken (2013)

7. Drego, V., Temkin, B., McInnes, A.: Social computing goes mobile - a social computing report. Forrester Research (2007)

8. Fernando, N., Loke, S., Rahayu, W.: Mobile cloud computing: a survey. Future Gener. Comput. Sys. **29**(1), 84–106 (2013)

9. Fleck, M., Frid, M., Kindberg, T., O'Brien-Strain, E., Rajani, R., Spasojevic, M.: From informing to remembering: ubiquitous systems in interactive museums. IEEE Pervasive Comput. **1**(2), 13–21 (2002)

10. Gentes, A., Guyot-Mbodji, A., Demeure, I.: Drive and share: efficient provisioning of social networks in vehicular scenarios. IEEE Commun. Mag. **48**(11), 90–97 (2010)

11. Gentes, A., Guyot-Mbodji, A., Demeure, I.: Gaming on the move: urban experience as a new paradigm for mobile pervasive game design. Multimedia Sys. **16**(1), 43–55 (2010)

12. Gerber, S., Fry, M., Kay, J., Kummerfeld, B., Pink, G., Wasinger, R.: PersonisJ: mobile, client-side user modelling. In: De Bra, P., Kobsa, A., Chin, D. (eds.) UMAP 2010. LNCS, vol. 6075, pp. 111–122. Springer, Heidelberg (2010)

13. Gerla, M., Kleinrock, L.: Vehicular networks and the future of the mobile Internet. Comput. Netw. **55**(2), 457–469 (2011)

14. Kuss, D., Griffiths, M.: Online social networking and addiction: a review of the psychological literature. Int. J. Environ. Res. Pub. Health **8**, 3528–3552 (2011)

15. López-Nores, M., Blanco-Fernández, Y., Pazos-Arias, J.: Cloud-based personalization of new advertising and e-commerce models for video consumption. Computer **56**(5), 573–592 (2013)

16. López-Nores, M., Blanco-Fernández, Y., Pazos-Arias, J., Gil-Solla, A.: Property-based collaborative filtering for health-aware recommender systems. Expert Syst. Appl. **39**(8), 7451–7457 (2012)

17. Malkin, G.S.: RIP: An Intra-Domain Routing Protocol. Addison-Wesley Longman, Boston (2000)

18. Natkaniec, M., Kosek-Szott, K., Szott, S., Gozdecki, J., Glowacz, A., Sargento, S.: Supporting QoS in integrated ad-hoc networks. Wireless Pers. Commun. **56**(2), 183–206 (2011)

19. Patil, R., Shah, S.R.: Cross layer based virtual node layer for reactive MANET routing. Int. J. Eng. Res. Technol. **1**(6) (2012)

20. Perkins, C.E., Royer, E.M., Das, S.: Ad hoc on-demand distance vector (AODV) routing (2003). http://www.ietf.org/rfc/rfc3561.txt

21. Ridong, F., Kun, Y., Xueqi, C.: A cooperative social and vehicular network and its dynamic bandwidth allocation algorithms. In: Proceedings of IEEE INFOCOM Workshop on Cognitive and Cooperative Networks, April 2011

22. Ryan-Collins, J., Stephens, L., Coote, A.: The new wealth of time: how timebanking helps people build better public services. http://www.timebankingwales.org/userfiles/NEW

23. Schuster, D., Rosi, A., Mamei, M., Springer, T., Endler, M., Zambonelli, F.: Pervasive social context: taxonomy and survey. ACM Trans. Intell. Syst. Technol. **4**(3), 46:1–46:22 (2013)

24. Sintoris, C., Yiannoutsou, N., Demetriou, S., Avouris, N.: Discovering the invisible city: location-based games for learning in smart cities. Interact. Des. Archit. **16**, 47–64 (2013)

25. Smaldone, S., Lu, H., Shankar, P., Iftode, L.: Roadspeak: enabling voice chat on roadways using vehicular social networks. In: Proceedings of Socialnets Workshop, in Conjunction with the IEEE 19th International Symposium on Personal, Indoor and Mobile Radio Communications (PIMRC), September 2008

26. Stock, O., Zancanaro, M., Busetta, P., Callaway, C., Krüger, A., Kruppa, M., Kuflik, T., Not, E., Rocchi, C.: Adaptive, intelligent presentation of information for the museum visitor in peach. User Model. User-Adap. Inter. **17**(3), 257–304 (2007)

27. Sun, J.Z.: Mobile ad hoc networking: an essential technology for pervasive computing. In: Proceedings of International Conference on Info-tech and Info-net (ICII), Beijing, China, vol. 3, October 2001

28. Tse, R.T.S, Dawei, L., Hou, F., Pau, G.: Bridging vehicle sensor networks with social networks: applications and challenges. In: Proceedings of International Conference on Communication Technology and Application (ICCTA), October 2011

29. Wang, Y., Stash, N., Sambeek, R., Schuurmans, Y., Aroyo, L., Schreiber, G., Gorgels, P.: Cultivating personalized museum tours online and on-site. Interdisc. Sci. Rev. **34**(2–3), 139–153 (2009)

30. Wu, J.: A simulation study on using the virtual node layer to implement efficient and reliable MANET protocols. Ph.D. Thesis (2011). http://groups.csail.mit.edu/tds/papers/Wu/JiangWuThesisFinal.pdf

31. Wu, J., Griffeth, N., Newport, C., Lynch, N.: Engineering the virtual node layer for reactive MANET routing. In: Proceedings of 10th IEEE International Symposium on Network Computing and Applications (NCA), Cambridge, MA, USA, pp. 131–138, August 2011

32. Xin, L., Zhuo, L., Wenzhong, L., Sanglu, L., Xiaoliang, W., Daoxu, C.: Exploring social properties in vehicular ad-hoc networks. In: Proceedings of 4th Asia-Pacific Symposium on Internetware, October 2012

33. Zhou, J., Sun, J., Athukorala, K., Wijekoon, D., Ylianttila, M.: Pervasive social computing: augmenting five facets of human intelligence. J. Ambient Intell. Humanized Comput. **3**(2), 153–166 (2012)

Energy Consumption Analysis of HPC Applications Using NoSQL Database Feature of EnergyAnalyzer

Shajulin Benedict[(✉)], R.S. Rejitha, and C. Bright

SXCCE, Nagercoil, India
{shajulin,rejitha,bency}@sxcce.edu.in
http://www.sxcce.edu.in/hpccloud

Abstract. A notion of increasing the energy efficiency of HPC machines or applications has reached the global HPC community forum in recent years. This has opened up several interesting possibilities that reduces the energy consumption of applications, including an energy consumption analysis mechanism which delves into the reason behind the energy consumption bottlenecks of applications. In order to easily analyze the energy consumption of applications (from machine to machine), a need for a dedicated energy consumption analysis tool has undoubtedly enthused application developers or users. In general, when applications were analyzed for performance bottlenecks in modern HPC architectures, such as, exascale machines which have more than tens of thousands of cores, a performance analysis tool might deliver a huge performance dataset. Querying such data in a short span of time can efficiently be done using document based NoSQL database systems. This paper proposes an online-based energy consumption analysis mechanism of HPC applications using EnergyAnalyzer Performance Database (EAPerfDB), a NoSQL-based performance database feature, of EnergyAnalyzer tool. The EnergyAnalyzer tool uses semantic agents in a distributed fashion to undergo the energy consumption analysis of HPC applications. In addition, the paper explores the findings of the energy consumption analysis of High Performance Computing Challenge (HPCC) benchmarks when NoSQL-based EnergyAnalyzer tool was used at the HPCCLoud Research Laboratory of our premise.

Keywords: Cloud storage · Energy analysis · HPC · NoSQL · Tools

1 Introduction

Solving energy consumption issue has been a crucial challenge in mobile computing domain since a long time. It is gaining importance in HPC architectures

This work is partially funded by the Department of Science and Technology of India under FAST Young Scientist Scheme - Engineering Sciences division (Grant No: SR/FTP/ETA-93/2011) and it is motivated by CIM-GIZ, Germany. For more details, visit www.sxcce.edu.in/hpccloud.

A. Al-Saidi et al. (Eds.): ICC 2014, LNCS 8993, pp. 103–118, 2015.
DOI: 10.1007/978-3-319-19848-4_7

as well since the electricity bill is increasing and there is a scarcity of electrical power to energize such machines especially in power scarce countries, such as, India. In fact, most of the current HPC architectures [18] or cloud data centres are operated in the range of megawatts. In addition, it is expected that the power bill for powering HPC supercomputer machines almost equals the costs of the machine over its entire life time [17]. This challenge has driven traditional HPC researchers to provide possible solutions which improve the energy efficiency of HPC applications.

In recent years, scientific application developers have started to use cloud technology for solving their applications [15]. The cloud based scientific applications are, in general, executed on HPC-as-a-service cloud infrastructures, such as, Amazon Supercomputing Service [1], enCore of UK, Appro's Xtreme-X Supercomputers, Penguin Computing on Demand (POD) [29], R-Cloud solutions [31] and so forth. To elegantly and energy efficiently run HPC applications, the cloud application developers, who work in diverse fields, including scientific domains, have also started characterizing [6,41], analyzing [35], and addressing the energy inefficiency problem of clouds [40].

In succinct, energy reduction techniques, in the capacity of an application developer, are conceivably accomplished using various approaches as follows:

1. Gaining enough knowledge about the energy consumption details of the individual code regions of applications when executed on an underlying architecture. The knowledge is gained by adopting techniques, such as, energy modeling techniques [37,39], energy estimation techniques [30], or energy monitoring techniques [36].
2. Adopting control mechanisms, such as, controlling idle resources [3], controlling compiler optimization switches [5], controlling CPU clock frequencies, and so forth.
3. Effectively utilizing programming languages, including parallelism constructs - for instance, reducing MPI wait times in MPI programming language [16], reducing double precision in programs, or considering various performance metrics such as Eflops, multitasking scalability, core availability, security index, SLA measures, temperature concerns, operational costs, and so forth.

In order to effectively adopt such available energy reduction mechanisms on applications, a dedicated energy consumption analysis tool is mandatory. The tool remains as an indispensable software component for application developers as the search for the energy inefficient codes of an application is a complicated process. The analysis process gets even worse when energy efficiency metrics, such as, number of threads, number of cores, or thermal index, showed varying results in different machines for the same application. The tool should, therefore, vividly assist user or application developer to figure out the energy inefficient code regions of an application. To do so, the tool, in principle, could generate hefty performance data, either via modeling or real measurements.

Recently, performance analysis tool developers' community has triggered the need for an intelligent scalable performance prediction/analysis system as they have gotten more interested in developing autotuning tools. An autotuning tool automatically [8] analyzes and tunes the energy consumption problems of applications. It requires a wide set of performance data relating to the runtime, compile time, and the behavioral aspects of an application in order to tune the application - i.e., these performance data would be useful for finding a proper match (an optimized code version) between code options and the executional configurations (number of threads, processors, and so forth) at the earliest time. At present, therefore, one of the most emerging challenge among these tool developers is to handle a large set of performance data which is possible when executed in future generation computer systems, such as, Many Integrated Core (MIC) architectures or exa-scale supercomputers which consists of 10000 to 100000 number of cores.

It is a proven research, notably, that the NoSQL-based database management systems are particularly useful [26] when a software uses statistical data or huge data, which probably could iteratively grow or shrink, in real time. This is due to the utility of key-value store mechanism which is often adopted in NoSQL databases. In addition, in recent years, HPC researchers have started to utilize NoSQL databases into their system for querying large datasets [19].

This paper has the following contributions:

1. It proposes an online based scalable energy consumption analysis mechanism using EAPerfDB, a NoSQL-based database management system, of Energy-Analyzer tool. An EnergyAnalyzer tool is an energy consumption analysis tool which is under development at the HPCCLoud Research Laboratory, India. The tool undergoes both the energy modeling approach and the real energy measurements (using Intel RAPL hardware counters [14,21]) for an application while executing it using semantic agents in a distributed fashion.
2. A few experiments were conducted and the results were explored when HPC Challenge (HPCC) benchmark was executed in the HPCCLoud Research Laboratory using the EnergyAnalyzer tool.

The rest of the paper is organized as follows: Sect. 2 describes the previous research works. Section 3 explains the design of EnergyAnalyzer tool and Sect. 4 explains how EAPerfDB is used in the EnergyAnalyzer tool. After the experimental results were discussed in Sect. 5, a few conclusions were given in Sect. 6.

2   Related Work

In fact, the performance analysis of applications is not a new concept - it is a mandatory step while developing HPC applications. In a few research works, the researchers have modeled performance constraints on parallel machines [32]. Additionally, there were notably a few leading HPC performance analysis tools in the market, such as, TAU [38], PAPI [20], Periscope [33], SCALASCA [27], HPCToolkit [13], IPM [28], and so forth.

The energy consumption issue of HPC applications and the corresponding analysis have magnified research notions in recent years among HPC researchers by developing energy-conscious applications, tools, or greener IT machines [2]. Even as traditionally available performance analysis tools are more robust in pointing out performance problems related to memory, MPI communication, timeline, and hardware counters, the tool developers are still working on to find out the energy consumption details of applications. For instance, TAU is working on energy analysis strategy using hardware counters via PAPI on SandyBridge processor machines; Periscope is implementing energy analysis with the help of power-aware hardware sensors supported by IBM on SuperMIG machines. Current performance analysis tools are in different flavors, such as, online vs. offline, distributed vs centralized, trace-based, profile-based, and so forth, due to the framework of those tools. A detailed survey of the current energy consumption analysis tools and their analysis methodologies for HPC architectures is discussed in [36].

Recently, most of the tool developers have strengthened the necessity of an automatic approach of tuning applications, as HPC architectures are varying atleast once in every couple of years. In addition, the available traditional tuning solutions are almost obsolete - i.e., traditionally, auto tuning approaches were held on specific applications [4] or were mostly blackbox [7]. Research growth in the autotuning research domain could be manifested - for instance, compiler researchers have designed auto tuning compiler optimizers considering multiple objectives [11], machine learning approaches, or compiler flag selection approaches.

Very rarely, tool developers have opted to utilize the relational database systems, such as, mySql or oracle in performance analysis tools. However, with the recent advances in NoSQL database systems, this paper suggests users/readers to using MongoDB for doing the energy consumption analysis of applications, as the performance data are, in general, very large when exa-scale and future computer machines were considered.

3   EnergyAnalyzer Design

EnergyAnalyzer tool is designed such that it uses semantic-based analysis agents in a distributed fashion to undergo analysis [34]. The analysis is online - while the application is running the analysis is done - so that the application developers can modify their code during next iterations or stop executing it considering energy inefficiency aspects of the code.

The EnergyAnalyzer consists of three major entities as listed below:

1. SSTranslator
2. Semantic-based Analysis Agents, and
3. Monitoring Manager

These entities are required to do energy consumption analysis of HPC applications. Figure 1 provides a pictorial representation of the EnergyAnalyzer tool architecture. The responsibilities of the entities are described in the following subsections.

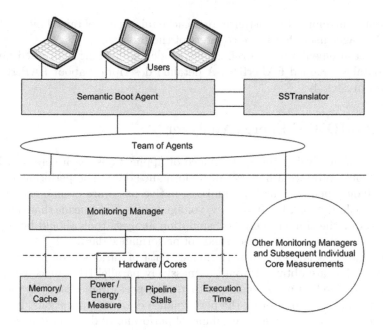

Fig. 1. EnergyAnalyzer tool architecture

3.1   SSTranslator

SSTranslator is a source-to-source translator which inserts some pre-defined functions of EnergyAnalyzer on HPC applications. The pre-defined functions include information about the code region, file name, and line number of an application. These functions are inserted before and after the code regions of the application.

3.2   Semantic-Based Analysis Agents

Semantic-based analysis agents entity of EnergyAnalyzer include Semantic Boot Agent and a team of analysis agents. The Semantic Boot Agent is a voluntary agent. This agent, at first, decides on the pre-defined parameters of the tool, such as, number of additional agents, tool overhead level, required measurements, and so forth, for the analysis. Later, the analysis agents of EnergyAnalyzer spawn applications on the available number of cores/machines. On execution, the application, which is linked to the Monitoring Manager entity of EnergyAnalyzer, invoke the required energy/hardware measurements to do the analysis in a distributed fashion.

3.3   Monitoring Manager

Monitoring Manager, the entity of EnergyAnalyzer, is kernel specific and it deals with hardware components for obtaining required measurements of agents.

For instance, memory stall instances and cache misses are obtained by the Monitoring Manager using hardware counters of the processors.

The measurement values are finally uploaded to a MongoDB based performance database named EAPerfDB. A detailed description about EAPerfDB is explained in Sect. 4.

4   EAPerfDB of EnergyAnalyzer

In general, on analyzing the performance of applications, each core of a HPC machine would produce a huge set of performance data. The performance data could include pipeline stalls, cache misses, native hardware events, energy consumption in Joules, or CPU frequency/voltage values. This means that the EnergyAnalyzer or the similar energy consumption analysis tools should be capable enough to handle the tens of thousands of performance data.

Investigating a large set of performance data of various code regions of an application that are obtained from the massively parallel HPC machines is not an easy task. The literature points out that a few performance analysis tools use file system approach for storing the performance data of applications. However, storing and retrieving such a huge volume of performance data via sequential file sharing mechanisms are not advisable, especially in the future HPC machines, including exa-scale machines; a few researchers have endeavored hash functions and keys to store performance data; and, recently, a few other researchers have adopted key-value pair implementation in order to store the possible large performance data of applications.

With the recent advances in NoSQL technologies and the growing number of processor cores in recent HPC machines, many researchers, who are working in the HPC Cloud research community domain, have tried to use NoSQL database technology. For instances, Google has announced the usage of NoSQL databases for servicing their infrastructures in Google Compute Engine [9]; the NoSQL databases were introduced with different insights to the global cloud market [25].

The EnergyAnalyzer Performance Database (EAPerfDB) of EnergyAnalyzer is the performance database of EnergyAnalyzer tool which is implemented using MongoDB. MongoDB is a NoSQL-based database system which is considered to be a more powerful database system, as it has the possibility of extending simultaneous connections to multiple servers. In addition, it has the capability of processing huge performance dataset which will be available via the Monitoring Manager entity of EnergyAnalyzer. Therefore, the earlier implementation of the Monitoring Manager of EnergyAnalyzer with a key-value pair implementation is upgraded with EAPerfDB. The following subsections explain how EAPerfDB is initialized and how the mongo clients communicate with server instances.

4.1   EAPerfDB Initialization

The EnergyAnalyzer uses C API of MongoDB where connection initialization, connection establishment check, and connection destruction processes are carried out. Before an application was executed, the semantic booter of EnergyAnalyzer initiates MongoDB database server connection using a specific system command as follows:

```
mongod --port \textit{portno} --bind\_ip \textit{DB-ipaddress}
    --dbpath \textit{path-to-db file}
```

where –port represents the port address, –bind_ip represents the ip address for binding purpose, and –dbpath is used to specify where the database should be stored.

4.2   EAPerfDB Clients

While executing a code region of an application, the semantic agents of Energy-Analyzer start Monitoring Manager entity for measuring the energy consumption value using energy modeling and real energy measurement approaches. The Monitoring Manager invokes the energy modeling approach to predict the energy consumption of an application for the underlying architecture immediately after the execution of a code region of an application was started. The estimated energy consumption value could even be gotten from some historical results that are available for the same application if executed earlier on the same architecture. The estimated value is uploaded to EAPerfDB.

The EAPerfDB clients are embedded in two entities of EnergyAnalyzer - Monitoring Manager and Semantic Agents. The mongo clients in the Monitoring Manager entity of EnergyAnalyzer are active at the start and end of the code regions of an application. The code region of an application can be an user-defined code region, main region, subroutine, or the other part of an application.

At the start of a code region, mongo clients initialize EAPerfDB with an unique id,

```
{ "_id" : { "$oid" : "53568760ba8c2f15365ff7a0" },
```

runtime specifications, and the corresponding values.

```
"0::0::1::656::Real::Energy" :0
"0::0::1::656::Real::ExecTime" :0
```

The values that are processed as a string and that are stored in the EAPerfDB include (i) process number, (ii) thread number, (iii) unique file number of applications, (iv) code region line number of the application, (v) real or model based measurement data, (vi) measurements (energy or execution time), (vii) measured value. Initially, the values are zero.

Later, at the end of the code region, the MonitoringManager entity updates the same unique id of EAPerfDB with the corresponding measured values. When the code region of the application was completely executed, the real measurement values that are obtained via RAPL hardware counter events are stored in the same database.

Subsequently, the embedded mongo clients of the Semantic Agents of EnergyAnalyzer could obtain those measurement values, as and when needed, to do further energy consumption analysis.

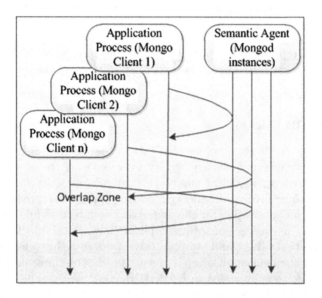

Fig. 2. Parallel Mongo clients adopted in the Monitoring Manager of EnergyAnalyzer

4.3   Parallel Mongo Clients

Mongo client processes, which are embedded in the Monitoring Manager of EnergyAnalyzer, are executed in parallel. In order to use EAPerfDB database system in parallel, EnergyAnalyzer initializes several *mongod* server instances with the required number of connections. Otherwise, when a new client connection was requested, the *mongod* server process shuts down its currently active client connection immediately and starts processing the new connection. Once the processing is complete, the server process terminates the current connection and resumes the previously preempted client process, which slows down the system.

The *mongod* server instances and a few application processes acting as a client are depicted in Fig. 2. However, there are possibilities for an overlap in such parallel implementations of EAPerfDB. For instance, consider mongo client 2 and mongo client n, which are embedded in the Monitoring Manager entity of EnergyAnalyzer, are updating EAPerfDB at the same time.

Hence, in order to ensure correctness, the MongoDB database, by default, has adopted reader-writer locks [22]. On ensuring the status of locks (see Fig. 3), Monitoring Manager shifts the overlapping zone and then enters the measured values, i.e., the value of the energy consumption of a code region, to EAPerfDB.

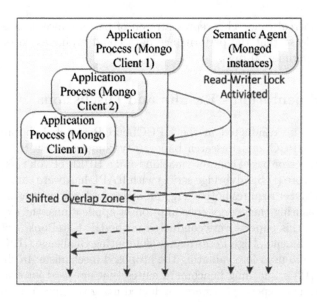

Fig. 3. Lock option - for protecting the performance data in EAPerfDB

4.4   Performance Data and Data Access Pattern

HPC applications run on more number of processors, mostly tens of thousands of processors. These processors need not be homogenous as the recent heterogeneous architectures have combined the advantage of both the GPU and the CPU technologies - GPU is focused on increasing throughput and power efficiency whereas CPU is focused on improving the memory access time. Interestingly enough, the top 10 systems of Green500 list had heterogeneous systems [10]. The heterogeneity results from combining standard multicore processors, Graphical Processing Units (GPUs), and co-processors within a node. Current heterogeneous systems deploy different version of General Purpose Graphics Processing Units (GPGPU)s, most frequently from Nvidia. Some HPC systems use, instead of GPGPUs, Intel's Xeon Phi processor [24]. While the GPGPUs deploy thousands of very specialized graphics cores and require programming in specialized programming interfaces, Intel's Xeon Phi has over 60 Intel standard cores enhanced with wide SIMD units that can be programmed in standard OpenMP. In addition, recently, researchers have endeavored ARM-based heterogeneous HPC system via the Mont-Blanc project [23].

In such scenarios, the application processes, running on numerous processors, upload various performance data including energy consumption values on the fly - i.e., when the application was executed the performance data would be loaded and queried.

The data access pattern model used in EAPerfDB is an embedded data model. This means that the related data are ordered in a single document style format in order to process the query related to the performance data of applications in real time. This representation of performance data is done in a document style so that the performance data could be increased or decreased during the experimental runs.

5   Experimentation - Results and Discussions

Experiments were conducted in the HPCCLoud Research Laboratory of our premise. The HPCCLoud Research Laboratory comprises of a HPProLiant 48 core AMD processor based compute machine and a HPEliteBook 8560w machine having 8 Intel core (i7 Sandybridge series) with RAPL hardware counter support. As EnergyAnalyzer requires both energy modeling and energy measurement approach for measuring the energy consumption of applications, the experiments - reported on in this paper - were conducted in the HP EliteBook 8560w.

In the experiments, High Performance Computing Challenge (HPCC or hpcc) benchmarks were used for evaluating the proposed mechanism. In short, HPCC benchmarks [12] are leading benchmark suites that are used for evaluating the architectures. The experiments were conducted using the hpcc 1.4.2 source code version which consists of matrix kernels.

The main C-based file of hpcc benchmark consists of 17 source code regions which could broadly be classified as 7 test domains, namely, hpl, latency/bandwidth, fft (single, star, mpi), stream (single, star), DGEMM (single, star), pTrans, and random access (single, star, mpi).

The hpcc test domains are explained as follows:

1. *hpl* is a Linpack benchmark. This benchmark measures the floating point rate of a set of linear equation code.
2. *latency/bandwidth* is another code region of hpcc. This code region of hpcc measures network latency and bandwidth of the code region. This code region represents different communication patterns in a machine.
3. *DGEMM* benchmark relates to the strength of the double precision values of codes. It measures the floating point rate of execution in a single and a star implementation styles of hpcc.
4. the *stream* code region of hpcc, as similar to DGEMM, has single and star implementation styles. This part of the hpcc benchmark measures the sustainable memory bandwidth and the relevant computation rate.
5. *pTrans* benchmark of hpcc uses parallel matrix transpose code in order to measure the total communication capacity of the network. This benchmark represents the strength of the underlying HPC networks.
6. *random access* benchmark measures the rate of integer random updates of memory system of HPC architectures. This code region of hpcc is implemented in three different implementation styles, namely, single, star, and mpi styles.
7. and, the *fft* benchmark of hpcc does fast fourier transform computations. This benchmark measures the floating point rate of the double precision values.

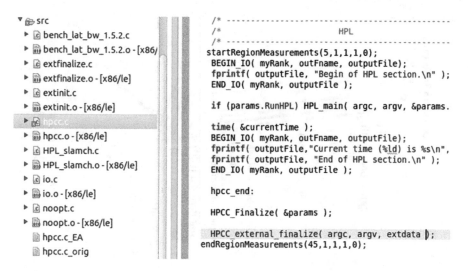

Fig. 4. HPCC - instrumented version of HPCC

The following subsections explain how the energy consumption of hpcc bench-marks was measured and analyzed using the EAPerfDB of EnergyAnalyzer - application was instrumented; EnergyAnalyzer uploaded the real energy measurement data of applications to EAPerfDB, a MongoDB based performance database of EnergyAnalyzer; finally, the Semantic Agents analyzed the available results and exposed the values to the user.

5.1   SSTranslator - HPCC Instrumentation

As mentioned earlier that the EnergyAnalyzer instruments applications with some pre-defined functions using the SSTranslator entity, the code regions of hpcc were instrumented using SSTranslator. The SSTranslator follows TAU [38] for instrumenting the code regions of applications. The instrumented code region of hpcc benchmark is depicted in Fig. 4.

Later, the executable of hpcc benchmarks was created with required compiler flags and it was kept ready for the Semantic Agents to do energy consumption analysis. The Semantic Agents, finally, started the application in four cores after the required number of agents were decided on the underlying machine.

5.2   Monitoring Manager and EAPerfDB

Once when the *startRegionMeasurements*() function (see Fig. 4), an instrumented statement from SSTranslator, was executed, the Semantic agents invoked energy modeling and real energy measurements of the code region. The energy modeling was done using Semantic agents itself. However, the real energy measurements were invoked via the Monitoring Manager entity which consequently invoked RAPL hardware counters.

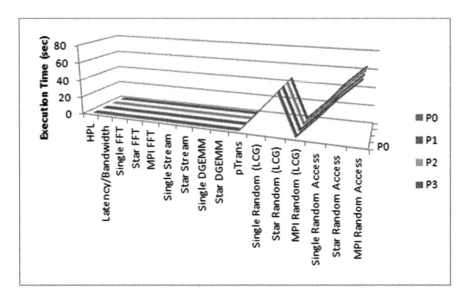

Fig. 5. HPCC - execution time results

The RAPL hardware counters are available in machine specific registers (msr) of the machine. These counters were accessed using the following function of the EnergyAnalyzer:

$$CreateAddRaplEvent();$$

When the *endRegionMeasurements()* function was executed, the Monitoring Manager stopped the measurements and uploaded the values to the EAPerfDB as C-based strings.

5.3   Energy Consumption and Execution Time - HPCC Results

The embedded mongo clients of semantic agents retrieved the results available in EAPerfDB and started to analyzing them for the code regions of hpcc benchmarks. As shown in Figs. 5 and 6, the EnergyAnalyzer identified the energy consumption and execution time for the code regions of hpcc.

A few findings from the obtained results are listed as follows:

1. The energy consumption values of MPI Random Access, Star Random Access, and Star Random Access (LCG) benchmarks were high (2795.85, 2292.048, and 1969.427 J respectively). The Random Access benchmarks check the integer update rate of the memory system for a HPC machine - the benchmarks do giga updates per second.
   The MPI Random Access benchmark does table initialization, table allocation, global table updation, and so forth using MPI while checking the

integer update rate of the memory system - MPI_allreduce and MPI_barrier constructs were used.

The Star Random Access and the Star Random Access (LCG) benchmarks observe the same integer update rate of the HPC memory system. However, the table initialization and updation approach of these benchmarks use single CPU process.

2. The single DGEMM benchmark of hpcc showed a considerably varying energy consumption values over the processes.
3. The execution time had a direct impact on the energy consumption of hpcc benchmarks. Clearly, this could be compared from Figs. 5 and 6. This assessment implies the necessity for improving performance on applications so that the energy consumption of an application is minimized. However, it equally significantly reveals the necessity for adopting energy reduction mechanisms on energy inefficient code regions such as Random Access with a compromise towards the other regions.

5.4   Online Analysis - EAPerfDB Capability

The analysis carried out while experimenting hpcc benchmarks was online - i.e., the analysis was done during the execution of hpcc. EAPerfDB, with the help of its on demand real time processing capability, supported semantic agents to independently query for results whenever the Monitoring Manager had uploaded the performance results to the database.

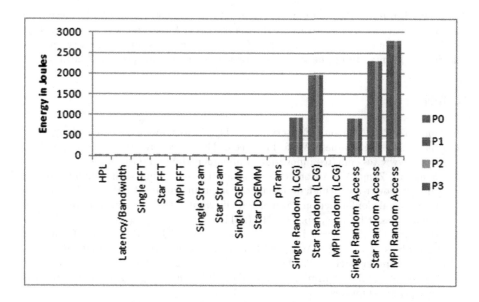

Fig. 6. HPCC - energy consumption values

6   Conclusion

The issue related to the energy consumption of HPC applications have reached the minds of energy conscious HPC programmers in recent years. Finding the energy consumption issues of HPC applications and thereby rectifying them by application programmers are not easy tasks due to to the complicated issues which inter-relate with one another.

To this end, many HPC application developers have started to rely on the energy consumption based performance analysis tools. HPC-based performance analysis tools could provide huge volume of performance data set which are cumbersome to deal with, in most of the cases.

This paper had expressed the design of the EnergyAnalyzer tool, a tool which analyzes the energy consumption of code regions of HPC applications using energy modeling and energy measurement approaches. The tool used NoSQL based MongoDB performance data management system named EAPerfDB. The EnergyAnalyzer tool development project, funded by the Department of Science and Technology of India, is under development at the HPCCLoud Research Laboratory of our premise.

After the design approach of EnergyAnalyzer was discussed, the paper showed the energy consumption analysis results of hpcc benchmarks which were experimented using a HP 8570w SandyBridge machine available at the HPC-CLoud Research Laboratory. In addition, the paper has listed a few research findings of hpcc benchmarks.

Acknowledgment. Shajulin Benedict thanks Prof. Michael Gerndt (TUM, Germany) for providing a research motivation. He thanks DST, India and Ms. Pragya Taneja (CIM-GIZ, Germany) for providing the financial and moral support to carry out this research work. In addition, he thanks the reviewers and organizers of ICC2014.

References

1. Amazon HPC, Amazon HPC services (2014). https://aws.amazon.com/hpc/
2. Anand Sivasubramaniam Make IT Green: The TCS way, Tech report, pp. 1–12 (2008). www.tcs.com/tcs_innovation_whitepaper_Make-IT-Green.pdf
3. Cheng, Y., Zeng, Y.: Automatic energy status controlling with dynamic voltage scaling in power-aware high performance computing cluster. In: Proceedings of 12th International Conference on Parallel and Distributed Computing, Applications and Technologies (PDCAT), pp. 412–416 (2011)
4. Whaley, R.C., Dongarra, J.J.: Automatically tuned linear algebra software. In: Proceedings of the 1998 ACM/IEEE Conference on Supercomputing (SC 1998). IEEE Computer Society, Washington, D.C., pp. 1–27 (1998)
5. Compiler, Compiler Optimization Switches (2014). http://gcc.gnu.org/onlinedocs/gcc/Optimize-Options.html
6. Conejero, J., Rana, O., Burnap, P., Morgan, J., Carrin, C., Caminero, B.: Characterising the power consumption of hadoop clouds - a social media analysis case study. In: Proceedings of CLOSER, pp. 233–243 (2013)

7. Cooper, K.D., Schielke, P.J., Subramanian, D.: Optimizing for reduced code space using genetic algorithms. In: Proceedings of the Conference on Languages, Compilers, and Tools for Embedded Systems (LCTES), p. 19 (1999)
8. Dagstuhl participants (2013). http://www.dagstuhl.de/program/calendar/partlist/?semnr=13401&SUOG
9. Google Compute Engine and NoSQL. http://www.infoq.com/news/2013/05/google-compute-engine
10. GreenLists, Top 500 List of Green Supercomputers (2014). http://www.green500.org/news/green500-list-november-2013
11. Herbert, J., Peter, T., Durillo, J.J., Simone, P., Philipp, G., Thomas, F., Moritsch, H.: A multi-objective auto-tuning framework for parallel codes. In: SC 2012 (2012)
12. hpcc. http://icl.cs.utk.edu/hpcc/
13. Adhianto, L., Banerjee, S., Fagan, M., Krentel, M., Marin, G., Crummey, J.M., Tallent, N.R.: HPCToolkit: tools for performance analysis of optimized parallel programs. Concurrency Comput. Pract. Exp. **22**(2), 685–701 (2010)
14. Intel In-built Sensors, Running Average Power Limit for Xeon Processors, July 2012. http://www.intel.com/xeon
15. Layton, J.: The Cloud's Role in HPC (2014). http://www.admin-magazine.com/HPC/Articles/The-Cloud-s-Role-in-HPC
16. Knobloch, M., Mohr, B., Minartz, T.: Determine energy-saving potential in wait-states of large-scale parallel programs. Comput. Sci. Res. Dev. **27**(4), 255–263 (2011)
17. Le, K., Ricardo, B., Zhang, J., Yogesh, J., Meng, J., Nguyen, T.D.: Reducing electricity cost through virtual machine placement in high performance computing clouds. In: Proceedings of 2011 International Conference for High Performance Computing, Networking, Storage and Analysis, SC 2011, pp. 1–22 (2011). doi:10.1145/2063384.2063413
18. LRZ Supercomputer Information. http://www.lrz.de/services/compute/supermuc/systemdescription/
19. LucidWorks, LucidWorks Integrates with MongoDB (2013). http://archive.hpcwire.com/hpccloud/2013-03-18/lucidworks_integrates_with_mongodb.html
20. Malony, A., Biersdorff, S., Shende, S., Jagode, H., Tomov, S., Juckeland, G., Dietrich, R., Poole, D., Lamb, C.: Parallel performance measurement of heterogeneous parallel systems with GPUs. In: International Conference on Parallel Processing ICPP 2011, Taipei, Taiwan, pp. 13–16 (2011)
21. Hahnel, M., Dobel, B., Volp, M., Hartig, H.: Measuring Energy Consumption for Short Code Paths Using RAPL, July 2012. www.sigmetrics.org/greenmetrics/Hahnel.pdf
22. MongoDB. http://docs.mongodb.org/manual/faq/concurrency/
23. MontBlanc Project (2014). http://www.montblanc-project.eu
24. Niels, B.: New Intel Xeon Phi Coprocessors to have Xeon CPUs On Board (2013). http://insidehpc.com/2013/05/24/new-intel-xeon-phi-coprocessors-to-have-xeons-on-board/
25. NoSQL. http://nosql-database.org/
26. NoSQL is useful. http://www.infoq.com/news/2013/04/gartner-technology-trends/
27. Geimer, M., Saviankou, P., Strube, A., Szebenyi, Z., Wolf, F., Wylie, B.J.N.: Further improving the scalability of the scalasca toolset. In: Jónasson, K. (ed.) PARA 2010, Part II. LNCS, vol. 7134, pp. 463–473. Springer, Heidelberg (2012)
28. Wright, N.J., Pfeiffer, W., Snavely, A.: Characterizing parallel scaling of scientific applications using IPM. In: The 10th LCI International Conference on High-Performance Clustered Computing, Boulder, pp. 1–21 (2009)

29. Penguin Computing, Penguin Computing on Demand (2014). http://www.penguincomputing.com/services/hpc-cloud/pod

30. PowerAdvisor, HP Power Advisor utility: a tool for estimating power requirements for HP ProLiant server systems, July 2012. http://h20000.www2.hp.com/bc/docs/support/SupportManual/c01861599/c01861599.pdf

31. RCloud, Rcloud from R-HPC (2014). http://www.r-hpc.com/

32. Sachs, K., Kounev, S., Buchmann, A.: Performance modeling and analysis of message-oriented event-driven systems. Softw. Syst. Model. **12**(4), 705–729 (2012). doi:10.1007/s10270-012-0228-1

33. Benedict, S., Gerndt, M.: Automatic performance analysis of OpenMP codes on a scalable shared memory system using periscope. In: Jónasson, K. (ed.) PARA 2010, Part II. LNCS, vol. 7134, pp. 452–462. Springer, Heidelberg (2012)

34. Benedict, S., Rejitha, R.S., Bright, C.B.: Energy consumption-based performance tuning of software and applications using particle swarm optimization. In: 6th IEEE CSI International Conference on Software Engineering (CONSEG) 2012, pp. 1–6 (2012)

35. Benedict, S.: Performance issues and performance analysis tools for HPC cloud applications: a survey. Computing **95**(2), 89–108 (2013). doi:10.1007/s00607-012-0213-0

36. Benedict, S.: Energy-aware performance analysis methodologies for HPC architectures - an exploratory study. J. Netw. Comput. Appl. **35**(6), 1709–1719 (2012)

37. Song, S., Grove, M., Cameron, K.W.: An iso-energy-efficient approach to scalable system power-performance optimization. In: Proceedings of the IEEE International Conference on Cluster Computing (Cluster 2011), Austin, Texas, pp. 262–271, September 2011

38. Shende, S., Malony, A.D.: The TAU parallel performance system. Int. J. High Perform. Comput. **20**(2), 287–311 (2006)

39. Do, T., Rowshdeh, S., Shi, W.: pTop: A Process-level Power Profiling Tool, July 2012. www.sigops.org/sosp/sosp09/papers/hotpower_13_do.pdf

40. Viswanathan, H., Lee, E.K., Rodero I., Pompili D., Parashar M., Gamell M.: Energy-aware application-centric VM allocation for HPC workloads. In: 2011 IEEE International Symposium on Parallel and Distributed Processing Workshops and Phd Forum (IPDPSW), pp. 890–897 (2011). doi:10.1109/IPDPS.2011.234

41. Simmhan, Y., Noor, M.U.: Scalable prediction of energy consumption using incremental time series clustering. In: BigData Conference, pp. 29–36 (2013)

Security

A Low-Overhead Secure Communication Framework for an Inter-cloud Environment

Ali Sajjad[1]([⊠]), Muttukrishnan Rajarajan[1], and Theo Dimitrakos[2]

[1] City University London, London, UK
[2] British Telecom Ltd, Adastral Park, Ipswich, UK
ali.sajjad@bt.com

Abstract. Most of the current cloud computing platforms offer Infrastructure as a Service (IaaS) model, which aims to provision basic virtualized computing resources as on-demand and dynamic services. Nevertheless, a single cloud provider may not have limitless resources to offer to its users, hence the notion of an Inter-Cloud environment where a cloud can use the infrastructure resources of other clouds. However, there is no common framework in existence that allows the service owners to seamlessly provision even some basic services across multiple cloud service providers, albeit not due to any inherent incompatibility or proprietary nature of the foundation technologies on which these cloud platforms are built. In this paper we present a novel solution which aims to cover a gap in a subsection of this problem domain. Our solution offers a security architecture that enables service owners to provision a dynamic and service-oriented secure virtual private network on top of multiple cloud IaaS providers. It does this by leveraging the scalability, robustness and flexibility of peer-to-peer overlay techniques to eliminate the manual configuration, key management and peer churn problems encountered in setting up the secure communication channels dynamically, between different components of a typical service that is deployed on multiple clouds. We present the implementation details of our solution as well as experimental results detailing the overheads of our solution carried out on two commercial clouds.

1 Introduction

Most of the currently available Cloud Computing solutions are mainly focused on providing functionalities and services at the infrastructure level, e.g., improved performance for virtualization of compute, storage and network resources, as well as necessary fundamental functionality such as Virtual Machine (VM) migrations and server consolidation etc. In the cases where higher-level and more abstract concerns like dynamic configuration and application level security are needed to be addressed, existing Infrastructure as a Service (IaaS) solutions tend to focus on functional aspects only. Furthermore, if a cloud's computational and storage infrastructure resources are overloaded due to increased workloads, its service towards it clients will degrade. The idea of an Inter-Cloud [1] has been gaining much traction to address such a situation, where a cloud can borrow the required

© Springer International Publishing Switzerland 2015
A. Al-Saidi et al. (Eds.): ICC 2014, LNCS 8993, pp. 121–136, 2015.
DOI: 10.1007/978-3-319-19848-4_8

infrastructure resources of other clouds. However, in order to progress from a basic cloud service infrastructure to a more adaptable cloud service ecosystem, there is a great need for tools and services that support and provide higher-level concerns and non-functional aspects in a comprehensive manner, e.g., automatic provisioning of value-added services like application and communication security.

The OPTIMIS project [2] has been a recently completed effort in this regard, which strived to provide a holistic approach to cloud service provisioning by offering a single abstraction for multiple coexisting cloud architectures. OPTIMIS addressed various high-level concerns in this domain like trust, risk, eco-efficiency and cost, however a major concern of high importance is the provisioning of a secure communication framework to the services utilizing the resources of different cloud IaaS providers. The usage pattern of these services is usually quite flexible. on one hand they might be directly accessed and managed by end-users, and on the other hand their access and management might be brokered and orchestrated by Cloud Service Providers (CSP) or third-party Cloud Brokers [3] for their customers.

There are three fundamental steps in the life cycle of a service in a cloud computing ecosystem; the construction of the service, the deployment of the service to one or more IaaS clouds and lastly the operational management of the service. In the resulting scenarios, the presence of multiple IaaS providers in the cloud ecosystem is the key issue that needs to be addressed by any inter-cloud security solution. A major goal of service owners is to select IaaS providers in an efficient way in order to host the different components of their services on appropriate clouds. In this respect, third-party cloud brokers [3] can play a major role in simplifying the use, performance and delivery of the cloud services. These brokers can also offer an inter-mediation layer spanning across multiple cloud providers to deliver a host of optimization and value-added services which take advantage of the myriad individual cloud services e.g., aggregation of different services or arbitration for a best-match service from multiple similar services. For the numerous interaction possibilities among these parties, whatever the usage scenarios maybe, the security of data and the communication between the consumers of the service and its multiple providers is of paramount importance.

In the light of the above discussion, it is advocated that an inter-cloud security solution is highly desirable that would provide a framework enabling seamless and secure communication between the actors of a cloud ecosystem over multiple cloud platforms. Such a solution, however, has to overcome a number of challenges because of architectural limitations. This is because most of the current cloud service platforms, and the multi-tenants environments they offer, make it difficult to give the consumers of their services flexible and scalable control over the core security aspects of their services like encryption, communication isolation and key management. Secure communication is also challenged by lack of dynamic network configurability in most cloud providers, caused by the inherent limitations of the fixed network architectures offered by these providers.

In this work we address the security concerns related to flexibility, scalability and overheads that in our view must be overcome in order to provide holistic provisioning of services to consumers from multiple cloud service providers. We present the design and architecture of an inter-cloud secure communication framework that offers the features of dynamic and scalable virtual network formation, efficient and scalable key management and minimal manual configuration. This framework enables secure and private communication between the components of a service utilising resources of multiple cloud platforms. Our peer-to-peer architecture provides a single virtual network to that service as an overlay of resources from multiple cloud providers and offers the capability to efficiently and transparently run services on top of this network while catering for the dynamic growth and shrinkage of the components of the service.

The rest of the paper is organized as follows: In Sect. 2 we present the background and related works that address the issues related to this domain. In Sect. 3 we elaborate on the detailed Inter-Cloud Virtual Private Network (ICVPN) architecture. In Sect. 4 we present our experimental setup and the analysis of the performance results and overheads of our solution. We conclude in Sect. 5 with the future directions of our work.

2   Related Work

Virtual Private Networks (VPN) have been a mainstay for providing secure remote access over wide-area networks to resources in private organizational networks for a long time. Well-known tools and softwares like OpenVPN [4] are used to create secure point-to-point or site-to-site connections for authenticated remote access. However, the main problem in client/server based approaches is that they require centralized servers to manage the life cycle of all the secure connections for the participating clients, hence suffering from a single point-of-failure. Another issue is the quite complex and error prone configuration problems especially if you want to construct and manage a large-scale network not having a relatively simple topology, as it would require customized configuration on every client and even more elaborate management and routing configuration on the server-side. Another major drawback is the complexity of key distribution among all the participating clients in a VPN, as the software itself does not provide any key distribution service and all keys have to be manually transferred to individual hosts. In case of the Public Key Infrastructure (PKI) model, an additional requirement of a trusted Certificate Authority (CA) exists that has to issue individual certificates to all the servers and clients constituting a VPN, which incurs an additional communication overhead when forming a virtual private network.

There have been some other VPN solutions for large-scale networks aimed at grid and cluster computing environments, such as VIOLIN [5] and VNET [6], that do not follow a strict client/server model based approach. VNET is a layer 2 virtual networking tool that relies on a VNET server running on a Virtual Machine Monitor (VMM) hosting a virtual machine in a remote network which establishes an encrypted tunnel connection to a VNET server running on a machine (called

Proxy) inside the users home network. All of the remote virtual machines communication goes through this tunnel and the goal of the Proxy is to emulate the remote virtual machine as a local host on the users home network, in effect presenting it as a member of the same LAN. The motivation of this approach is to tackle the users lack of administrative control at remote grid sites to manipulate network resources like routing and resource reservations etc. but it suffers from the previously discussing problem of complex and manual configuration though going for the simplicity of a private LAN. Also the scalability will be a big issue for the Proxy as the number of remote virtual machines grows as each will require a secure tunnel connection and corresponding virtual network interface mapped to the Proxys network interface by the VNET server software.

VIOLIN is a small-scale virtual network with virtual routers, switches and end hosts implemented in software and hosted by User-Mode Linux (UML) enabled machines as virtual appliances. It allows for the dynamic establishment of a private layer 3 virtual network among virtual machines, however, it doesnt offer dynamic or automatic network deployment or route management to setup the virtual network. Virtual links are established between the virtual appliances using encrypted UDP tunnels that have to be manually setup and are not self-configuring, making it cumbersome to establish inter-host connections in flexible and dynamic fashion.

P2P VPN solutions like Hamachi [7] and N2N [8] have come up as peer-to-peer alternatives to centralized and client/server model based VPNs. Hamachi is a shareware application that is capable of establishing direct links between computers that are behind NAT firewalls. A backend cluster of servers are used to enable NAT traversal and establish direct peer-to-peer connections among its clients. Each client establishes and maintains a control connection to the server cluster. It is mainly used for internet gaming and remote administration but suffers from scalability issues as each peer has to maintain the connection with the server as well as any other peers it wants to communicate with, ending up with the overhead of a mesh-topology. It therefore offers limited number of peers (16 per virtual network) and limited number of concurrent clients (50 per virtual network). The keys used for connection encryption and authentication are also controlled by the vendors servers and individual users do not initially control who has access to their network.

N2N is a layer 2 VPN solution which doesn't require a centralized back-end cluster of servers like Hamachi but it uses a peer-to-peer overlay network similar to Skype, where a number of dedicated super-nodes are used as relay agents for edge nodes that cannot communicate directly with each other due to firewall or NAT restrictions. The edge nodes connect to a super-node at start-up and pre-shared TwoFish [9] keys are used for link encryption. As it operates on layer 2, the users of the overlay have to configure their IP addresses etc. It also assumes node membership as relatively static with edge nodes rarely leaving or joining the network over their life cycle.

More recently, some commercial cloud computing services have been made available by different vendors that provide a virtual private network inside their public cloud offering and offering the customers some limited degree of control over this network, which is called a Virtual Private Cloud (VPC). Prime examples in this domain are Amazon Virtual Private Cloud [10], Google Secure Data Connector [11] and CohsiveFT VPN-Cubed [12]. These are aimed at enterprise customers to allow them to access their resource deployed on the vendor's cloud over an IPSec [13] based virtual private network. Although these products allow the possibility of leveraging the cloud providers' APIs to flexibly grow and shrink their networks, the management and configuration is as complex as a traditional network as components of the VPC such as internet gateways, VPN servers, NAT instances and subnets have to be managed by the customers themselves. Furthermore, the customers are required to setup an IPSec device on their premises that connects to an IPSec gateway in the VPC running as a virtual appliance which integrates the enterprises network with the VPC subnet in the cloud. Most importantly, with the exception of [12], these solutions are locked to single cloud vendor and [12] provides use of a selective set of cloud providers by placing its virtual appliances as VPN gateways in these cloud infrastructures and allowing the customers to join these gateways in a mesh topology manually.

3   Design and Architecture

In this section we present the design and architecture of our inter-cloud secure communication framework, the Inter-Cloud VPN (ICVPN). The architecture is inspired by two main techniques, namely Peer-to-Peer (P2P) Overlays [14] and VPNs [15]. Network virtualization techniques like VPNs and P2P Overlays have been shown to provide their users legacy communication functionalities of their native network environments, despite the topology, configuration and management architecture of the actual underlying physical network. This fits perfectly with our goal of providing a secure virtual private network as a service to the consumers operating on top of multiple cloud providers. All complications and complexities of managing a physical network can be handled by the overlay network, enabling the services deployed on multiple clouds to benefit from a customized communication network typically only available in physical local-area environments.

3.1   Peer-to-Peer Overlay

The core technique employed by the ICVPN is the use of two tiers of P2P overlays. A Universal Overlay (UO) forms the higher tier overlay and is used to provide a scalable and secure service infrastructure to initiate and bind multiple lower tier VPN overlays (VO) to different cloud services. The universal overlay can be initiated either by the service owner, a cloud broker or the cloud service providers. Its main purpose is to help with the bootstrapping activity of VPN peers of the VPN overlay. It also provides other functionalities such as service advertisement, service discovery mechanisms, and service code provisioning, with minimal requirement for manual configuration and administration.

This approach acts as an aggregation service for the peered overlay resources (which in this case are virtual machines) span across multiple cloud domains to help form a virtual private network. The peers of the universal overlay act as super peers for the nodes of the underlying VPN overlays and let new nodes enrol, authenticate, bootstrap and join a particular VPN overlay based on the cloud service requiring a VPN service.

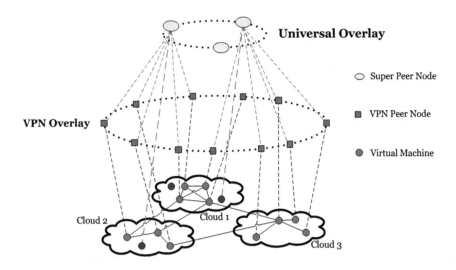

Fig. 1. Two-tiered overlay architecture for the Inter-Cloud VPN solution

As depicted in Fig. 1, the service owner/provider or the cloud broker could itself be a peer in the universal overlay and a subset of the universal overlay peers can act as super-peers for the peer nodes of the VPN overlay for a particular cloud service. This enables the service owner/provider or the cloud broker to publish and propagate configuration and other data throughout the universal overlay. This is done by using its super peer as the initial dissemination point and then taking advantage of the scalable content-sharing capabilities of the Distributed Hash Table (DHT) feature of the overlay. The universal overlay peers can join and leave the system dynamically and additional VMs from the cloud providers can be provisioned to act as the universal overlay peers as well.

To join the universal overlay, each peer needs to acquire a unique identification number (PID). This is generated by the peer itself on its first initialization on a VM as a unique 160-bit random number. It also needs some bootstrapping data to validate itself with a super peer for admission into the overlay. The bootstrapping data consists of the IP addresses of the super peers, the ID of the service that this particular VM belongs to and some security-related parameters described later. This data is embedded in a secure cache on the VM by a VM contextualization service [16] when it is provisioned for the service deployment and the same contextualization service is used to install the peer-to-peer client in the VM.

Once the peer has joined its overlay, it needs to discover its neighbours and gather additional configuration data to establish secure tunnels with them so that the deployed service can communicate securely with its different components deployed on different cloud platforms. In order to achieve this, we use the following scheme based on the Functional Encryption predicates.

3.2 Secure Service Based Resource Discovery

After joining a peer-to-peer overlay, each peer needs to discover its neighbours for the resources they provide to achieve the secure communication goals of the application using the overlay. Most commonly these resources are configuration and credentials data and the secure communication goals of a typical application pertain to encryption of traffic associated with specific ports and protocols. In most structured P2P systems, the peers must maintain lists of neighbours to achieve this goal efficiently. To populate these lists, peers in a structured overlay usually use distributed trackers or IP Multicast [17]. Although IP multicast offers the feature of scalable group communication needed for efficient resource delivery, it is not suitable for use in our system architecture, this is mainly due to its very limited deployment by ISPs and network carriers as well as the complexity of its architectural design [18]. A P2P tracker is a specialised service that introduces other peers of an overlay to the requesting peer. In order to perform this function, a tracker keeps track of peers as soon as they make a request. A tracker may be deployed as a dedicated server or distributed among the peers of an overlay it self. At first glance the distributed trackers based approach looks very suitable for use in our system architecture as it maps nicely with the functionality of the peers of the universal overlay i.e. well known bootstrapping points. However, this approach is vulnerable to malicious attacks like Denial-of-Service (DoS) and Sybil attacks [19], in which the attacker can subvert the functioning of a peer-to-peer overlay by creating and using a large number of false identities. For ICVPN we focus on the Sybil attack where a malicious attacked can impersonate a number of the Universal Overlay peers to subvert the process of resource discovery.

A common way of dealing with this issue is to use some trusted authority to allocate peer IDs to the participating peers and the peers validate each other by querying the central authority with a validation request. In our model, it can work by designating a set of super peers as the Certificate Authorities (CA) for the overlays other peers. The CA can assign peer IDs to the peers and signs a certificate that binds the serviceID of the cloud service making use of our solution and peer ID within the public certificate of the peer for a limited time duration. The peer then can use this signed certificate to authenticate itself with other peers in the overlay. However, using this Trusted Third Party (TTP) model to validate peers and allocate them their identities can introduce substantial communicational and computational overhead, especially as the number of peers in the overlay increases. We propose a decentralized solution that overcomes the above mentioned scalability problems by utilizing a functional encryption based scheme [20].

In a generic functional encryption scheme, a decryption key describes a function of the encrypted data to the user. This function $F(\cdot, \cdot)$ is modelled as a Turing Machine [21] and an authority possessing a master secret key (msk) can generate a key skk that can be used to compute the function $F(k, \cdot)$ on some encrypted data. Identity-Based Encryption [22–24], Searchable Encryption [25] and Attribute-Based Encryption [26] are some examples of a Functional Encryption scheme. To describe it more formally but briefly, A functional encryption scheme (FE) for a functionality F dened over (K, X) is a sequence of four algorithms (setup, keygen, encryption, decryption) satisfying the following correctness condition for all $k \in K$ and $x \in X$ is given in Table 1.

Table 1. Four-tuple functional encryption

Sequence	Explanation
$setup(1) \rightarrow (pp, msk)$	Generate a public and master secret key pair
$keygen(mk, k) \rightarrow sk$	Generate secrekt key for k
$enc(pp, x) \rightarrow c$	Encrypt message x
$dec(sk, c) \rightarrow y$	Use sk to decrypt c

For ICVPN, we employ a special case of Functional Encryption which falls under the category of systems known as the predicate encryption schemes with public index. For our scheme we make use of the system defined in [26] as Attribute-Based Encryption (ABE), where the decision that which users can decrypt a ciphertext is based on the attributes and policies associated with the plaintext message and the user. In this scheme an authority creates secret keys for the users of the system based on attributes or policies for each user and anyone can encrypt a plaintext message by incorporating the appropriate attributes or policies in the scheme. We describe the simplified step-wise description of our version of this scheme as follows:-

i. A super peer sets up its own Master Secret ms and Public Parameters pp
ii. The super peer generates a private key for itself using the attributes $ServiceID$ and $SuperPeerID$ as the public key i.e. $Pub_{SP} = ServiceID \wedge SuperPeerID$, for each service the super peer is managing
iii. After bootstrapping, the VPN peer sends a provisioning request to the super peer encrypted by the super peers public key (Pub_{SP})
iv. The super peer issues a private key to the VPN peer encrypted by its own private key, against the public key with attributes $Pub_{VPN} = VMID \wedge PeerID \wedge ServiceID$
v. The super peer inserts the VPN peers public key in the universal overlay DHT to keep a record of issued private keys, against the $key(ServiceID) = value(List\ of\ VMID)$ and for each peer; $key(VM_{ID_i}) = value(Pub_{VPN_i})$

vi. The VPN peer query the universal overlay DHT for lists of other peers and gets the result of $key(ServiceID)$ encrypted using $Pub_{VPN_x} = PeerID \wedge ServiceID$

In Sect. 5 we show the evaluation results of the performance overhead of using our secure resource discovery scheme as compared to that using a PKI-based approach described earlier in this section.

3.3   Secure Virtual Private Connections

The key feature of our ICVPN is establishing a secure communication network between the peers of the overlay formed over a collection of cloud providers infrastructure. Therefore, after successfully joining the overlay network to become part of a service, a VPN peer starts the process of creating secure tunnels to the other peers of the service it wants to communicate with, according to the functional operations of that particular service. To achieve this, we make use of IPSec [13] to authenticate and encrypt each IP packet of a communication session between the peers, thus creating end-to-end tunnels which provide protection against eavesdropping, message tempering and message forgeries. For establishing mutual authentication between peers at the beginning of the session and negotiation of cryptographic keys to be used during the session, we employ the Internet Key Exchange protocol [27], which can make use of standard cryptographic primitives like public key cryptography [28] and AES [29]. In our approach, we make use of an authenticated Diffie-Hellman based scheme to derive a secure session key which is used in the AES-CBC mode to ensure the confidentiality of the traffic exchanges between the peers using the tunnel [30]. The session keys generated for the IPSec communication are valid for a short period of time and when the keys expire the protocol is run again to come up with new session keys to maintain the IPSec tunnels.

Another practical advantage of this approach is the reuse of existing frameworks and tools which have been thoroughly tried and tested in a myriad of different domains, are widely used and have been adopted in both academic and commercial domain. The main components of the peer-to-peer client used to construct a virtual private network in our model are shown in Fig. 2. These include the standard components required to form a structured peer-to-peer overlay like the Distributed Hash Table (DHT) service, which basically acts as the command-and-control channel for the ICVPN solution, key-based routing, peer discovery, bootstrapping service and overlay maintenance service. All of these services are provided by a modified Kademlia implementation. In addition to these peer-to-peer specific components, we have a secure content storage for the client where sensitive data like keys, passwords, and security tokens etc. are stored. The configuration component is integrated with the overlays DHT so that the clients behaviour can be modified dynamically by push new configurations to it from the super peers. The configuration component manages both the peer-to-peer related configurations as well as the policies used to configure the IPSec tunnels between the peers for the use of the higher-level services using the client to provide the secure communication framework.

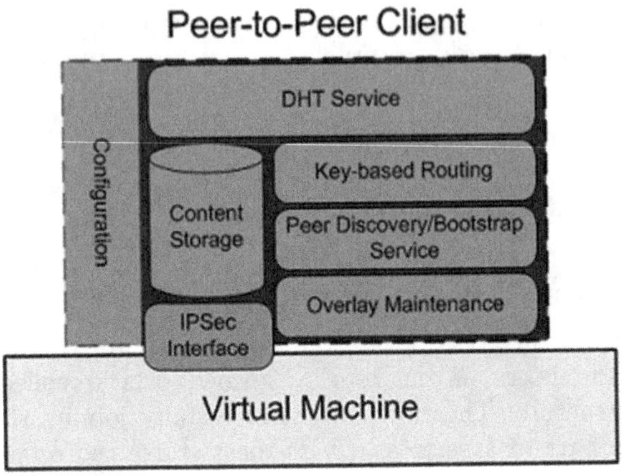

Peer-to-Peer Client

Fig. 2. Architecture of a P2P client in the VPN overlay

The P2P client software sets up and configures the IPSec security associations according the service network security policy, which is advertised by the service owner through the DHT of the Universal Overlay. The peers of the underlying VPN overlay periodically check for any update in the security policy and apply and enforce any changes on the kernel of the VM through the P2P client's IPSec interface.

4   Implementation

We implement a working prototype of ICVPN using the Java programming language on virtual machines running the Linux operating system. Our implementation is built using open source libraries and APIs. Specifically, we use the BouncyCastle library [31] for most of the cryptographic operations, the cpabe library [32] for the Functional Encrytion based secure resource discovery, and the TomP2P library [33] for its implementation of the Kademlia [34] peer-to-peer protocol and the overlay DHT. In addition, we use BT Compute Cloud [35] and Flexiant Cloud [36] as our cloud service providers.

5   Evaluation

In this section we present the results of a series of experiments we conducted to evaluate the effect of our prototype ICVPN solution upon the network performance of a service deployed on two different cloud IaaS providers. We use a 3-tier web service comprising of database, business logic and presentation components deployed on nine virtual machines hosted on the clouds of British Telecom Ltd. and Flexiant Ltd., our partners in the EU OPTIMIS project. The purpose of these experiments is to evaluate the architecture being proposed, in terms of service latency and service throughput, in a practical scenario with a service deployed over a real wide-area network, with the BT cloud geographically located in Ipswich, England and Flexiant cloud located in Livingston, Scotland.

5.1 Service Latency

We define service latency as the inter-cloud round-trip time taken by a HTTP request, issued by a service component on one cloud, to get a response from the target service component on a different cloud. We compare the latency between the components of the service deployed on different cloud providers, as the latency between the components in the same cloud is almost negligible as they are usually hosted on the same hyper-visor. We measured the latency by using the round-trip delay of an HTTP HEAD request/response pair, as the components of the web service communicate with each other using HTTP protocol and ICMP, the de facto latency measurement protocol, is blocked in the networks of our cloud providers. We measured the latency readings by running 10 experiments very hour for a period of 24 h, firstly without using the ICVPN solution and then with it.

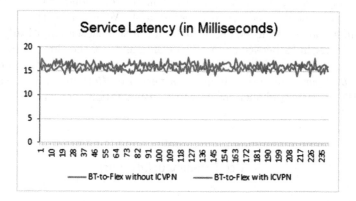

Fig. 3. Service latency of 240 round-trip time experiments from BT to Flexiant clouds

Looking at the results shown in Figs. 3 and 4 we can see that using our solution only has a small impact on the HTTP latency, increasing it just by about 5 %. For ease of analysis, we collect the network traffic dump when running our experiments, using the tcpdump packet sniffer. We found out from the traffic dumps that the increased delay we encountered is mostly due to the additional packets transmitted and received by the peers for the purposes of key exchange and cryptographic primitives negotiation when establishing an IPSec tunnel. After this initial handshake phase is over, the latency performance is almost same in the comparative experiments.

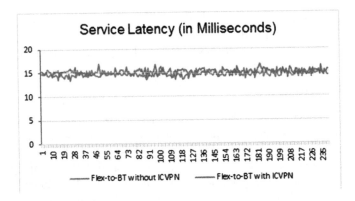

Fig. 4. Service latency of 240 round-trip time experiments from Flexiant to BT clouds

5.2   Service Throughput

We define service throughput as the inter-cloud network throughput between service components deployed on different clouds. We measure the throughput between components of the service deployed on different cloud providers by using Iperf [37], a commonly used network testing tool. We measured the throughput in both directions by transferring 30 MB data, a size chosen empirically to saturate the WAN links between the components and get the throughput results representing realistic conditions. We obtained the throughput measurements by running *10* experiments every hour for a period of *10* h, firstly without using the ICVPN solution and then applying the security policy to tunnel the traffic through IPSec.

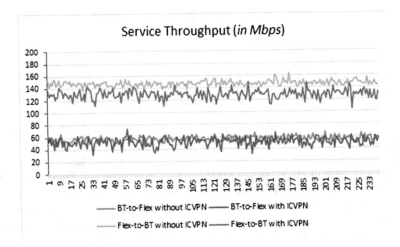

Fig. 5. Service throughput of 240 data transmission experiments in both directions between BT and Flexiant clouds

From the throughput results shown in Fig. 5, the first thing that stands out is the difference in the throughput values depending on the direction of transferring the data. Although we don't have the detailed knowledge of the underlying physical wide-area network connectivity between the two cloud service providers, such readings are not unheard of in this domain and are usually due to differences in upstream and downstream traffic conditions, different routes chosen by the IP packets or network configuration issues. Irrespective of that, by looking at the comparative results it is clear that we just incur a small overhead in the throughput, of about *10 %*. By analysing the traffic dumps generated from the throughout test, we can attribute this overhead to the IKE and IPSec handshakes in addition to the extra time taken by the VM kernel in encrypting and encapsulating 30 MB of data for each throughput test.

5.3 Secure Resource Discovery Overheads

One of the main overheads in peer-to-peer overlays related to the cost of the resource discovery after the peers have bootstrapped. Securing this process further adds to this overhead but in an effort to characterise the effect of our secure resource discovery mechanism, we compare it with an alternate design of a PKI-based system where the super peers have the functionality of a Certificate Authority (CA), each peer is issued a signed certificate upon authenticated completion of the bootstrapping process and queries the Universal Overlay DHT for resource discovery and gets the resulting data back which is encrypted by the owning peer using its private key.

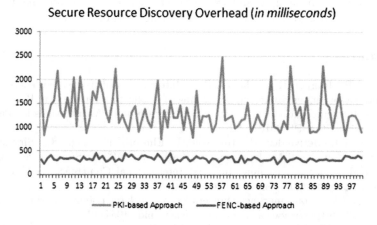

Fig. 6. Secure resource discovery for 100 runtime analysis between PKI and functional encryption approaches

We remove the cost of the DHT lookups from our measurements as their theoretical complexity is known to be $O\ log(n)$ for Kademlia DHT but due to the nature of actual runtime measurements they can add unhelpful noise to the data. We define the runtime cost for both designs as the time duration between the start and end of the secure resource discovery process.

From the results shown in Fig. 6, the mean runtime of the PKI-based design is *1313.52* ms whereas that for our Functional Encryption based scheme is *338.81* ms. This shows that our scheme incurs about *74.2* % less overhead than a PKI based scheme.

6   Conclusion

In this paper, we present a secure communication framework for services deployed in an inter-cloud environment. We employ the robustness and scalability afforded by structure peer-to-peer overlays to join virtual machines running on different cloud IaaS providers with each other using IPSec tunnels, hence providing confidentiality, authentication and integrity for all the data exchanged between different components of a cloud service. Our solution needs minimal manual configuration as peers are automated to discover the information needed to perform their operations from the Universal Overlay. We also provide a distributed and scalable key management solution for the consumption of the virtual machines to set-up the secure communication channels. Our solution supports the dynamic addition and removal of nodes from the VPN overlay as we use the peer-to-peer DHT not just as a command and control channel for managing the VPN peers but also for the churn management of peers in the VPN overlay. We have evaluated a prototype implementation based on experiments conducted in realistic conditions, over multiple cloud infrastructure environments and found minimal latency, throughput and security overheads of creating and maintaining the ICVPN connections among the participating VMs of a service.

References

1. Buyya, R., Ranjan, R., Calheiros, R.N.: Intercloud: utility-oriented federation of cloud computing environments for scaling of application services. In: Proceedings of the 10th International Conference on Algorithmsand Architectures for Parallel Processing (ICA3PP 2010) (2010)
2. Ferrer, A.J., Hernandez, F., Tordsson, J., Elmroth, E., Zsigri, C., Sirvent, R., Guitart, J., Badia, R.M., Djemame, K., Ziegler, W.: OPTIMIS: a holistic approach to cloud service provisioning. In: First International Conference on Utility and Cloud Computing, December 2010
3. Gartner: Cloud consumers need brokerages to unlock the potential of cloud services, July 2009. http://www.gartner.com/it/page.jspid=1064712
4. Yonan, J.: OpenVPN - an open source SSL VPN solution. http://openvpn.net
5. Jiang, X., Xu, D.: VIOLIN: virtual internetworking on overlay infrastructure. In: Proceedings of the 2nd International Symposium on Parallel and Distributed Processing and Applications (2003)
6. Sundararaj, A.I., Dinda, P.A.: Towards virtual networks for virtual machine grid computing. In: Proceedings of the 3rd USENIX Virtual Machine Research and Technology Symposium (2004)

7. LogMeIn: Hamachi - a zero-configuration virtual private network. https://secure. logmein.com/products/hamachi2
8. Deri, L., Andrews, R.: N2N: a layer two Peer-to-Peer VPN. In: Hausheer, D., Schönwälder, J. (eds.) AIMS 2008. LNCS, vol. 5127, pp. 53–64. Springer, Heidelberg (2008)
9. Schneier, B., Kelsey, J., Whiting, D., Wagner, D., Hall, C., Ferguson, N.: The Twofish Encryption Algorithm: A 128-bit Block Cipher. John Wiley & Sons Inc, New York (1999)
10. Amazon: Virtual private cloud. http://aws.amazon.com/vpc
11. Google: Secure data connector. http://code.google.com/securedataconnecto
12. CohesiveFT: VPN-Cubed. http://www.cohesiveft.com/vpncubed
13. Doraswamy, N.: IPSec : The New Security Standard for the Internet, Intranets, and Virtual Private Networks, 2nd edn. Prentice Hall, Englewood Cliffs (2003)
14. Andersen, D., Balakrishnan, H., Kaashoek, F., Morris, R.: Resilient overlay networks. SIGCOMM Comput. Commun Rev. 32(1), 66 (2002)
15. Tanenbaum, A.S., Wetherall, D.J.: Virtual private networks. In: Computer Networks, 5th edn, pp. 821. Prentice Hall, October 2010
16. Armstrong, D., Djemame, K., Nair, S.K., Tordsson, J., Ziegler, W.: Towards a contextualization solution for cloud platform services. In: CloudCom, pp. 328–331 (2011)
17. Deering, S.E., Cheriton, D.R.: Multicast routing in datagram internetworks and extended lans. ACM Trans. Comput. Syst. 8(2), 85–110 (1990)
18. Diot, C., Levine, B., Lyles, B., Kassem, H., Balensiefen, D.: Deployment issues for the ip multicast service and architecture. Netw. IEEE 14(1), 78–88 (2000)
19. Douceur, J.R.: The sybil attack. In: Druschel, P., Kaashoek, M.F., Rowstron, A. (eds.) IPTPS 2002. LNCS, vol. 2429, pp. 251–260. Springer, Heidelberg (2002)
20. Boneh, D., Sahai, A., Waters, B.: Functional encryption: a new vision for public-key cryptography. Commun. ACM 55(11), 56–64 (2012)
21. Turing, A.M.: On computable numbers, with an application to the entscheidungsproblem. Proc. London Math. Soc. 42, 230–265 (1936)
22. Shamir, A.: Identity-Based cryptosystems and signature schemes. In: Blakely, G.R., Chaum, D. (eds.) CRYPTO 1984. LNCS, vol. 196, pp. 47–53. Springer, Heidelberg (1985)
23. Boneh, D., Franklin, M.: Identity-Based encryption from the weil pairing. In: Kilian, J. (ed.) CRYPTO 2001. LNCS, vol. 2139, p. 213. Springer, Heidelberg (2001)
24. Cocks, C.: An identity based encryption scheme based on quadratic residues. In: Honary, B. (ed.) Cryptography and Coding 2001. LNCS, vol. 2260, pp. 360–363. Springer, Heidelberg (2001)
25. Boneh, D., Di Crescenzo, G., Ostrovsky, R., Persiano, G.: Public key encryption with keyword search. In: Cachin, C., Camenisch, J.L. (eds.) EUROCRYPT 2004. LNCS, vol. 3027, pp. 506–522. Springer, Heidelberg (2004)
26. Hohenberger, S., Waters, B.: Attribute-Based encryption with fast decryption. In: Kurosawa, K., Hanaoka, G. (eds.) PKC 2013. LNCS, vol. 7778, pp. 162–179. Springer, Heidelberg (2013)
27. Kaufman, C.: Internet key exchange protocol version 2 (ikev2). In: RFC 5996 (2010)
28. Diffie, W., Hellman, M.: New directions in cryptography. IEEE Trans. Inf. Theor. 22(6), 644–654 (1976)
29. 197, F.I.P.S.P.: Announcing the advanced encryption standard (aes) (2001)
30. Housley, R.: Using advanced encryption standard (aes) ccm mode with ipsec encapsulating security payload (esp) (2005)

31. Legion of the Bouncy Castle: Bouncy castle java cryptography apis (2013). http://www.bouncycastle.org/java.html
32. Bethencourt, J., Sahai, A., Waters, B.: Advanced crypto software collection: the cpabe toolkit (2011). http://acsc.cs.utexas.edu/cpabe
33. Bocek, T.: TomP2P: A P2P-based high performance key-value pair storage library (2012). http://tomp2p.net
34. Maymounkov, P., Mazières, D.: Kademlia: a Peer-to-Peer information system based on the XOR metric. In: Druschel, P., Kaashoek, M.F., Rowstron, A. (eds.) IPTPS 2002. LNCS, vol. 2429, pp. 53–65. Springer, Heidelberg (2002)
35. BritishTelecom: BT Compute Cloud (2013). https://cloud.btcompute.bt.com
36. Flexiant: Flexiant, your cloud simplified (2013). http://www.flexiant.com
37. Ajay Tirumala, L.C., Dunigan, T.: Measuring end-to-end bandwidth with iperf using web100. In: Web100, Proceedings of Passive and Active Measurement Workshop (2003)

Analysing Virtual Machine Security in Cloud Systems

Taimur Al Said$^{(\boxtimes)}$ and Omer F. Rana

School of Computer Science and Informatics, Cardiff University, Cardiff, UK
{alsaidts,ranaof}@cardiff.ac.uk

Abstract. The cloud computing concept has significantly influenced how information is delivered and managed in large scale distributed systems today. Cloud computing is currently expected to reduce the economic cost of using computational and data resources, and is therefore particularly appealing to small and medium scale companies (who may not wish to maintain in-house IT departments). To provide economies of scale, providers of Cloud computing infrastructure make significant use of virtualisation techniques – in which processes of various *tenants* sharing the same physical resources are separated logically using a *hypervisor*. In spite of its wide adoption in Cloud computing systems, virtualisation technology suffers from many security and privacy issues. We outline security challenges that remain in the use of virtualisation techniques to support multiple customers on the same shared infrastructure. We also illustrate, using an experiment, how *data leakage* occurs when multiple VMs are executed on the same physical infrastructure, leading to unauthorised access to (previously) deleted data.

1 Introduction

Although the general ideas behind Cloud computing are not new, their recent adoption by significant portions of the information systems industry (both users and providers), have introduced new challenges in scalability, security and economic models. Cloud computing is a concept which promotes the economic use of resources among clients by employing the "pay-per-use" revenue model, such that clients will pay only for the resources they use (often advertised on a per hour or per month basis). Cloud computing leverages on the significant investment being made in internet and communications infrastructure between the Cloud consumer and the provider. There are many companies offering Cloud services of different flavours, e.g. Amazon through its AWS suite[1]. Similarly, Google has also recently considered providing metered Cloud services. Despite the various benefits of Cloud computing, many potential consumers in different sectors have been reluctant about migrating to a public Cloud. Some of them, instead, have adopted the use of a private Cloud instead of public offerings, especially in industry sectors such as oil and gas [24]. This is mainly because

---

[1] Amazon Web Services - http://aws.amazon.com.

© Springer International Publishing Switzerland 2015
A. Al-Saidi et al. (Eds.): ICC 2014, LNCS 8993, pp. 137–151, 2015.
DOI: 10.1007/978-3-319-19848-4_9

of the security and privacy concerns associated with the use of public Clouds. In a Cloud computing environment, the physical infrastructure of the Cloud provider is shared amongst (potentially) hundreds of consumers (tenants) using the concept of virtualisation. As tenants use the virtual space given to them by the Cloud provider, there may be a possibility that several tenants access the same physical disk space (over which their shared, virtual partition is hosted). When the virtual machine is turned off or deleted, the same disk space could be given to a new tenant who can, in principle, use various software tools to recover data belonging to the previous tenant. This may lead to the disclosure of a consumers' private data. This paper focuses on this particular aspect by first surveying various virtualisation security issues currently prevalent in many commercial virtualisation systems and by exploring the process of recovering permanently deleted data from virtual machines. It tries to answer the following questions: (i) what are the key security issues associated with the use of virtualisation in multi-tenancy environments; and (ii) can permanently deleted data be retrieved successfully out of the virtual machines? The rest of this paper is organized as follows: Sect. 2 introduces the concept of Cloud Computing, Sect. 3 introduces virtualisation technology and Sect. 4 covers Cloud privacy issues. Section 5 discusses virtualisation security issues and Sect. 6 covers covers various aspects of the problem introduced by virtualisation and highlights related work, while Sect. 7 describes the experiments we carry out to demonstrate limitations with an existing, widely used, virtualisation system. Section 8 provides a discussion of the results and highlights some future research directions then it concludes the paper.

2   Cloud Computing

Cloud computing is a concept which has gained considerable attention recently in a variety of fields, e.g. academia, research and enterprises. Consumers in each field have different motivations for migrating their systems to the Cloud [28]. According to [2], Cloud computing refers to both the applications delivered as services over the internet and the hardware and systems software in the data centers that provide these services. If that data center is accessed as a pay-per-use service over the internet then it is called "public". If it is not made available to the public then it is called "private". The use of data centre based hosting of system and data therefore has significant similarities with the Cloud-based deployment (in some instances, they are in practice synonymous). In [13], the authors suggest that "the cloud computing concept offers dynamically scalable resources provisioned as a service over the internet." According to NIST (the U.S National Institute of Standards and Technology), Cloud computing has three service models: SaaS (Software as a Service), PaaS (Platform as A Service) and IaaS (Infrastructure as A Service) [22]. Examples of SaaS are email services like Gmail, Hotmail, etc. An example of the PaaS service model is the Google App Engine which enables users to deploy and scale Python and Java-based web applications[2]. An example of IaaS is Amazon Web Services (AWS) which allow consumers to rent pre-configured virtual machines and pay for these per use only. While web browsers are used to access SaaS, web services are used to access IaaS. Both web services and web browsers may be used to access PaaS [13]. Notable benefits of Cloud computing are: universal data access from anywhere using the internet, automated storage management, avoiding the capital expenditure on hardware, software, personnel, etc. According to [24], Cloud computing offers deployment flexibility and speed to implement for small businesses. Hybrid cloud is a combination of one or more clouds (private, community or public) that remain a unique entity but are bound together by standardized or proprietary access interfaces, enabling data and application portability [4]. A community Cloud serves a group of consumers who have shared concerns such as mission objectives, security, and privacy and compliance policy [22].

3   Virtualisation

3.1   Overview

Virtualisation technology lets a single machine simultaneously run multiple operating systems (OSs) or multiple sessions of a single OS [31]. By freeing developers and users from traditional interface and resources constraints, Virtual Machines (VMs) provide software interoperability, system impregnability and platform versatility [15,29]. VMs are usually classified into two categories: (i) System virtual machines: provide a complete system platform which supports the execution of a complete OS. For example, it provides a platform to run programs where the real hardware is not available, e.g. legacy systems. Another aspect in the use of VMs is to improve utilisation of computing resources – the key reason for use in Cloud computing. (ii) Process virtual machines: are designed to run a single program (supports a single process) and are built with the main purpose of providing program portability and flexibility. In virtualisation, the physical server is called the host whereas the virtual servers are called guests. The VM manager or Hypervisor makes different VMs independent of each other. There are three types of server virtualisation: Full Virtualisation, Para-Virtualisation and OS-level virtualisation, as described in Table 1.

3.2   Hypervisor

The hypervisor or virtual machine monitor (VMM) is the basic abstraction layer that sits directly on the hardware of the physical server (Type 1 hypervisor). The Hypervisor is responsible for scheduling and partitioning memory of the various VMs running on the physical device [33]. If the hypervisor is installed on top of the host operating system, then it is said to be 'type 2 hypervisor'.

In addition to abstracting the hardware for the virtual machine, the hypervisor controls the execution of VMs as they share a common processing environment, as illustrated in Fig. 1. The hypervisor has no knowledge of networking,

---

[2] Google App Engine - https://console.developers.google.com/start/appengine.

Table 1. Types of server virtualisation&comparisons

	Full virtualisation	Para virtualisation	OS-level virtualisation
Availability of the hypervisor?	Yes	Yes	No
Guests knowledge of each other?	Unaware	Aware	Must be of the same OS type
Independence of guest servers	Yes	Yes	Yes
Description	The hypervisor interacts directly with the physical server's CPU and disk space	As each guest is aware of the others and their demands, the hypervisor does not need more processing power	Virtualisation capability is part of the host OS which performs the operations of a fully virtualised hypervisor
Limitations	Physical server must reserve some processing power and resources to the hypervisor; this can impact server performance and slow down operations	The guest OS must be tailored specifically to run using the hypervisor	Guest servers must run the same OS

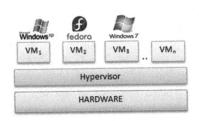

Fig. 1. Location of the hypervisor (type 1)

external storage, video, or any other common I/O functions. It serves as a platform for the VMs hosted on the physical server. This allows running various types of operating systems which are not compatible with each other independently. A list of potential VM management software includes:

– VMware workstation: VMware is the leading product in desktop virtualisation. It acts as a virtual computer on which any OS can be installed.
– Virtual Box: is an open source application to manage and run VMs. It can be used to run a virtual (guest) OS on any host machine that runs Windows, Linux, Mac OS X or Solaris operating system.
– Microsoft Virtual PC: Microsoft Virtual PC allows a complete "virtual computer" to be created – and is free to download and use.
– Citrix XenServer: is an open source virtualisation platform for managing Cloud deployments, server and desktop virtual infrastructures. It is based on the Xen hypervisor.

3.3   Virtualisation in Cloud Computing

Virtualisation is the basis of Cloud computing because it simplifies the delivery of services by providing a platform for optimizing complex IT resources in a scalable manner [12]. It can be applied to memory, networks, storage, hardware, OS, and application. In a typical scenario, we can imagine having a powerful physical machine with large amounts of storage, memory and a fast processor. Using a VMM, several virtual servers can be hosted on the machine. Storage, memory and processing will be divided among the virtualised servers. If a certain VM required additional storage, then it will be easily acquired from the host machine. Until recently, Graphics Processing Units (GPUs) could not be virtualised.

4   Cloud Privacy

Privacy is one of the most cited concerns in cloud security literature. Sharing resources within a Cloud computing environment could result in unexpected side and covert channels being created [5]. An example is the effect of cross user de-duplication, which happens when Cloud service providers tend to save only one single copy of a file to avoid redundancy. Harnik et al. [11] have covered de-duplication privacy implications in detail. Whereas in [26], the authors focus on techniques hackers may use to ensure co-residence i.e. injecting a VM on the same physical machine as the targeted VM. Although the process of ensuring physical co-residence with a given VM is not trivial, they were successfully able to monitor some activities of the target VM using a covert side channel. Activity patterns may be visible to users of the same shared resource. Divulging activity patterns could lead to reverse-engineering a Cloud consumers' confidential information [5]. Zissis et al. in [35] argue that data privacy could be breached unintentionally due to data remittance which is the residual representation of data.

The Amazon.com Cloud system allows users to create and share VM images with other users in addition to the ones provided by Amazon itself. In [3], the authors developed an automated system to download and analyze instances of those public images. The authors discovered that some of these VM images issue unsolicited connections to suspicious sites. Also, they discovered backdoors and left out credentials. Some of the VM images had malware which monitor the browsing habits of the user. Recovery of deleted data from public user images was possible even from Amazon.com images. The researchers used NMap, a network port scanning tool, to find out the number of running instances. In [32], the authors mentioned that OpenNebula (an open source Cloud system) had a bug which leaves user passwords accessible by anyone on the entire network. The Cloud Security Alliance mentioned in its "2013 Cloud Security Top Threats" document that if the user encrypts data before uploading it to the cloud but loses the encryption key, then the data will be lost as well. Amazon Web Services (AWS) has recently launched 'CloudTrail'[3] which is intended to to give the owner

---

[3] Amazon Cloudtrail - http://aws.amazon.com/cloudtrail.

of an AWS account details of how the Amazon API was used, by whom, which source IP address were used,etc. However, it does not tell the user how the data inside his VMs were used or (potentially) modified.

5   Virtualisation Security

According to [2], virtualisation is the primary security mechanism in the Cloud – intended to isolate the system and data of one user from another. However, not all resources are virtualised and not all resources are bug free. In [31], the authors argue that organizations are facing the challenge of securing virtualised systems which are vulnerable to the same threats as physical systems including intrusions and malware. Despite being also a security mechanism, there exist many security issues which are associated with virtualisation. There is significant literature which covers some of these issues in detail such as [1, 7, 10, 18, 20, 23, 25, 31]. According to [9], the threats that work in a physical world could also work in a virtualised world and could be more devastating. The reason is that those threats could propagate much more rapidly within a virtualised environment to affect the other guests of the physical host. In the discussion of virtualisation security, one has to consider two aspects. The first aspect to be considered is the whole virtualisation environment which includes the physical host, the Host OS, the hypervisor, the VM and the guest OS. In [1], the authors suggest that the security of any virtualisation solution is heavily dependent on the individual security of each component, from the hypervisor and host OS to guest OS, applications and storage. Some researchers argue that the security of the Cloud provider in general also needs to be considered [16]. The second aspect to be considered is the important role of the hypervisor in such a virtualised environment. To provide a focused discussion on virtualisation-specific issues, the following sections will focus on three components which are: the hypervisor, Virtual Machine (VM) and Guest OS. Common attacks on these components will be described.

5.1   Hypervisor-Related Attacks

In any virtualisation system, the hypervisor allocates the host machine's resources to each virtualised operating system or to each program running on a virtualised OS. It emulates a hardware device for each VM and handles the communication between the CPU, the storage medium, and the network via the OS [31]. In the IaaS model, attacking the hypervisor would mean compromising all the running VMs (managed by the hypervisor). Perhaps the biggest threat to virtualisation security is that hypervisors have more privileged access to hardware resources than typical applications [31]. One hypervisor hijacking technique, "hyperjacking", involves an attacker running a very small footprint hypervisor that takes complete control over the host OS [25]. An example of hyperjacking is the 'blue-pill' malware that executes as a hypervisor to gain control of a computer's resources [27]. The bluepill starts a thin hypervisor under the main OS which can still maintain reference to the devices but has no control over it. The same concept was demonstrated by a group of researchers under the term 'Virtual Machine Rootkits (VMBR)' [17]. According to [1], some virtualisation products offer multiple ways to manage hypervisors, so if the management interface is not secured, the hypervisor will be under threat. Also, if the management console is accessed remotely, communications must be protected. In December 2013, the openSSL website was breached[4]. Instead of attacking the website itself, the attackers targeted the hosting company which stored the website in host machine with insecure management console to access the hypervisor. In [20], the authors suggest that poor isolation or inappropriate access control policy will cause an inter-attack between VMs or between VMs and the hypervisor. A group of researchers successfully demonstrated that it is possible to reconstruct private keys of certain VM from another VM in the same host using side channel attacks [34].

There were bugs which allow virtualised code to break loose to some extent. The authors in [30] provide an overview of the use of virtualisation and demonstrate that the widely used VMM or the hypervisor cannot be considered fully secure. They argue that bad configuration or design flaws in the VMM could lead to a denial of service, system halt or VM *escape*. In a denial of service attack, the VM uses all the computing capacities of the host preventing other VMs from running correctly. System halt may cause a VM to crash. VM escape is an exploit in which the attacker runs code on a VM that allows an operating system running within it to break out and interact directly with the hypervisor [20]. Hence, in the VM escape threat, an attacker may gain access to the memory located outside the region allocated to the corrupted VM in an environment which has access to the host OS. Many bugs which allow escaping from a VM have been found in famous virtualisation software such as: Microsoft Virtual PC/Virtual Server, VMware and Xen [10]. All of these attacks are possible because there is a possibility to detect whether there is a hypervisor running underneath the OS and also its type. In [25], the authors demonstrate how an attacker could take control of the VMware and Xen virtualisation software when moving a virtual machine from one physical computer to another (referred to a VM migration). A security assessment done on Rackspace - a famous cloud provider- indicated that some virtual servers contained data processed earlier on other virtual servers. This was due to the improper wiping of disks and to the way the hypervisor was configured to read/write from the disk [14].

5.2   VM-Related Attacks

In virtualisation, if the host is not secure, then the virtual machine is not necessarily secure [5], even if the latter was patched effectively. In addition, managing VM migration could add another level of complexity to the security process especially when the VM is migrated to an unsecure host. It is suggested in [9] that virtualisation is very dynamic, with systems constantly creating and shutting down VMs or moving them to different hosts – so the entire security process

---

[4] OpenSSL website defacement - http://tinyurl.com/luugk25.

must be dynamic. VM sprawl is considered another issue in a virtualisation environment. It happens when the number of VMs is continuously growing, while most of them are idle or never return back from sleep mode [20]. According to a study by Commvault[5], about 30–40 percent of the VMs created end up being unused and about 10 percent of them have impact on cost as well. This could lead to the overuse of the infrastructure. Another dimension of complexity is the security configuration for large numbers of VMs on multiple host computers within an organization which can be very difficult.

5.3   Guest OS-Related Attacks

It is widely observed that traditional operating systems have vulnerabilities – hence attacks which exploit these vulnerabilities may also work against virtualised OSs with the same vulnerabilities [31]. However, securing VM operating systems cannot be performed in the same way as securing a typical OS. For example, typically, security for a system of machines is enforced over the network by placing physical hardware, such as firewalls, between devices [9]. In contrast, in a virtual environment, hardware cannot be placed between VMs. Securing the host OS and the guest OSs against malware infections is very important. However, since antivirus products which run in virtualised environments use agents to scan each VM instead of the individual instance of the product, this can slow the performance of a VM by creating antivirus storms [9].

6   Data Recovery in VMs

To demonstrate vulnerability of a VM when used within a multi-tenancy architecture, we demonstrate how permanently deleted data from a VM may be recovered. Such vulnerability continues to exist in many real VM deployments in Cloud systems. In [3], for example, an automated system to download VMs from Amazon EC2 was implemented. However, no detailed description was provided as to how analysis was carried out or how the virtual disk images were taken. In [26], the work involved some analysis on the underlying VMs, however, it was not clear how this was done. In [8], several acquisition tools were evaluated against the retrieval of volatile and non-volatile data. However, the discussion was at a higher level and did not go into details of the extracting or imaging processes. In the following sections we describe how VMs can be imaged and analyzed by dividing the process, and various software tools that can be used at each stage.

7   Experiment Methodology

On a disk, data is generally stored on the surface of a platter in sectors and tracks. A sector is a subdivision of track which has a fixed number of bytes. Sectors are often grouped together into clusters. When files are deleted from any machine,

---

[5] Commvault: VM Sprawl - http://tinyurl.com/nxukpm4.

only details like: path on cluster, sector information, creation date, modification date, etc. will be erased but the actual physical file may still be there if it was not overwritten. This means that there is a possibility that data which has been deleted could be retrieved again from the unallocated space but is that also possible with virtual disks? To provide a clear answer, we divide our experiment methodology into phases where each phase is independent of the other. In each phase, the process can be performed in various ways. The phases are:

– Preparation Phase: Setting up of the VMs and preparing the files.
– Deletion phase: the permanent removal of files from the VM.
– VM Imaging Phase: extracting an exact disk image to be analyzed.
– Mounting Phase: mounting the image as a drive for analysis (optional)
– Recovery Phase: using some tools to recover deleted data.

The next section covers the technical experiment and the described phases. It will also highlight the tools used, briefly, in each phase.

7.1   The Preparation Phase

VMware was used to run a WinXP virtual machine. 12 GB was allocated for the VM. Five files were chosen from the internet: two Word documents, one PDF file, one WMV file and one XLS file. The files and their sizes appear in Fig. 2.

Name	Date modified	Type	Size
Wildlife	14/07/2009 06:32	Windows Media A...	25,631 KB
eps	15/07/2013 19:00	Microsoft Excel 97...	31 KB
dubai-travel-plan-3-nights	15/07/2013 18:54	Microsoft Word 9...	173 KB
PrivateCloudForDummies	15/07/2013 18:51	Adobe Acrobat D...	3,427 KB
oscar_winning_films	15/07/2013 18:41	Microsoft Word 9...	73 KB

Fig. 2. List of chosen files and their sizes

7.2   Deletion Phase

The mentioned files were deleted from their stored locations using (Shift-Del) which is supposed to delete any file permanently from the machine.

7.3   VM Imaging Phase

The aim of this phase is to create an exact copy of the VM disk containing all the allocated or unallocated disk space (bit-by-bit copy). There exist many imaging software tools for Windows and Linux, using a command line or graphical interface. The Linux dd tool is the most widely used and allows imaging of any type of storage medium. It is also used as a disk wiping/erasing tool. The problem with dd is that it creates an exact replica of the source drive in the destination including the file system type; meaning that the destination drive will lose other stored files unless it was reformatted again. In this experiment, Helix bootable CD was used. Helix provides an easy to use interface (as illustrated in Fig. 3) which allows acquiring raw images of drives and storing them in small chunks in the required destination. It also allows verifying the resulting disk image by calculating a hash value. The purpose of verifying the hash was to ensure that the image has not been altered during the image creation process. The VM's C:Drive was selected as the source and an external hard disk was selected as the destination after specifying a new folder name in the external hard disk. In addition, the option of verifying the hash was selected.

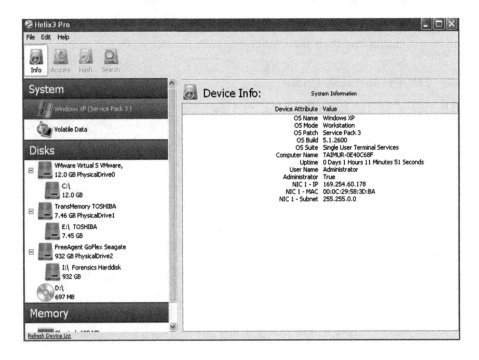

Fig. 3. Helix interface

The whole imaging process for the 12 GB VM drive took about 17 min and the execution time of the verification process was approximately 34 min. Of course, as the size of the volume increases, the process tends to take considerable amount of time.

7.4 Mounting Phase

This phase can be optional if the recovery tool in the next phase accepts raw images as input. In this experiment, the recovery tools require a mounted drive.

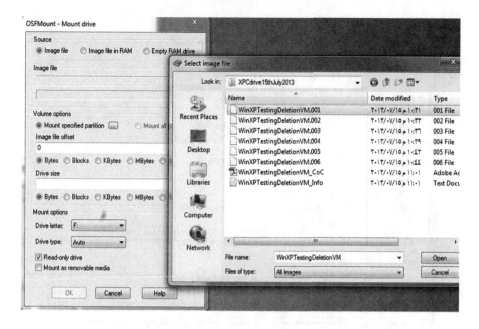

Fig. 4. Disk image partitions being loaded to OSFMount

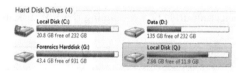

Fig. 5. Demonstrating a successful disk mount

OSFMount[6] is a free and easy to use software tool which allows mounting raw disk images to the Windows operating system (Fig. 4). The mounted disk image will appear exactly as any normal external drive. Moreover, it allows mounting as a read-only mode. In this phase, the saved raw disk images were loaded to the OSFMount software and a drive letter 'Q' was chosen. Read-only mode was chosen because we do not want to alter the disk contents. Hence, a new drive Q was added to the list of drives in the host computer (Fig. 5).

7.5   Recovery Phase

Again, there exist many software tools which allow the retrieval of deleted files out of raw disks. The RecoverMyFiles tool was used for its easy to use interface the support for many file types. The tool takes the drive location as input and allows choosing between several search modes (Fig. 6). In order to minimize the

---

[6] OSFMount tool- http://www.osforensics.com/tools/mount-disk-images.html.

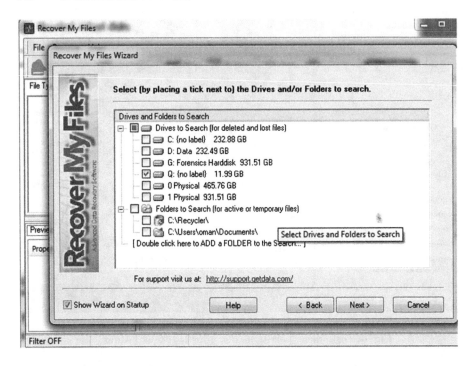

Fig. 6. Selecting drive Q – containing the VM disk image

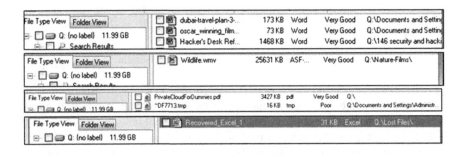

Fig. 7. Recovered deleted files

search time, specific file types were chosen: doc, PDF, WMV, XLS. All the recovered files, except the spread sheet XLS file, kept their original file name and size and were successfully recovered, as illustrated in Fig. 7.

8   Discussion and Conclusion

After describing the key concepts in virtualisation and the associated security limitations with existing VM management software, we demonstrate how permanently deleted files can be recovered from deleted VM disk images. The whole experiment scenario was to demonstrate what happens in a multi-tenancy Cloud computing environment, as tenants may extract VM images and issue various analysis tasks on them. One of the tests is to recover deleted data. The DOS and Windows file systems use fixed-size clusters so even if the actual data being stored requires less storage than the cluster size, an entire cluster is reserved for the file. This unused space is called the slack space. The slack space may have data which had been deleted in the past. Since the allocated space for any new VM is not necessarily given in successive disk locations, there could be a possibility for previous data to be within the allocated space. This data may not be related to the VM itself. It could be left out of past VMs.

As the retrieval of deleted data from virtual disk images was possible, a question can be asked about whether encryption of files or virtual machines may solve the problem of data privacy. In [21] the authors argue that cryptographic techniques are essential to provide information separation and data confidentiality in a Cloud environment. Data may be encrypted at rest in the cloud provider's storage or in motion while it is being used by the consumer. Consumers are recommended to encrypt the data before moving them to the Cloud. There are a variety of commercial products which offer encryption of files before moving them to the Cloud such as BoxCryptor, Viivo, CloudFogger, etc. In [15], the authors discuss a novel security scheme for encrypting virtual disk images in the cloud computing environment. When performing the encryption, a key to encrypt the data will be generated and the same key can be used for decryption. Although encryption of cloud files is essential and had many benefits, it has some drawbacks as well. Data encryption restricts the user's ability to perform keyword search and thus makes the traditional plaintext search methods unsuitable for cloud computing [19]. Another issue is the effect on performance as the encryption and decryption processes require complex computation power. In [6], estimates are provided for the cryptographic costs of some encryption algorithms. The authors find that making use of cloud storage as a simple remote encrypted file system is extremely unfeasible if considering only core technology costs. Managing the encryption/decryption keys is a very important issue in the application of encryption concept that needs to be addressed. In this paper we also describe Cloud privacy issues and their relevance in the context of virtualisation techniques. We identify the lack of literature regarding VM imaging and the recovery of deleted data from such images. We have carried out a practical experiment to demonstrate this.

References

1. Anand, R., Sarswathi, S., Regan, R.: Security issues in virtualization environment. In: 2012 International Conference on Radar, Communication and Computing (ICRCC), pp. 254–256. IEEE (2012)
2. Armbrust, M., Fox, A., Griffith, R., Joseph, A.D., Katz, R., Konwinski, A., Lee, G., Patterson, D., Rabkin, A., Stoica, I., et al.: A view of cloud computing. Commun. ACM **53**(4), 50–58 (2010)

3. Balduzzi, M., Zaddach, J., Balzarotti, D., Kirda, E., Loureiro, S.: A security analysis of amazon's elastic compute cloud service. In: Proceedings of the 27th Annual ACM Symposium on Applied Computing, pp. 1427–1434. ACM (2012)
4. Chaves, S., Westphall, C., Westphall, C., Geronimo, G.: Customer security concerns in cloud computing. In: The Tenth International Conference on Networks, ICN 2011, pp. 7–11 (2011)
5. Chen, Y., Katz, R.H.: Glimpses of the brave new world for cloud security (2011), http://www.hpcinthecloud.com/hpccloud/2011-02-22/glimpses_of_the_brave_new_world_for_cloud_security.html
6. Chen, Y., Sion, R.: On securing untrusted clouds with cryptography. In: Proceedings of the 9th Annual ACM Workshop on Privacy in the Electronic Society, pp. 109–114. ACM (2010)
7. Christodorescu, M., Sailer, R., Schales, D.L., Sgandurra, D., Zamboni, D.: Cloud security is not (just) visualization security: a short paper. In: Proceedings of the 2009 ACM Workshop on Cloud Computing Security, pp. 97–102. ACM (2009)
8. Dykstra, J., Sherman, A.T.: Acquiring forensic evidence from infrastructure-as-a-service cloud computing: exploring and evaluating tools, trust, and techniques. Digital Invest. **9**, S90–S98 (2012)
9. Garber, L.: The challenges of securing the virtualized environment. Computer **45**(1), 17–20 (2012)
10. Gurav, U., Shaikh, R.: Virtualization: a key feature of cloud computing. In: Proceedings of the International Conference and Workshop on Emerging Trends in Technology, pp. 227–229. ACM (2010)
11. Harnik, D., Pinkas, B., Shulman-Peleg, A.: Side channels in cloud services: deduplication in cloud storage. Secur. Priv. IEEE **8**(6), 40–47 (2010)
12. Hurwitz, J., Bloor, R., Kaufman, M., Halper, F.: Cloud Computing for Dummies, vol. 1. Wiley, Hoboken (2009)
13. Jensen, M., Schwenk, J., Gruschka, N., Iacono, L.L.: On technical security issues in cloud computing. In: IEEE International Conference on Cloud Computing, CLOUD 2009, pp. 109–116. IEEE (2009)
14. Jordon, M., Forshaw, J.: Dirty disks raised new questions about cloud security (2012). http://www.contextis.com/resources/blog/dirty-disks-raise-new-questions-about-cloud/
15. Kazim, M., Masood, R., Shibli, M.A.: Securing virtual machine images in cloud computing (2013)
16. Kazim, M., Masood, R., Shibli, M.A., Abbasi, A.G.: Security aspects of virtualization in cloud computing. In: Saeed, K., Chaki, R., Cortesi, A., Wierzchoń, S. (eds.) CISIM 2013. LNCS, vol. 8104, pp. 229–240. Springer, Heidelberg (2013)
17. King, S.T., Chen, P.M.: Subvirt: implementing malware with virtual machines. In: 2006 IEEE Symposium on Security and Privacy, pp. 314–327. IEEE (2006)
18. Li, J., Li, B., Wo, T., Hu, C., Huai, J., Liu, L., Lam, K.: Cyberguarder: a virtualization security assurance architecture for green cloud computing. future Gener. Comput. Syst. **28**(2), 379–390 (2012)
19. Li, J., Wang, Q., Wang, C., Cao, N., Ren, K., Lou, W.: Fuzzy keyword search over encrypted data in cloud computing. In: 2010 Proceedings IEEE INFOCOM, pp. 1–5. IEEE (2010)
20. Luo, S., Lin, Z., Chen, X., Yang, Z., Chen, J.: Virtualization security for cloud computing service. In: 2011 International Conference on Cloud and Service Computing (CSC), pp. 174–179. IEEE (2011)

21. Martucci, L.A., Zuccato, A., Smeets, B., Habib, S.M., Johansson, T., Shahmehri, N.: Privacy, security and trust in cloud computing: the perspective of the telecommunication industry. In: 2012 9th International Conference on Ubiquitous Intelligence & Computing and 9th International Conference on Autonomic & Trusted Computing (UIC/ATC), pp. 627–632. IEEE (2012)
22. Mell, P., Grance, T.: The NIST definition of cloud computing. Natl. Inst. Stand. Technol. **53**(6), 50 (2009)
23. Pearce, M., Zeadally, S., Hunt, R.: Virtualization: issues, security threats, and solutions. ACM Comput. Surv. (CSUR) **45**(2), 17 (2013)
24. Perrons, R.K., Hems, A.: Cloud computing in the upstream oil & gas industry: a proposed way forward. Energy Policy **56**, 732–737 (2013)
25. Ray, E., Schultz, E.: Virtualization security. In: Proceedings of the 5th Annual Workshop on Cyber Security and Information Intelligence Research: Cyber Security and Information Intelligence Challenges and Strategies, p. 42. ACM (2009)
26. Ristenpart, T., Tromer, E., Shacham, H., Savage, S.: Hey, you, get off of my cloud: exploring information leakage in third-party compute clouds. In: Proceedings of the 16th ACM Conference on Computer and Communications Security, pp. 199–212. ACM (2009)
27. Rutkowska, J.: Subverting vistatm kernel for fun and profit. Black Hat Briefings, Las Vegas (2006)
28. Sehrawat, A., Bishnoi, N.: Security: a key requirement of cloud. Int. J. Adv. Res. Comput. Sci. Softw. Eng. (IJARCSSE) **3**(6), 1044–1048 (2013)
29. Smith, J.E., Nair, R.: The architecture of virtual machines. Computer **38**(5), 32–38 (2005)
30. Studnia, I., Alata, E., Deswarte, Y., Kaâniche, M., Nicomette, V., et al.: Survey of security problems in cloud computing virtual machines. In: Proceedings of Computer and Electronics Security Applications Rendez-vous (C&ESAR 2012) (2012)
31. Vaughan-Nichols, S.J.: Virtualization sparks security concerns. Comput. **41**(8), 13–15 (2008)
32. Wang, L., Tao, J., Kunze, M., Castellanos, A.C., Kramer, D., Karl, W.: Scientific cloud computing: early definition and experience. In: HPCC, vol. 8, pp. 825–830 (2008)
33. Xen: How does xen work? (2009). http://www-archive.xenproject.org/files/Marketing/HowDoesXenWork.pdf
34. Zhang, Y., Juels, A., Reiter, M.K., Ristenpart, T.: Cross-VM side channels and their use to extract private keys. In: Proceedings of the 2012 ACM Conference on Computer and communications security, pp. 305–316. ACM (2012)
35. Zissis, D., Lekkas, D.: Addressing cloud computing security issues. Future Gener. Comput. Syst. **28**(3), 583–592 (2012)

Cloud Computing: Security Issues Overview and Solving Techniques Investigation

Yu Yang[✉], Chenggui Zhao, and Tilei Gao

Yunnan University of Finance and Economics, Kunming 650211, China
yeongyuk@126.com

Abstract. Cloud computing is a new computing model which uses virtualization technology, distributed computing, parallel computing and other existing technologies to achieve cloud service virtualization and economies of scale, whilst increasingly overwhelming cloud security issues has brought great challenges and concerns to the cloud services providers and cloud users, especially trust and privacy issues with regard to cloud computing and cloud shared storage associated security issues. In the paper, we expound the basic concepts of cloud computing, deployment models, service models and key features, analyze and outline the currently highlighted cloud security issues, report the status quo of cloud computing security, investigate the prevalent and typical cloud computing security problem key solving techniques, and thus render a comprehensive cloud computing security technical reference model, which is composed of associated cloud security solving techniques that result from inevitably multi-faceted cloud security issues. The model is expected to alleviate prominent cloud security issues. This paper generalizes cloud security technology research directions and further development space of cloud security technology and standardization.

Keywords: Cloud computing · Security issues · Trusted cloud computing solving techniques · Shared storage security solving techniques · Cloud security technical reference model

1 Introduction

Cloud computing is a promising novel computing model, for the sake of economies of scale, which harnesses the existing distributed computing, grid computing and virtualization technology and so forth to abstract a large number of hardware and software resources into a shared resources pooling. Cloud computing is defined as a model for enabling convenient, on-demand network access to a shared resource pooling of configurable computing resources (e.g., networks, servers, storage, applications, and services) that can be rapidly provisioned and released with minimal management effort or service provider interaction [23]. It provides the virtualized resources through the network and, computing tasks are assigned to resource pooling that gather abundant resources so that different computing tasks to obtain the corresponding computing power, storage

© Springer International Publishing Switzerland 2015
A. Al-Saidi et al. (Eds.): ICC 2014, LNCS 8993, pp. 152–167, 2015.
DOI: 10.1007/978-3-319-19848-4_10

space and application services, aligning with different Cloud Service User (CSU) diverse needs. Therefore, cloud computing can solve remarkably time-consuming and memory-consuming computational problems, such as: calculating large-scale high-dimensional data, analyzing the petabyte scale web log, etc. Depending on the application whether it is running in a shared infrastructure or on a proprietary infrastructure, cloud computing usually is classified as four kinds of deployment models: public cloud, private cloud, community cloud and hybrid cloud [13,31,34].

Cloud computing is defined three types of service models: Software as a Service (SaaS), Platform as a Service (PaaS), Infrastructure as a Service (IaaS).

SaaS: The CSUs use on-demand applications and provisioned computing resource services. They only manage application profile settings, and almost not merely manage or control the underlying cloud infrastructure (basic network management, storage, servers and other cloud infrastructure), thus reducing the maintenance and operation costs of hardware and software development. SaaS success cases have: Salesforce's Sales cloud and Service Cloud; Microsoft's Live, Hotmail, Office Web App; Google's Gmail and Google Docs; IBM's Lotus Live, Blueworks Live; Apple's Mobileme; Oracle's Oracle On Demand; AdventNet the Zoho, etc.

PaaS: The CSUs leverage the provided on-demand computing platform to develop and deploy their own applications. They only manage their application deployment and possible hosting application configuration, without managing basic cloud infrastructure, thus reducing the hardware and software used for platform costs of purchase, rental and maintenance. PaaS success cases have: Salesforce's Force.com, Heroku and Database.com; Microsoft's Azure; Google's Google App Engine; IBM's CloudBurst Appliance and Ensembles; Aptana the Aptana Cloud and others.

IaaS: The CSUs impose on-demand memory, network, and other provisioned computing infrastructure services to develop and run applications. They need manage operating systems, storage and deployed applications, etc., but needn't manage fundamental cloud infrastructure, thus reducing the hardware and software costs of purchase, rental and maintenance. IaaS success cases have: Amazon's EC2 (Elastic Compute Cloud), S3 (Simple Storage Service), Simple Queue Service and SimpleDB; IBM's SmartCloud and Drop box of DropBox; NYSE of Rackspace; GoGrid's Cloud Servers; Sun's Cloud Service; Decho's Mozy and so forth.

Cloud computing services exist six kinds of essential characteristics, they demonstate the discrimination against the traditional computing model [19]:

Virtualized resource pooling: The CSP leverage virtualization technology to dynamically assigned computing resources to the CSUs.

On-demand self-service: The CSUs use provision computing capabilities when required by business demands.

Measurable provision: The CSP control and manage resource use by leveraging a metering capability at some level of abstraction of provisioned services, to ensure the effective management of billing services.

Broad network access: The CSUs access to cloud services through network.

Rapid elasticity and scaling: Allowing cloud services, resources and infrastructure to be automatically provisioned as the CSUs' business requirements change.

Multi-tenant: According to the CSUs' business requirements dynamically allocate different physical and virtual resources for multiple the CSU usage.

To summaries, virtualization technology is of importance cloud computing technology that abstract cloud resources, application services and infrastructure as available separate virtual resources for the CSUs usage. According to previous studies, cloud computing model is shown in Fig. 1.

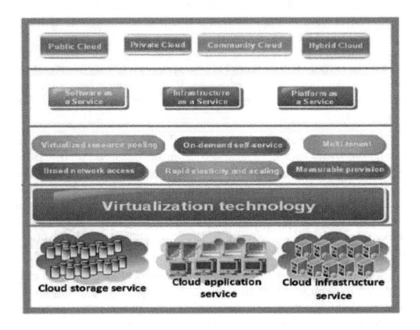

Fig. 1. Cloud computing model

In this paper, we try to systematically investigate the issues of cloud computing security with the following contributions:

- We analyze and elaborate currently highlighted cloud computing security issues and sum up imperative cloud computing security problem solving techniques.
- We present a comprehensive cloud computing security technical reference model through studying associated cloud security solving techniques.
- We generalize a few urgency cloud security technology research directions and indicate the further development space of cloud security technology and standardization.

The rest of this paper is organized as follows: Sect. 2 analyzes and elaborates the currently utmost urgency cloud security issues; Sect. 3 investigates the representative solving techniques with regard to prevalent and typical cloud computing security issues, including audit and Service Level Agreement (SLA) management technique, trusted cloud computing technology, shared storage security technology, virtualization security technology, network application security technology, authentication and access control technology; Sect. 4 renders a comprehensive cloud computing security technical reference model; Sect. 5 succinctly summarizes the paper and, exhausts and focus on cloud computing security issues solving techniques directions and standardization techniques.

2 Analysis of Cloud Computing Security Issues

Currently, cloud computing security issues and state-of-the-art solving technical spark widespread interests in the field of information technology. With the growing popularity of cloud computing applications, cloud security has become a vital factor, which restricts the development of cloud computing. The continuing occurrence cloud computing security incidents exacerbate the CSUs' concerns on data security and privacy. For example, in February 2009 and July 2009, Amazon S3 encountered twice interrupts, and caused a single service that depends on the network to crash [4]; In March 2009, Microsoft Azure service suffered an outage; In January 2010, Salesforce service paralyzed; In April 2011, Amazon infrastructure configuration error, resulting in Amazon EC2 service is not available, including Reddit news service, Hootsuite, Quora, Foursquare answer service and a number of prominent cloud-based websites stay offline [5]; In June 2011, the UK's National Healthcare System (NHS) was hacked and so on. Cloud computing security issues stem from inherent security problems and the associated with what technologies are used. According to the quantitative analysis of current cloud computing security concerns of Nelson et al. [18]: multi-tenant access security of the entire cloud computing security concerns ratio is 7 %, 2 % of access control, 3 % of authentication, 5 % of network application security, 1 % of security framework, 2 % of component safety, 4 % of port security, 5 % of virtual environment safety, 34 % of shared storage security, 6 % of audit and compliance risk, 19 % of legal issues, 2 % of the CSU management, 6 % of authorization management, 5 % of SLA management and 2 % of redundant and others.

The CSP and the CSUs share responsibility for security risks in cloud computing environment. We focus on SaaS security issues, PaaS service security issues, IaaS service security issues, along with audit and compliance security issues in cloud computing environment and, briefly shed light on the more prominent issues.

2.1 Analysis of SaaS Service Security Issues

Multi-Tenant Access Security: Leveraging multi-tenant environment that achieves the economies of scale in cloud computing. There exist various levels of trust relationships between different tenants with the CSP, which some certain tenants perhaps are malicious attacker. Due to shared and multi-tenant environment, once multi-tenant isolation failure, tenants can access each other's data and applications, thereby affecting others access security.

Access Control: Imperfect access control direct impact confidential information safety. On one hand, foreign governments have legal right to surveil the data stored in the cloud, so they can access to confidential information under some circumstances. On the other hand, internal IT staff have highly privileged access to the CSU's sensitive information under some CSP inadequate security mechanisms and vetting [30].

Authentication and Authorization: The CSP provides the authorized CSU with a mechanism of authentication and authorization through Application Program Interfaces (APIs) in the form of password. There is a risk of username and password might have been hijacked. In the registration process, the CSP's fragile authentication mechanism may bury hidden trouble and caused security risks: anonymous users, spammers, malicious code developers and cyber criminals attack.

Network Application Security: In the cloud computing environment, network application security refers the related security issues about network communications and network cloud infrastructure configuration. Virtual network enhances the Virtual Machines (VMs) interconnectivity and VM Hypervisor access virtual networks through bridging and routing, resulting in the isolation between VMs easily failure, causing DDoS (Distributed Denial of Service), DoS, virtual network sniffer, virtual network spoofing, Address Resolution Protocol (ARP) spoofing, redirect packets and other network application security issues.

2.2 Analysis of PaaS Service Security Issues

Framework Securitty: Cloud computing based on virtualization technology and VM Hypervisor multi-tenant framework, virtualization technology enables infrastructure and resources as available isolated VMs to the CSUs, which security tremendous depends hypervisor robustness. The VMs isolation failue triggers an attacker can bypass the hypervisor to manipulate other CSUs' virtual machines under framework vulnerability circumstance.

APIs Security: Cloud computing commonly uses APIs on cloud service configuration, management, service surveillance, and interaction between the CSP and CSUs. The APIs are responsible for the CSU authentication and access control, its vulnerability is likely to cause anonymous access network, clear text authentication and inadequate detection and limited service monitoring, impertinent authorization.

2.3 Analysis of IaaS Service Security Issues

Virtual Environment Security: VM Hypervisor and VM Monitor are virtualization software components. Virtual environment security issues involve in management procedures and monitor vulnerabilities. The VM snapshot likely restore to enable previously disabled accounts and password, attack among VMs after virtualization isolation failure.

Shared Storage Security: Cloud computing shared storage security mainly refers to the cloud data security, including data storage security, data encryption, data isolation and data destruction. Data security primarily ensure their confidentiality, integrity and availability. Data storage security focus on data loss or leakage and data transmission and migration security. Under the strategic of destruction and outside the jurisdiction, cloud computing may lead to informative data loss; Storage and management deficiencies may also lead to data loss and leakage. Data loss or unauthorized disclosure to third parties is the most serious cloud computing security threats. For instance, Encrypting the data are being processed may hinder the data retrieval, resulting in non-normal data access. Data transmission and migration security issues should prioritize transfer data encryption algorithm vulnerabilities, data plagiarism risk in the process of network transmission, data lockin issues in the process of data migration, data location, data flow border-crossing of jurisdiction and other issues. Besides, owing to immature cloud data processing strategy, data destruction technology cannot thoroughly delete the CSU's data and even the CSP cannot recover data.

2.4 Analysis of Audit and Compliance Security Issues

Audit: Inspect and verify records in the process of authentication and authorization. Its purpose is to check whether or not comply with the predetermined safety standards and policies. Auditing ensure data integrity and enable data owners to believe that their data do not occur without trace operations. Audit failure will lead to disclosure of sensitive information.

Compliance Risk and Legal Issues: Compliance refers to the effectiveness of cloud services and related audit policies. Data storage and usage policies require periodic archiving and auditing in cloud computing environment. Compliance risk arises from the lack of auditing and assessment of industry-standard, the CSP not incapably prove to the CSUs that they comply with the necessary regulations. Furthermore, given different jurisdictions have multifarious laws, it is burdensome and lengthy to ensure cloud computing compliance with all legislations.

The CSU Management: Malicious insiders are more destructive and serious than external accidents because of the insiders's own access privileges. The CSP's access control strategic decides the management efficiency of the CSUs. The CSU management failure causes the destruction of information resources, information eavesdropping and different types of fraud issues.

Authorization Management: Once authorizing success, the CSU becomes legally privileged user. The authorization management failure direct give rise to the unauthorized access to cloud services and even confidential data. In addition, insufficient or missing authorization management easily come into being the CSU privacy risk and information leakage.

SLA Management: Service Level Agreements (SLA) ensures the validity of the CSU requested service and the implementation of fundamental safety regulations. Cloud SLA emphasizes service availability, data integrity, privacy and other aspects. SLA management security vulnerability maybe prohibit vulnerability assessment and intrusion detection.

3   Cloud Computing Security Issues Key Solving Technology Research

Cloud computing security solving is the current primary and imperative research missions. Based on the aforementioned overview, we investigate the trusted cloud computing security solving techniques, shared storage security solving techniques, virtualization security solving techniques, network application security solving techniques, identity authentication and access control security solving techniques, audit and SLA management and compliance security solving techniques. We manifest cloud security services technologies and standards in Fig. 2, enforcing appropriate security techniques to solve the above-mentioned discussion cloud computing security issues. The Fig. 2 illustrates Cloud storage services, cloud application services and cloud infrastructure services rely on cloud

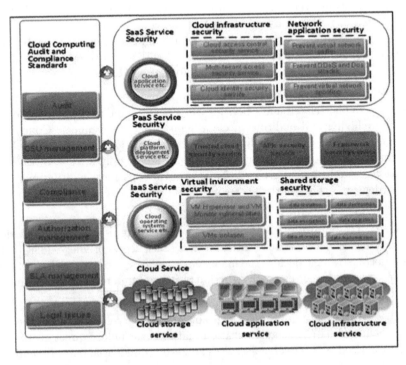

Fig. 2. Cloud security services technologies and standards

computing audit and compliance, and vice versa, audit and compliance promote cloud services unremittingly improved.

3.1   Trusted Cloud Computing Technology

The trusted cloud computing techniques attract abundant interests in cloud computing security research fields, which solve the trust relationship between the CSUs and CSP. Trust Management Model Based on Fuzzy Set Theory (TMFC) [38], by trust evaluation sets, the CSUs make their decision on whether or not to use the services. Shantanu et al. [29] propose a new trusted and collaborative agent-based two-tier framework to protect network communications security. The end-to-end Service Discovery Method (SDM) in Interoperable Cloud Computing Environments (ICE) renders trusted computing [21]. Moreover, the trusted Third Party Auditor (TPA) is one effective way to realize the security trusted computing.

3.2   Shared Storage Security Technology

Guaranteeing cloud computing shared storage data security is one of the important cloud measurement of Quality of Service (QoS). Kawser et al. [16] proposed cloud data storage security model. The Cloud Computing Background Key Exchange (CCBKE) designed to effectively deal with high-dimensional scientific applications data encryption [3]. Threshold secure data sharing scheme is aimed at solving data transmission security issues in Federated Clouds [15]. Server management algorithm assure data consistency and secured storage in the untrusted cloud [2]. P. Syam et al. [24] proposed an effective and flexible distribution verification protocol to address data storage security in cloud computing. The protocol uses Sobol Sequence to verify the integrity of erasure coded data and prevent unauthorized data modification attacks, and even cloud server colluding attacks. A. AlZain et al. [17] rendered Multi-clouds Database Model, which uses shared key algorithm to ensure data security and privacy between the CSPs, thus reduce the risk of data loss and leakage and effectively avoid attack from malicious insiders. Based on an anonymous privilege control scheme AnonyControl to address not only the data privacy issues in a cloud storage, but also the CSU identity privacy problems in existing access control schemes [33]. P. Naga et al. [20] proposed effective fuzzy keyword search over encrypted cloud data while maintaining keyword privacy. They exploited edit distance to quantify keywords similarity and then protect key privacy of sensitive information wildcard-based and gram-based techniques. Huiqi et al. [11] proposed the Random Space Perturbation approach to ensure secure and efficient range query and kNN query services for protected data in the cloud. Under data encryption condition, there are not access restriction and lose authorization of the TPA privacy protection architecture [1]. Gansen et al. [7] designed Separation Model, Availability Model, Migration Model, Tunnel Model and Cryptography Model respectively to manage the CSU's applications and data control, service interruptions, data lock, data confidentiality and integrity problems.

In conclusion, the academia and industry are active in shared storage security technology research all the time always. Besides, Proofs of Retrievability (PORs) will become further research and development tendency of data integrity.

3.3 Virtualization Security Technology

Virtualization is the key technology to build cloud computing, which abstracts infrastructure and resources as separate virtual resources pooling to the CSUs, meanwhile, the CSP must provide safe and isolation virtual environment. Based on the Chinese Wall [32] security policy to forbid deploying and running the competitors VMs on the same physical machines. Hanqian et al. [10] proposed a novel virtual network framework aimed to control the intercommunication among virtual machines deployed in physical machines with higher security. The Virtualization Security Framework [28] contains two parts: virtual system security and virtualization security management, which the former is responsible for virtualization security problems and the latter for virtualization security management settles the question that various VM managements bring. Online Penetration Suite [26] performs pre-rollout scans of virtual machines for security vulnerabilities using established techniques and prevents execution of flawed virtual machines.

To summarize, virtualization technology is cloud computing environments foundation and important aspects that becomes important research direction in cloud computing security domain.

3.4 Network Application Security Technology

In the process of implementation of cloud computing, virtual machine yields network application security vulnerabilities. Firewall Gateway is the first line of defense of cloud computing environment security, it can prevent any port and unknown IP addresses remote access to private LAN by simply losing packets. Unfortunately, once the intruder eavesdrop the CSU's account and passwords, they can bypass the firewall to intrude entire network. Pardeep et al. [22] proposed Hidden Markov Model and data mining clustering techniques to detect any kind of intrusion detection in the network. Steganographic encryption can protect cloud service network communication security [36]. The Integrated Intrusion Detection and Prevention System (IDPS) [9] detects and can prevent diverse types of intrusion.

To sum up, network application security issues are plausibly more prominent. And, attract more people to study network application security technology.

3.5 Identity and Access Control Technology

Identity and Access Management (IAM) provides authentication, authorization and auditing for the CSU to access cloud services. The CSP should implement robust authentication and access control, correctly implement the IAM, ensure the CSU's data security. Jung et al. propose Adaptive Access Control Algorithm that determines the security level to achieve protected resource access control. Extend popular Extended Xml Access Control Markup Language model [35] significantly by integrating flexible access control decisions and data access in a seamless fashion to resolve authorization technology problem. The eXACML+ [37] achieves the fine-grained cloud data access control. Multidimensional password generation technology can protect identity authentication [8].

All in all, identity and access control is the imperative technology for cloud computing implementation. Currently, significant research achievements not present and merely extend the existing technology. In addition, IDM mechanism is competent at protecting the CSU's privacy and sensitive information processing.

3.6   Audit and SLA Management Technology

Examine and verify the CSU authentication and authorization records and check whether or not meet predefined security standards and policies. Security management must realize service description and introduce service features in cloud computing environment. Under not violating the CSP strategy and satisfying SLA, seeking the best operating configuration and service integration. Utilizing the public key based homomorphism authenticator and uniquely integrate it with random mask technique to achieve a privacy-preserving public auditing system for cloud data storage security [6]. Based on trusted TPA security mechanisms to resolve data integrity and privacy issues [12]. Chaves et al. [27] summarized the SLA of the cloud computing security management and proposed SLA safety monitor architecture Sec-Mon.

In summary, audit and SLA management play an important role in cloud computing. Currently, a viable research direction is that the CSP how to provide a trusted TPA for the CSUs.

3.7   Compliance Standards and Risk Technology

At current, many governments and corporations have noticed compliance standards risk issues, and actively to establish a common standard and to promote the popularity of cloud computing. The CSP should monitor internal audit process to ensure compliance. The mature compliance security standards have: Amazon Web Services IAM standard PCI DSS Level 1, ISO 27001; Salesforce system status, privacy management commitment standard ISO 27001, SysTrust, SAS 70 Type II; Microsoft Access Control, CSU data isolation standard PCI DSS, HIPAA, SOX, ISO 27001, SAS 70 Type I and Type II; IBM compliance security service standards ISO 27001; Google access control, CSU data isolation standard SAS 70 Type II, FISMA. Compliance Certification analysis algorithm (Comcert) effectively detect possible violations compliance events [25].

Summing up, when using cloud computing, we need to consider compliance standards and risk, legal and jurisdiction issues, the CSP service evolution right of knowing and so forth.

4   The Proposed Cloud Security Technology Reference Model

Cloud computing security solving techniques are of vital importance in cloud computing research field. Such as, RSA encryption algorithm cannot ensure communication security in cloud data storage; Collaborative agent-based two-tier framework confirms the CSU privacy information access control, however, when the CSP information is unknown, it cannot prevent unauthorized access and malicious behavior; Based on Hidden Markov Model data mining clustering techniques and multidimensional password generation technology could easily lead to cloud environment load imbalance; Sec-SLAs encounters security matrix definition and SLA scalability issues; eXACML+ has only made some innovative research and breakthroughs in theory, but put into practical application still need some distance. Therefore, it is of emergency to build a comprehensive cloud computing security technology model. Based on the aforementioned cloud security issues analysis and cloud computing security issues key solving technology investigations, the Fig. 3 displays a novel comprehensive cloud security techniques reference model.

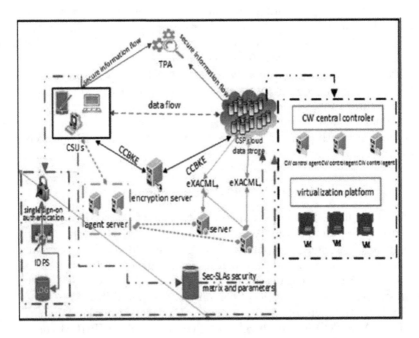

Fig. 3. Comprehensive cloud security techniques reference model

The reference model is described as following:

Trusted TPA Services: Trusted TPA is on behalf of the CSU to monitor cloud data storage security risks. We will employ Sobol Sequence to guarantee cloud data storage integrity and privacy in the model. In addition, TPA also provide technical assurance for trusted cloud computing and support forensic for solving SLA conflict.

Data Encryption Services: Data encryption technology is research hotspot in cloud computing area. We study state-of-the-art encryption technologies and use CCBKE in the model since it can improve the encryption efficiency, and avoid the cloud environment load imbalance.

Virtual Environment Security Services: The CSP should ensure virtual environment safety and isolation. We employ the graph coloring algorithm to achieve the correct deployment of VMs and physical isolation.

Authentication and IDPS Services: Relatively mature technologies for the CSU authentication and IDPS services, including authentication system with multi-dimensional generation technology, IDPS systems, based on clustering HMM detection technology. We impose single sign-on authentication since it can reduce the cost of security enforcement, avoid cloud computing overloading. The IDPS not only detects diverse types of intrusion, but prevents them, not limited to alert.

Access Control Services: We enforce eXACML+ in the proposed reference model because its fine-grained access control feature and effective detecting misconfigurations of access policy.

SLA Management Services: SLA management is committed to ensuring the availability of cloud services, data integrity and privacy and security protection and other aspects. Effective and efficient SLA management services can decrease unnecessary conflicts between the CSUs and CSP. We exploit Sec-Mon that Chaves et al. proposed SLA monitoring framework in the reference model. In addition, we summarize several imperative cloud security technology, standardization and cloud security technology research directions:

(1) The CSUs through APIs for authentication and access the cloud services. Although the software stack make important contributions to interoperability between different cloud platforms, but the provided APIs are still incompatible proprietary technologies, which to be solved is standardization of the APIs. To solve expected data lockin problem and to develop and deploy SaaS services of federated cloud. Enhance the availability and interoperability of cloud computing.

(2) When the CSU requested service exceeds the load peak, although hybrid cloud allow to public cloud for requesting intensive resources, but virtualized dynamic load balance management and cloud resource allocation methods still need algorithms and key technical support to improve the QoS of cloud computing.

(3) Lacking of trust between the CSP and CSUs hamper cloud computing on-demand services and the globalization process. Trust is not just technical issues but also social issues. Gratifyingly, the problem can be solved through technology research and development [14]. How to establish trust between the CSP and CSUs through SLA and credibility system is a hotpoint in cloud security research field.

(4) Cloud shared storage security technology is of importance and intractability cloud security technology research field, referring research sharing data from malicious modify, delete, lockin and secure transmission and migration security, research the integrity and confidentiality of sharing sensitive and confidential information against intrusion and fine-grained access control policy and so forth.

(5) Besides the traditional network attacks, the new introduction challenges and attacks are partly attributed to using virtualization key technologies, much-needed comparative research insight into virtual environment security technology.

(6) Cloud computing SLA is imperative to cloud security technology research domain, including laws liability transfer issues, unpredictable the CSU's demand for services, frequent hardware and software failures and signed SLA conflicts between the CSUs and CSP. In addition, trust negotiation is usually defined in the process of SLA, thus directly affecting trusted cloud computing application.

(7) Owing to the cloud platform through virtualization distribute data storage to different servers in the world. Thus, global cloud computing compliance standardization being required to resolve many of the CSU's copyrighted data and jurisdiction issues.

5   Conclusion and Future Works

Cloud computing has made a significant contribution for the information industry and information technology in the information field. We review the more prominent issues as well as SLA, compliance and legal issues and, study the trusted cloud computing technology, shared storage security technology, virtualization security technology, network application security technology, authentication and access control technology, audit and SLA management technologies, and compliance risk technology. We attempt to render a comprehensive cloud computing security technical reference model. Further research still needs to prove reasonable and practical of the model. Cloud computing is provided with overwhelming characteristic and remarkably limitless development space. However, with the cloud computing research of academia and industry, we face manifold critical issues, particularly, security issues. Therefore, the increasingly prominent and burdensome cloud computing security issues need to be jointly solved by academia, industry and government. And, exploring and developing comprehensively practical and effective security solving techniques.

Acknowledgements. This work is supported by the Natural Science Foundation of Yunnan Province, China, under Grant No. 2010ZC095, and the Natural Science Foundation of Education Department of Yunnan Province, China, under Grant No. 2012Z064.

References

1. Mana, A., Munoz, A., Gonzlez, J.: Dynamic security monitoring for virtualized environments in cloud computing. In: International Workshop on Securing Services on the Cloud, pp. 1–6. IEEE Press (2011)
2. Dinesh, C.: Secured data consistency and storage way in untrusted cloud using server management algorithm. Technical report 1111.2412, ArXiv e-prints (2011)
3. Liu, C., Zhang, X., Chen, J., Yang, C.: An authenticated key exchange scheme for efficient security-aware scheduling of scientific applications in cloud computing. In: Ninth International Conference on Dependable, Autonomic and Secure Computing, pp. 372–379. IEEE Press (2011)
4. Feng, D., Zhang, M., Zhang, Y., Xu, Z.: Cloud computing security research. J. Softw. **22**, 71–82 (2011)
5. Doelitzscher, F., Reich, C., Knahl, M., Passfall, A., Clarke, N.: An agent based business aware incident detection system for cloud environments. J. Cloud Comput. **1**(1), 1–19 (2012)
6. Vidhisha, G., Surekha, C., Rayudu, S.S., Seshadri, U.: Preserving privacy for secure and outsourcing for linear programming in cloud computing. Technical report 1211.1457, ArXiv e-prints (2012)
7. Zhao, G., Rong, C., Jaatun, M.G., Sandnes, F.E.: Deployment models-towards eliminating security concerns from cloud computing. In: International Conference on High Performance Computing and Simulation, pp. 189–195. IEEE Press (2010)
8. Dinesha, H.A., Agrawal, D.V.: Multi-dimensional password generation technique for accessing cloud services. Int. J. Cloud Comput.: Serv. Archit. **2**(3), 31–39 (2012)
9. Alsafi, H.M., Abduallah, W.M., Pathan, A.S.K.: IDPS: an integrated intrusion handling model for cloud computing environment. Int. J. Comput. Inf. Technol. **4**(1), 1–16 (2012)
10. Wu, H., Ding, Y., Winer, C., Yao, L.: Network security for virtual machine in cloud computing. In: International Conference on Computer Sciences and Convergence Information Technology, pp. 18–21. IEEE Press (2010)
11. Xu, H., Guo, S., Chen, K.: Building confidential and efficient query services in the cloud with rasp data perturbation. In: IEEE Transactions on Knowledge and Data Engineering (2013)
12. Gul, I., Islam, M.H.: Cloud computing security auditing. In: The 2nd International Conference on Next Generation Information Technology, pp. 143–148. IEEE Press (2011)
13. Yang, J., Chen, Z.: Cloud computing research and security issues. In: International Conference on Computational Intelligence and Software Engineering, pp. 1–3. IEEE Press, 2010
14. Hwang, K., Dongarra, J.J., Fox, G.C.: Distributed and cloud computing. Elsevier/Morgan Kaufmann, Amsterdam, London (2012)
15. Venkataramana, K., Padmavathamma, M.: A threshold secure data sharing scheme for federated clouds. Technical report 1209.2614, ArXiv e-prints (2012)

16. Wazed Nafi, K., Shekha Kar, T., Anisul Hoque, S., Hashem, M.M.A.: A newer user authentication, file encryption and distributed server based cloud computing security architecture. Technical report 1303.0598, ArXiv e-prints (2013)

17. AlZain, M.A., Soh, B., Pardede, E.: MCDB: using multi-clouds to ensure security in cloud computing. In: International Conference on Dependable, Autonomic and Secure Computing, pp. 784–791. IEEE Press (2011)

18. Gonzalez, N., Miers, C., Redígolo, F., Simplício, M., Carvalho, T., Näslund, M., Pourzandi, M.: A quantitative analysis of current security concerns and solutions for cloud computing. In: Third International Conference on Cloud Computing Technology and Science, pp. 231–238. IEEE Press (2011)

19. National Institute of Standards & Technology (NIST). http://csrc.nist.gov/groups/SNS/cloudCcomputing/cloud-def-v15.doc

20. Aswani, P.N., Shekar, K.C.: Fuzzy keyword search over encrypted data using symbol-based Trie-traverse search scheme in cloud computing. Technical report 1211.3682, ArXiv e-prints (2012)

21. Goyal, P.: Application of a distributed security method to End-2-End services security in independent heterogeneous cloud computing environments. In: Services, pp. 379–384. IEEE Press (2011)

22. Kumar, P., Sehgal, V., Shah, K., Shukla, S.S.P., Chauhan, D.S.: A novel approach for security in cloud computing using Hidden Markov model and clustering. In: World Congress on Information and Communication Technologies, pp. 810–815. IEEEPress (2011)

23. Srivastava, P., Singh, S., Pinto, A.A., Verma, S., Chaurasiya, V.K., Gupta, R.: An architecture based on proactive model for security in cloud computing. In: Recent Trends in Information Technology, pp. 661–666. IEEE Press, Chennai (2011)

24. Syam Kumar, P., Subramanian, R., Thamizh Selvam, D.: Ensuring data storage security in cloud computing using Sobol sequence. In: International Conference on Parallel Distributed and Grid Computing, pp. 217–222. IEEE Press (2010)

25. Accorsi, R., Lowis, D.I.L., Sato, Y.: Automated certification for compliant cloud-based business processes. Bus. Inf. Syst. Eng. 3(3), 145–154 (2011)

26. Schwarzkopf, R., Schmidt, M., Strack, C., Martin, S., Freisleben, B.: Increasing virtual machine security in cloud environments. J. Cloud Comput. 1(1), 1–12 (2012)

27. de Chaves, S.A., Westphall, C.B., Lamin, F.R.: SLA perspective in security management for cloud computing. In: International Conference on Networking and Services, pp. 212–217. IEEE Press (2010)

28. Luo, S., Lin, Z., Chen, X., Yang, Z., Chen, J.: Virtualization security for cloud computing service. In: International Conference on Cloud and Service Computing, pp. 174–179. IEEE Press (2011)

29. Pal, S., Khatua, S., Chaki, N., Sanyal, S.: A new trusted and collaborative agent based approach for ensuring cloud security. Technical report 1108.4100, ArXiv e-prints (2011)

30. Pearson, S., Benameur, A.: Privacy, security and trust issues arising from cloud computing. In: Second International Conference on Cloud Computing Technology and Science, pp. 693–702. IEEE Press (2010)

31. Ramgovind, S., Eloff, M.M., Smith, E.: The management of security in cloud computing. In: Information Security for South Africa, pp. 1–7. IEEE Press (2010)

32. Tsai, T.H., Chen, Y.C., Huang, H.C., Huang, P.M., Chou, K.S.: A practical chinese wall security model in cloud computing. In: Asia-Pacific Network Operations and Management Symposium, pp. 1–4. IEEE Press (2011)

33. Jung, T., Li, X.Y., Wan, Z., Wan, M.: AnonyControl: control cloud data anonymously with multi-authority attribute-based encryption. Technical report 1206.2657, ArXiv e-prints (2012)
34. Bhraguram, T.M., Sumesh, M.S.: Cyber security information exchange based on data asset de-coupling factor in cloud computing. In: Recent Advances in Intelligent Computational Systems, pp. 89–95. IEEE Press (2011)
35. Dinh, T.T.A., Wenqiang, W., Datta, A.: City on the sky: extending xacml for flexible, secure data sharing on the cloud. J. Grid Comput. **10**(1), 151–172 (2012)
36. Mazurczyk, W., Szczypiorski, K.: Is cloud computing steganography-proof? In: International Conference on Multimedia Information Networking and Security, pp. 441–442. IEEE Press (2011)
37. Wang, W.Q., Anh, D.T.T., Lim, H.B., Datta, A.: Cloud and the city: facilitating flexible access control over data-streams. In: Jonker, W., Petković, M. (eds.) SDM 2012. LNCS, vol. 7482, pp. 58–74. Springer, Heidelberg (2012)
38. Sun, X., Chang, G., Li, F.: A trust management model to enhance security of cloud computing environments. In: Second International Conference on Networking and Distributed Computing, pp. 244–248. IEEE Press (2011)

Author Index

Printed in the United States
By Bookmasters